There are centuries of pastoral wisdom packed in the pages of this book. Like his mentor Jonathan Edwards, Clotfelter knows how to shepherd sensitive souls through difficult Calvinist doctrines.
  —Douglas A. Sweeney,
      Associate Professor and Chair, Department
      Church History and the History of Christian Thought
      Trinity Evangelical Divinity School

Dr. Clotfelter tackles a volatile subject with diligence and sensitivity. Juxtaposing the theologies of Jonathan Edwards and George McDonald, the author elucidates the different doctrines of divine judgment and predestination, reconciling these oftentimes unpopular doctrines with the biblical witness regarding divine mercy and grace. Thoroughly saturated with Scripture, this book stands as a welcome affirmation of a classic theological position for today's reader.
  —Richard Weber,
      Assistant Professor, Theology
      Moody Bible Institute

DAVID CLOTFELTER

Sinners
IN THE HANDS OF A
GOOD God

RECONCILING DIVINE JUDGMENT AND MERCY

MOODY PUBLISHERS
CHICAGO

All Scripture quotations, unless otherwise indicated, are taken from *The Holy Bible, English Standard Version.* Copyright © 2000; 2001 by Crossway Bibles, a division of Good News Publishers. Used by permission. All rights reserved.

Scripture quotations marked NIV are taken from the *Holy Bible, New International Version®. NIV®.* Copyright © 1973, 1978, 1984 by International Bible Society. Used by permission of Zondervan Publishing House. All rights reserved.

Scripture quotations marked NKJV are taken from the *New King James Version.* Copyright © 1979, 1980, 1982, 1992 by Thomas Nelson, Inc. Used by permission. All rights reserved.

Library of Congress Cataloging-in-Publication Data

Clotfelter, David.
   Sinners in the hands of a good God : reconciling divine judgment and mercy / David Clotfelter.
      p. cm.
   Includes bibliographical references and indexes.
   ISBN 0-8024-8160-4
   1. God—Righteousness. 2. God—Mercy. 3. Sin. I. Title.

BT145.C56 2004
234'.3—dc22

2004013342

1 3 5 7 9 10 8 6 4 2

Printed in the United States of America

To Lisa,
my partner in the pursuit of God

CONTENTS

Avoid profaneness; come not here:
Nothing but holy, pure, and clear,
Or that which groaneth to be so,
May at his peril further go.

✝GEORGE HERBERT
The Church Porch

ACKNOWLEDGMENTS

THIS BOOK HAS BEEN SEVERAL YEARS in the writing, and without a summer's sabbatical leave from the pastoral ministry, it might never have been finished. To the leaders and people of Chinese Christian Alliance Church I offer my heartfelt thanks.

I am also grateful to Richard Webber, assistant professor of theology at Moody Bible Institute, and to Jim Vincent, general editor at Moody Publishers, for their careful reading of the entire manuscript and excellent suggestions for its improvement. I am, of course, responsible for the remaining flaws.

In addition, I wish to thank my parents and sisters, who played a greater role in the development of my theology than they realize. Perhaps only another person who has anguished over God's character can understand just how much it has meant to me to come from a happy home. There are dark times when one says, "No matter how deep my confusion and how great my fear, I know that a God who could put such wonderful people in my life must be good."

Finally, thanks to my children, Daniel and Sarah. What a joy it is to be your father! How much I have learned from you!

THE STRUGGLE
TO UNDERSTAND
GOD'S JUSTICE

*'Twas grace that taught my heart to fear,
and grace my fears relieved.*

+JOHN NEWTON
"Amazing Grace"

*What is required [for finding theological answers] is a pure
heart, eyes that have been opened, child-like obedience, a life in
the Spirit, rich nourishment from Holy Scripture. . . .*

+KARL BARTH
Anselm: Fides Quarens Intellectum

AS A YOUNG TEENAGER I used a simple argument to convince my-self that God does not exist. A good, all-powerful God would never permit the evil and suffering we experience in this world. A being who was only good *or* powerful—or one who was neither—would not be God. The simplest and most reasonable conclusion for a thinking person to draw was that there is no God and that all that exists, including suffering and what we call "evil," is the product of mindless and amoral natural forces.

I was in college before I began to seriously question this logic, and in graduate school before God drew me, much astonished, into trust in Jesus Christ. But even then the problem of God's relationship to human suffering continued to dog me. I was no longer so troubled by the existence of suffering in general, since I could see that a good God might well permit evil in the short run for the eternal good He could bring from it.] Instead, what now bothered me was the evidence, *from the Bible,* that God Himself brings suffering on people, and that in the case of the impenitent He intends to continue doing so forever. Worse yet, [I found passages in the Scriptures that appeared to state that it is God who ultimately determines who will and who will not believe and be saved.]

This was staggering. Could it really be possible that God brings certain human beings into this world for the sole purpose of damning them?

I had had a taste of God's goodness and a glimpse of His glory in the face of Jesus Christ; I knew that He is incapable of doing wrong. Yet there were times early in my Christian life when I was so horrified by the doctrines of hell and predestination that I found myself near despair. From that despair, God seemed to be a demon, human freedom a grotesque illusion, and life a charade. It took me several years to find peace.

It is because of the intensity of my own struggle over the justice of God's dealings with human beings that I have chosen to write on this topic and to do so in a more personal way than is common for theological books. I do not wish to arouse doubts about God's goodness in the Christian reader who has not already felt them; indeed, if what I have written thus far strikes no chord in your heart, I suggest you put this book aside and forget it. Again, the non-Christian who thinks me a fool for even worrying about such matters would be well advised to return the book to the shelf and find something more interesting to read. But I know from my own hard experience that for the person who *has* wondered seriously about the goodness of God, essays that gloss over the difficulties do not bring satisfaction. The reader who struggles wants help from a writer who has struggled. If I can assist one such person to make progress in understanding the ways of God, I will give thanks for the privilege.

FROM GEORGE MACDONALD TO JONATHAN EDWARDS

While I discuss many authors in this book, two names are especially prominent. This is because for me the men behind them have come to represent two radically different ways of thinking about the justice of God. The first man, George MacDonald, may possibly be known to the reader as the author of many delightful novels and fantasies and the man whom C. S. Lewis viewed as his teacher, although he never knew him personally. MacDonald is justly acclaimed for his Christian fiction, but I encountered him first as a preacher and theologian in an edited edition of his "Unspoken Sermons," called *Creation in Christ,* which came into my hands a year or so after my conversion to Christ. Because I loved C. S. Lewis, it was natural for me to turn with an eager and open heart to the man Lewis claimed to have quoted in every one of his books. The second man, Jonathan Edwards, is probably known to most people only as the author of the most famous sermon in American history, "Sinners in the Hands of an Angry God," although among scholars he is also recognized as undoubtedly the greatest theologian and philosopher America has yet produced. I found my way to him largely through the writings of John Piper.

George MacDonald despised the theology of Jonathan Edwards. In fact, as far as I know, Edwards was the only writer whom MacDonald censured by name in print:

> I desire to wake no dispute, will myself dispute with no man, but for the sake of those whom certain believers trouble, I have spoken my mind. I love the one God seen in the face of Jesus Christ. From all copies of Jonathan Edwards's portrait of God, however faded by time, however softened by the use of less glaring pigments, I turn with loathing. Not such a God is He concerning whom was the message John heard from Jesus, that He is light, and in Him is no darkness at all.[1]

Since Edwards died sixty-eight years before MacDonald was born, we have no rebuttal from his pen. But it is clear from the overall tenor of Edwards's writings, as well as from the many places where he directly refutes opinions that would later be espoused by MacDonald, that Edwards would have been no more appreciative of MacDonald's ideas than MacDonald was of his.

How Can We Understand God?

My struggle to come to grips with the justice of God can be described as a long and difficult journey from George MacDonald to Jonathan Edwards. MacDonald introduced me to a God whose ways with human beings were understandable and reasonable. MacDonald's theological method was simple: He took any attitude or action that might be attributed to God and asked whether it seemed compatible with God's self-revelation in Jesus or with the image of a heavenly Father. Would a good and loving father ever condemn his children to endless punishment? Of course not! Well then, neither would God. God might well punish people, but only out of love and in order to bring them to repentance; His sole concern would always be to draw His creatures out of their sins and into His embrace.

Again, would a good father ever punish one child for the guilt of another, meanwhile letting the second go free? Heaven forbid! Well then, the traditional understanding of the Atonement must be mistaken, for it portrays God as transferring the guilt of sinners to the sinless Son of God and punishing Him for what He had not done. MacDonald's way of constantly measuring traditional ideas against what he understood to be God's revelation of Himself in Jesus and in ordinary human behavior impressed me, and for several months I found myself a wholehearted follower of his method and of his theology.

Soon, however, I ran into difficulty. As much as I liked MacDonald's view of God, I couldn't see that it really squared well with Scripture. MacDonald himself seemed to have been convinced that he was interpreting the Bible correctly, but I increasingly found points of conflict. I wanted him to be right. Indeed, I wanted it so badly that for a while I preferred his sermons to the Bible. And I vastly preferred them to such a book as J. I. Packer's *Knowing God,* which I read for the first time at about this point. MacDonald's God was easy to understand; one had only to reason from human fatherhood or from the behavior of Jesus in the Gospels to know what He would or would not do. Packer's God was complex; to know Him one had to approach Him from all different angles, looking at His attributes one at a time and accepting a considerable amount of apparent contradiction among them.

The Priority of Scripture

The problem—the irritating problem—was that Packer's view seemed more biblical. And, in the end, I knew that I could build a Christian life only on the Scriptures of the Old and New Testaments.

As attractive as MacDonald's ideas were, if they didn't match the teaching of the Bible, they would have to go.

After much turmoil and with a great sense of loss, I laid aside my copy of his sermons and turned back to the Bible and the hard work of making sense of God's justice in its pages.

In that task many writers were of help to me, but none so much as Jonathan Edwards. Edwards's work, like that of MacDonald or of any other thinker or writer, must itself be judged against the Bible. Edwards was certainly not infallible. But what came to impress me about him was the clarity of thought he brought to the problem of divine justice and his boldness in following the teaching of Scripture even when it led far from common human understanding.

That is why Edwards represents the other end of the spectrum from MacDonald: not because their theology differs on every point (indeed, it does not), but because their approaches to God are diametrically opposed.

Although he would deny it, MacDonald sought to accommodate the justice of God to the sentiments of man. He was confident that he knew what a good God *ought* to do, and he was not greatly disturbed by the existence of biblical passages that contradicted his theories. Confronting such passages, his usual response was to insist that whatever they might mean, they obviously could not mean what they appeared to mean! Edwards's approach was quite different. He recognized that man's sense of justice has not been completely destroyed by the Fall and is therefore in some measure a guide to the ways of God, but Edwards sought always to subordinate human reasoning and feeling to the teaching of Scripture. MacDonald told me to trust my instincts about God; Edwards told me to distrust those instincts and cast myself on the Bible.

Because the tension between the theological positions of MacDonald and Edwards was so important in my own efforts to think through the justice of God, I have quoted both of them fairly liberally, especially in parts 1 and 3. Their words remain powerful proclamations of two vital positions today, so much so that beginning with chapter 2 I will speak of them in the historical present tense. I quote MacDonald because he has stated powerfully and memorably the positions I found I needed to reject, and I quote Edwards because he gave me the keys I needed to make sense of the Bible. Yet I do not assume that the reader has any prior knowledge of these writers, and I am not primarily interested in the contrast between them. My concern is with the teaching of Scripture; I bring MacDonald, Edwards, and other writers into the discussion purely as a means to the goal of elucidating the Bible's own presentation of divine justice and mercy.

I like to think that in heaven, at some point since the death of George MacDonald in 1905, MacDonald and Edwards have met one another and made peace. I envision MacDonald humbly asking Edwards's forgiveness for maligning him. I also envision MacDonald admitting that Edwards's theology was sounder than his own, and Edwards expressing appreciation for MacDonald's superior imaginative powers. I see the two men embracing and joyously moving further in and higher up into the beatific vision. In heaven there are no more rancorous theological disputes. But that is heaven.

Here in this world we continue to struggle to know the truth and to discard falsehood. And the stakes are high. Is there an eternal hell? Can a good God really send people there and *leave* them there? Doesn't He have the power and the goodness to save all people? If so, *then why doesn't He do it?* These are the concerns of this book. My answers are not new. The path I have traveled is old and well worn. But it is a path that each new generation of Christians must walk, and so I have tried to leave a few marks along the way to help those who may be just a few steps behind.

REVIVAL AND THE HOLINESS OF GOD

I have already said that I am writing to help people who, like myself, find the biblical presentation of divine justice difficult to understand or accept. I must now add another purpose for this book. We evangelicals—and especially we evangelical pastors—yearn for revival. We have read of times when the church has been powerful, when conversions have occurred in the thousands and all of society has been transformed by the power of the gospel, and we want to see the same thing happen in our own day. And so we have, quite properly, focused much attention on calls to fasting and prayer.

Looking for the Key

In addition, though, many of us have also entered into a frustrating and fruitless quest for the "key" to revival. We have attended conferences and learned to market our churches. We have imitated the cell-church movement. We have spoken in tongues, listened to self-proclaimed prophets, and pursued signs and wonders. We have changed our worship styles to cater to our culture's impatience with doctrine and its desire for immediate emotional gratification. We have studied the art of communication and learned to craft sermons that provide well-balanced doses of humor, insight, and comfort. We have incorporated drama and multimedia presentations into our worship, taking at face value the claim that only by doing so can we minister effectively to modern, visually oriented, television-conditioned church attendees.

But it seems to me that there is one thing we have not generally done, and it is the most crucial thing of all. We have not, by and large, exerted great effort to make sure that the message we are preaching is really the gospel. We are good marketers and good moralists, but too often we are shallow theologians. We are fearful of preaching the doctrines that offend, in part because we don't wish to drive people away and in part because we have never felt the power of those doctrines ourselves.

God, as David Wells has argued, seems "weightless" in the modern world and even in the modern evangelical church.[2] His hatred of sin does not pierce us. His wrath does not terrify us. His sovereignty does not humble us. And so, instead of presenting His truth in all of its shocking angularity, we massage the gospel to smooth its way in our world. Instead of giving people strong doctrine, powerfully presented and closely applied, we give them tips for successful living. Instead of confronting them with the hard fact that they are headed for perdition, we flatter them that they are very fine people who lack only faith to make their lives full. And yet, in spite of this failure to understand and proclaim the gospel, we continue to hope that somehow, by means of some new insight or book or technique, we will "release" God's power for revival.

The truth is that there is no key to revival. Charles Finney and all who have followed him have been utterly mistaken: Revival is not something we create or even something we "pray down"; it is a sovereign work of God, given in His timing and for His purposes and glory. We are more likely to produce rain by dancing than to produce revival by the use of our methods and techniques. If we really desire revival, we must turn to God. And that means both that we must pray to Him earnestly and humbly, recognizing that there is no power in our prayers but only in the God to whom we pray, and that we must be certain that it is the gospel we believe and the gospel we preach.

Sin . . . and Grace

When God has given revival in the past, it has generally been preceded and attended with preaching that sounded the depths of human sin and divine grace. During the First Great Awakening, Jonathan Edwards discovered that it was his sermons on the sovereignty and righteous wrath of God that seemed to do most to promote God's work among his hearers. Decades later, in the Second Great Awakening, that same truth was rediscovered by a new generation of preachers.[3] We may be sure that if God chooses to send revival today, it will be both accompanied and encouraged by a greatly deepened awareness of His implacable hatred of sin and His astounding, free love for sinners. These emphases stand in complete contradiction not only to the spirit of liberal Christianity but also to most of what passes for evangelicalism, in which the love of God is often so sentimentalized as to be utterly devalued. Yet without these emphases, the gospel is not rightly known.

The grace that is truly amazing is a grace that first causes hearts to fear and then brings relief—not one that persuades them that there was never anything to be afraid of in the first place. The love of Christ as expressed in His death on the cross is a love that is inevitably misunderstood until it is seen against the backdrop of the crushing issues of sin, wrath, hell, and divine sovereignty.

My hope, then, is that this book can make some small contribution to the efforts of Christians to come to grips with the holiness of God, and to the efforts of their leaders to do the kind of preaching that has historically been found most conducive to the revival of the church, the awakening of the lost, and the promotion of the Christian missionary drive.

THE SCOPE AND ARGUMENT OF THE BOOK

This is not a book for professional theologians, who will surely feel that I cover too many topics and cover them too lightly. Instead, I am writing for the ordinary believer who wants to see how the Bible's teachings on divine justice and divine mercy may be brought together and harmonized. And so I make no apology for covering a lot of ground. That is the only way the job can be done! We can never be at peace about God's ways with us until we have thought about a range of matters: God's attitude toward our sin, His plan to punish the guilty forever, the relationship between His grace and our faith, the meaning of Christ's death, the change in our status that occurs when we believe, and God's original purposes in creation. At least, in my mind, these issues are so closely related that they simply must be viewed together. It is that conviction that explains the structure of the book.

Part 1 sets forth the truth that God regards us as guilty sinners and defends eternal punishment against the theories of universal salvation and annihilation of the lost. Part 2 takes up the topic of predestination. I first consider some alternatives to the Calvinistic view of election and then explain why that view is the one most consistent with the Bible. Part 3 then examines the meaning of the Cross in the light of our guilt and God's sovereignty. I argue that by His life and death Jesus fully satisfied the justice of God for His chosen people, so that those who believe are not only forgiven but also given a title to eternal joy.

The final chapter of the book attempts to draw all the threads of the discussion together by considering God's ultimate purposes in creating the universe and establishing this strange, wonderful drama of salvation.

A final word: The prayers at the ends of the chapters represent the cries and yearnings of my own heart as I have meditated on the topics discussed. I include them for just one purpose: to emphasize the truth that the study of theology—and especially the study of the vexing, soul-wrenching issues considered in this book—should never be undertaken without prayer. Unless the Holy Spirit enlightens us, we can never truly understand God's ways—no matter how much we may study. And unless our growth in the knowledge of God leads to a deepening of our love for Him and for other people, it is fruitless.

Regardless of whether you agree with my theology, I hope you will pray for greater light on the subjects discussed and for an ever-increasing hunger to know God and seek His kingdom.

Father, You have graciously brought me to a point in life where there is nothing so important to me as to know You. I wish to give myself to You wholly and without reservation, and I want to trust perfectly in Your perfect goodness. Give me courage to face hard questions about Your ways with Your creatures. Make me too tough-minded to settle for simplistic answers. Strengthen my powers of reasoning that I may make sense of Your self-revelation in Christ and in the Bible.

Grant, too, that as I grow in knowledge of You, I may also grow in knowledge of myself. Open my eyes to my pride and rebellion; deepen my repentance, my humility, my dependence on Your saving grace, my gratitude, and, above all, my love. In Jesus' name, amen.

NOTES

1. George MacDonald, *Creation in Christ*, ed. Rolland Hein (Wheaton, Ill.: Shaw, 1976), 81. MacDonald's protest is reminiscent of a similar comment attributed to the poet John Milton: "I may go to hell, but such a God [as that of the Calvinistic teaching] will never command my respect," as quoted by Karl Barth, *Church Dogmatics*, vol. 2, bk. 2, trans., ed. Geoffrey W. Bromiley et al., (Edinburgh: T & T Clark, 1957), 13.

2. David Wells, *God in the Wasteland* (Grand Rapids: Eerdmans, 1995), 88–115.

3. My favorite author on the theology of revival is Iain H. Murray. See especially his *Pentecost Today? The Biblical Basis for Understanding Revival* (Edinburgh: Banner of Truth, 1998).

PART ONE

Under His Judgment

They who are in a natural condition,
are in a dreadful condition.

+JONATHAN EDWARDS
"Natural Men in a Dreadful Condition"

If we take the testimony of Scripture seriously, and if we base
our doctrines on its teaching—as indeed we should—we are
compelled to believe in the eternal punishment of the lost.
To be sure, we shrink from this teaching with all that is within
us, and do not dare to try to visualize how this eternal
punishment might be experienced by someone we know.
But the Bible teaches it, and therefore we must accept it.

+ANTHONY HOEKEMA
The Bible and the Future

1

THE SOUL
THAT SINS,
IT SHALL DIE

I will punish the world for its evil, and the wicked for their iniq-uity; I will put an end to the pomp of the arrogant, and lay low the pompous pride of the ruthless.

+ISAIAH 13:11

WHEN HE WAS FIVE YEARS OLD, my son came to me one day with a tearful confession: "Daddy, do you remember a long, long time ago, when the VCR broke? Please forgive me, Daddy; I'm the one who put that piece of plastic inside. I'm so sorry."

I had known all along who was responsible for the problem with the video cassette recorder, yet my son's confession brought me a great deal of joy. It was gratifying to see him owning up to his action and confessing that he had done wrong. I took him up into my lap, thanked him for being honest with me, and reassured him of my love and forgiveness. It never occurred to me to punish him for his action; it was more than sufficient that he had come clean.

It is tempting to extrapolate from this sort of everyday parental experience and develop a theology in which God's only concern with our sin is with the harm it does to us or to our relationship with Him.

Isn't He, after all, a God of love? And doesn't He present Himself to us as a loving Father who, though He may at times chastise His children, does so only for their good?

In this view, God may well hate sin but always loves the sinner, and so His goal must always be to bring the sinner to repentance. If punishment can be of assistance in bringing about this repentance, then God in His love will punish. But He will punish only as long as is necessary to bring about the desired change. An everlasting punishment, or one with no reformative or preventive value, would be merely cruel and so cannot possibly be part of a loving God.

MacDonald on Divine Punishment

Destroying Sin

This is precisely the kind of theology George MacDonald preached. For him, God's justice was not His determination to punish sinners but to make them good: "Primarily, God is not bound to *punish* sin; He is bound to *destroy* sin. If He were not the Maker, He might not be bound to destroy sin—I do not know. But seeing He has created creatures who have sinned, and therefore sin has, by the creating act of God, come into the world, God is, in His own righteousness, bound to destroy sin."[1]

MacDonald was not saying that God is the author of human sin, but that because He is our Father He can never be satisfied with anything less than our complete restoration to holiness. The traditional understanding of hell—that it consists of the everlasting punishment of the impenitent—was in MacDonald's view ridiculous and pernicious:

> Take any of those wicked people in Dante's hell, and ask wherein is justice served by their punishment. Mind, I am not saying it is not right to punish them; I am saying that justice is not, never can be, satisfied by suffering—nay, cannot have any satisfaction in or from suffering. . . .
>
> Such justice as Dante's keeps wickedness alive in its most terrible forms. The life of God goes forth to inform, or at least give a home to victorious evil. Is He not defeated every time that one of those lost souls defies Him? God is triumphantly defeated, I say, throughout the

hell of His vengeance. Although against evil, it is but the vain and wasted cruelty of a tyrant.[2]

It seemed evident to MacDonald that if God could not bring His creatures to repentance, His only possible option would be to annihilate them. Yet MacDonald was equally certain that this would not be necessary, but that one way or another—even by a punishment that would last for eons—God would have His way and restore all people to Himself.

Trying to Understand the Heart of God

Before criticizing MacDonald's views, we need to admit that they are attractive. There is indeed, for many Christians, real difficulty in accepting certain parts of the orthodox explanation of the gospel. Does God really view all people as sinners and hold them responsible for their sins, regardless of the opportunities they have had to learn of His truth? Does His justice really demand that *payment* be made for sins, such that we must either pay the price ourselves or else have it paid by Christ? Is it actually possible that someone *can* pay for another's wrongs? And does it make sense to think that a loving God would requite those whose sins are not paid for by Christ with a punishment that has no end and no power to reform?

These are serious and difficult questions, and a theology like MacDonald's, which angrily brushes them aside as based on grievous misunderstandings of the heart and mind of God, has deep emotional appeal. I would like very much to think that God views all people as His children. I would like to believe that the only punishment any person will receive is that which is tailored to promote his or her repentance. I would like to believe that all finally will be saved. I find, however, that the Bible keeps getting in my way.

MORE THAN A FATHER

The Biblical Principle of Being God's Child

The fundamental problem with MacDonald's theology is his insistence that the analogy of fatherhood provides a sufficient basis for understanding God's relationship to human beings: "Men cannot, or will not, or dare not see that nothing but His being our Father gives Him any right over us—that nothing but that could give Him a perfect right."[3] Scripture does not back him up at this point. While God is acknowledged to be the creator of all (Isa. 45:12) and the judge of all (Gen. 18:25), the analogy of the parent-child relationship is almost always restricted in the Bible to God's relationship with Jesus, His relationship with Israel, and His relationship with the individual Christian believer.

It is when we trust in Jesus that we are given the right to become children of God (John 1:12) and to speak to Him as children to a Father (Matt. 6:9). To be able to call ourselves His children is not our privilege by nature but a sign of the immense love that God has lavished on those He has chosen (1 John 3:1).

To be sure, God could not become the Father of believers if He were not inherently of a loving and fatherly character. And the psalmist affirms that God is "kind in all his works" (Ps. 145:17). But to say that God treats all people as His children goes far beyond the actual assertions of the Bible and undermines Scripture's teaching about the special status and privileges of believers.[4]

Sinners Before a Judge

But if human beings, apart from faith in Christ, do not stand before God in the relationship of children before a Father, then what is our status? The core biblical answer is that we stand before Him as sinners before a judge. Despite MacDonald's angry assertions to the contrary, and despite our own natural distaste for this aspect of the Bible's teaching, most of the language used in Scripture to describe our natural standing before God, as well as most of the language used to explain what Christ has done for those who believe, is *legal* language, the language not of the family but of the courtroom. Human beings are viewed in the Bible as convicted criminals awaiting a punishment that is both just and severe. God is presented—He presents Himself—as a judge who will by no means leave the guilty unpunished (Ex. 34:7) and as One who pours out wrath (not just corrective chastisement) on evildoers. And His ultimate answer to our plight is to inflict on Jesus the punishment that we ought to have had:

But he was wounded for our transgressions; he was crushed for our iniq-
uities; upon him was the chastisement that brought us peace, and with his
stripes we are healed. All we like sheep have gone astray; we have turned
every one to his own way; and the Lord has laid on him the iniquity of
us all. (Isaiah 53:5–6, emphasis added)

We will return shortly to develop this thought. Much hangs on our
ability to see that God holds all people to be guilty of sin and deserving
of punishment, *regardless of whether that punishment leads to repentance.*
But first let us pause to note that while MacDonald's view of God is
based upon a biblical truth and has a certain logical consistency to
it, it can be maintained only by affirming that one truth at the expense
of other truths also taught in the Bible. [We are attracted to MacDonald's
theology in part because of this very fact: It seems so logical, so self-
consistent. But what if that logic is a faulty logic?] What if God is big-
ger than that logic? What if He is, in fact, not *only* a father, but a father
and more?

The truth, I believe, is that we can rightly understand God only
if we forswear the temptation to draw our own extended conclusions
from the analogies He gives us, and stick as close as possible to what
He has actually said. MacDonald's ideas, according to one of the re-
viewers quoted on the back cover of my copy of MacDonald's sermons
(*Creation in Christ*) have about them "a translucence, even a quality
of radiating light." I would have to add that they also have about them
a certain hubris. As we continue our inquiry into God's justice, we
do well to keep in mind that the person who is esteemed by God is
not the one who waxes eloquent as he develops one biblical idea to
the detriment of others, but the one who is humble and contrite in
spirit and who "trembles" at God's word (Isa. 66:2).

We may not always find it easy to reconcile the various truths of
the Bible. Nevertheless, we must humbly keep in check both our desire for logical consistency and our outrage at truths we do not like.
God will no doubt reward our search by giving us ever-greater insight into the relationships among the truths He has revealed about
Himself. We may be quite sure that all that God does is, in fact, logical and self-consistent. But we should not presume to reject that
which we have not had the patience or humility to accept on God's
own terms.

The Wages of Sin

We have said that apart from Christ, fallen human beings stand before God as convicted criminals deserving nothing more than punishment, and that God is not obligated to limit a sinner's punishment to that which will lead to his or her repentance. What is the biblical evidence for these assertions?

The evidence is overwhelming, so much so that it is hard to see how any serious student of the Bible could come to any other conclusion. It is plain, first of all, that all human beings are regarded as sinners: "All have sinned and fall short of the glory of God" (Rom. 3:23); "None is righteous, no, not one" (Rom. 3:10); "God made man upright, but they have sought out many schemes" (Eccl. 7:29).

The Bible's Statements of Our Liability

In addition, it is also plain that the commission of sin brings a just liability to punishment. This may be shown in several ways. First, there are explicit statements of the Scriptures. Consider these five:

The soul who sins shall die. (Ezekiel 18:4)

Then he will say to those on his left, "Depart from me, you cursed, into the eternal fire prepared for the devil and his angels." (Matthew 25:41)

Though they know God's decree that those who practice such things deserve to die. (Romans 1:32)

The wages of sin is death. (Romans 6:23)

. . . inflicting vengeance on those who do not know God and on those who do not obey the gospel of our Lord Jesus. (2 Thessalonians 1:8)

Such statements can be multiplied, but these are sufficient to make the point. What is promised to sinners, as sinners, is *punishment*. There is in none of these statements any hint that the purpose of that punishment is the reformation of the sinner. The plain implication of them all is that sinners will be punished because it is *just* for them to be punished.

Our Liability Implied in Calls for Discipline and Punishment

A second way of proving that Scripture views all human beings as guilty of sin and liable to punishment is by observing the language used to describe God's attitude toward sin and sinners. We learn in Hebrews 12:5–11 that God "chastises" or "disciplines" those whom He regards as His children. This terminology is quite consistent with the idea that God uses hardships or troubles to promote the spiritual growth of Christians. But consider for a moment passages such as these: "I will take vengeance on my adversaries and will repay those who hate me" (Deut. 32:41); "Vengeance is mine; I will repay, says the Lord" (Rom. 12:19); "But for those who are self-seeking and do not obey the truth, but obey unrighteousness, there will be wrath and fury" (Rom. 2:8); "For if we go on sinning deliberately after receiving the knowledge of the truth, there no longer remains a sacrifice for sins, but a fearful expectation of judgment, and a fury of fire that will consume the adversaries" (Heb. 10:26–27).

This is hardly the language of fatherly reproof. As Jonathan Edwards wrote in his response to views similar to those later championed by George MacDonald, "To say that vengeance, wrath, fury, indignation, fiery indignation, wrath without mixture, mean a mere wholesome, fatherly discipline, designed for the good only of the subjects, is to say that the inspired writers were grossly ignorant of the proper and common use of language."[5]

I think we must agree with Edwards. If God intended that we should understand from these passages that He punishes only to bring about repentance, one cannot help feeling that He expressed Himself very poorly. And if it should be argued that God threatens more than He actually delivers—that He uses the frightening terminology of *wrath*, *fury*, and *fire* only to move us to repentance but has in fact no intention of inflicting such punishment—then we must ask whether God really is so weak that He cannot get His way without making empty threats. No, the clear implication of these passages is that God fully intends to punish sinners, and there is nothing at all to suggest that the punishment is reformative in nature.

We may go further. The universal guilt and liability to punishment of human beings is implied in all that is said in Scripture about salvation. If we do not deserve punishment, then it should be possible

33

for us to be saved on the basis of justice rather than mercy. Indeed, we should not have to speak of being "saved" at all, since the idea of salvation implies that we are justly exposed to something bad. Because of our sins, we are subject to God's wrath (Eph. 2:3; Rom. 5:9). Because of our inability to keep God's Law, we stand under a curse (Gal. 3:10).

It is because we are guilty—because we have no right to expect anything from God but punishment—that we speak of redemption through Christ as a work of mercy and grace.

Punishment and Repentance

But perhaps we may introduce an objection at this point: Even if we concede that all human beings deserve punishment from God, can't we still hold to the idea that the punishment they deserve is nothing more nor less than that which God, in His divine wisdom, knows will bring them to repentance? In other words, perhaps we may retain our conception of God as always working for the restoration of people, even while we admit the justice of divine wrath. Could we not even agree with MacDonald that it is *because* the punishment is intended for the sinner's good that it may be called just?

I do not believe we can. Note first that this whole line of reasoning, which sees divine punishment as intended for the sinner's good, is foreign to the passages we have already considered. Nor does such reasoning address those passages that declare people who die impenitent are "thrown away," "lost," "destroyed," or that they "suffer the punishment of eternal destruction" (Matt. 13:48; Luke 9:25; John 17:12; Matt. 10:28; Heb. 10:39; 2 Peter 3:7; 2 Thess. 1:9). Although it comes naturally to us to hope that all divine punishment is disciplinary in nature, the Bible does not give us much encouragement in that direction.

Furthermore, the moment we assert that the punishment or curse threatened to the unrepentant is the very thing needed to bring the person to repentance and faith, we find ourselves in impossible logical difficulties; since this implies that Christ died to save sinners from the one thing (punishment) that can bring about their salvation. Indeed, it would not make sense to call a disciplinary punishment a "curse" at all; we should instead call it a blessing and say that Christ saves some people (who repent in this lifetime) by delivering them from the curse and saves all others by inflicting the curse on them! But there is, of course, nothing in the New Testament of any such double work of Christ; we are told only that He came to redeem "us" (believers) from the curse (Gal. 3:13).

The logical problems deepen. If we say that the *only* punishment that a sinner deserves is that which will bring him to repentance, then we must admit that after he has suffered that punishment and repented, he must be admitted to heaven on the basis of justice rather than of mercy. Any further punishment beyond that point would be unjust. Yet the Bible says nothing of a salvation that is earned or secured through suffering: It is by grace alone that anyone can be admitted to eternal joy. MacDonald's position is hopeless.

WHY DOES GOD PUNISH SIN?

I do not see any alternative but to believe that God punishes sin because sin deserves punishment. It is *just* for Him to punish sin, and because it is just, there is no need to add the element of reformation or discipline in order to make it just.

MacDonald writes, "Primarily, God is not bound to *punish* sin; He is bound to *destroy* sin." But where is the biblical proof of this assertion? MacDonald's problem is that he cannot see any good coming out of punishment that does not reform. Punishment cannot undo the sin or make atonement for the wrong done; if it also cannot effect a change in the one being punished, then a good God would respond by annihilating the sinner. To continue the punishment with no hope of its ever bringing about good would be pointless.

In part we must agree with MacDonald. If there really is *no* good to be derived from the punishment of the wicked, then it is hard to see how such punishment could ever be considered just. It does not follow, however, that the good that comes from the punishment of the wicked must be a good *to them*. What if God punishes the wicked (whose deeds deserve punishment) for the good that comes thereby to the universe as a whole? Suppose that through their punishment God displays His holiness and authority, and enhances the joy of the redeemed by drawing attention to the greatness of His mercy toward them.

This would seem to be the point of Romans 9:22–23: "What if

God, desiring to show his wrath and to make known his power, has endured with much patience vessels of wrath prepared for destruction, in order to make known the riches of his glory for vessels of mercy, which he has prepared beforehand for glory . . . ?" In this case, those being punished do not derive any good from their punishment, but the universe as a whole does.

Crime and Punishment

Perhaps we can clarify this idea by thinking for a moment about human justice. Some believe the state should not punish wrongdoers unless by so doing it can either bring about their reformation or protect the community from further injury. In most people, however, there is an ineradicable notion that underlying these two legitimate aims of punishment is a deeper and more basic one, namely, the fact that bad deeds *deserve* punishment. They believe that in inflicting punishment the state is making an important and necessary moral statement. Of course, our sense of justice can easily be corrupted by something lower, such as bloodthirstiness or a desire for revenge. But even so, when a criminal is punished and people express pleasure and say, "Justice has been served," they are generally saying more than that their personal feelings have been satisfied; they are saying that in some significant way the moral order and the authority of the state and the law have been upheld.

In the same way, God's punishment of the wicked can be said to "glorify" Him: It reveals His character, reinforces the sanctity of the moral law that has been broken, and counterbalances the damage done to His honor and majesty by the disobedience of His creatures. As such, the punishment of the wicked is good in and of itself, regardless of whether it results in their repentance and salvation.[6]

Punishment Delayed

For the biblical writers, and especially the psalmists, the real problem of God's justice is not why He punishes the wicked but why He is taking so long to do so! When the authors of the Psalms cry out for justice, they are crying for God to end His patient endurance of evil and wreak vengeance on His enemies:

How long, O God, is the foe to scoff?
Is the enemy to revile your name forever?
Why do you hold back your hand, your right hand?
Take it from the fold of your garment and destroy them! (Psalm 74:10–11)

We may well feel nervous about praying such prayers ourselves, knowing how easily we can confuse God's cause with our own and how readily we sin against the biblical command to love our enemies. The point, however, is that the idea that God cannot justly punish without simultaneously reforming is alien to the Bible, while the notion that wickedness deserves God's wrath is found all the way from Genesis to Revelation.

HOW DID WE GET INTO THIS MESS?

For three years in the early 1980s, I taught English at a university in Taiwan, and for a portion of that time I had the opportunity to teach the Bible to English majors. One of the most interesting and revealing moments in my first Bible class came while we were discussing the story of Adam and Eve. My students wanted to know why the first couple disobeyed God and ate the forbidden fruit. I could answer only that they really had no reason to do so; God had clearly warned them of the consequences of such a deed, and they had nothing to gain and everything to lose by sinning. Their action was completely without any possible justification.

My students, dissatisfied and approaching the problem from a background of Confucian morality, saw the matter quite differently: They insisted that the Fall must properly be blamed not on Adam and Eve but on God. If God had rightly educated His creatures, they reasoned, then the first couple never would have sinned; the fact that they did sin was proof that God had failed in His responsibility to His pupils.

This response to the Fall left me dumbfounded, yet as I thought about it later, I realized that it was not entirely unlike my attitude toward God's justice as a whole. Surely God could have prevented Adam and Eve from sinning, I thought. And if He could, shouldn't He have? Somehow it did not seem fair for Him to hold me responsible for my sin when I never had a choice about being born a sinner!

37

Was not God in some way responsible for making me what I am, I reasoned, and shouldn't He bear the guilt of the things I do wrong? It seems once we admit that we are sinners and that as sinners we deserve punishment, we begin to look for a way of shifting blame to God.

An Outcome of Our Evolution?

Of course, for many modern people (and the overwhelming majority of liberal theologians), the problem itself is not to be taken seriously. They assume that modern scientific knowledge of the origins of the human race has rendered obsolete the whole story of Adam, Eve, and the Fall; and they insist that we must instead understand human "fallenness" as reflecting our evolutionary heritage.[7] That is, we are selfish, dishonest, proud, ruthless, lustful, and murderous; not because our first ancestor disobeyed God, but because a whole chain of ancestors were helped by those traits to survive and reproduce.

Although we need not include here an extended discussion of the difficult scientific and theological issues raised by the question of the Fall, a couple of points may be in order. First, scientists know much less than many people seem to think they do about the origins of our race. The study of skeletal remains will never tell us whether their owners were fully human, created in the image of God as we are; nor will it reveal to us anything about their innocence or guilt before God. The naturalistic assumptions that underlie much scientific study of human origins may make the biblical account of an original innocence *seem* implausible, but it is most unlikely that paleontology can ever either prove or disprove its truth.[8] Those who have accepted the Bible's authority and trustworthiness[9] on other grounds have no reason to abandon its teaching at this point.

The Reality of the Fall

Second, the biblical account of a real, historical fall into sin is so intimately tied to the rest of the Christian faith that its abandonment is disastrous. If we can no longer believe Paul when he tells us that sin and death entered the human race through one man, then why should we believe him when he tells us that now God's grace overflows to the many through Christ, the second Adam (see Rom. 5:12–19)?

Even more seriously, if our present sinful state is not the result of the Fall but is simply the condition in which God made us, then our problems with His justice become truly intolerable. As hard as it may be to understand why He allowed the whole human race to incur guilt and fall into a sinful condition as a result of the sin of one man, it is harder still to see how He could justly *create* us as sinners and still hold us responsible for our own actions. It is no coincidence that theologians who abandon the idea of the Fall generally also move either to depersonalize God or to strip Him of His omnipotence, viewing Him as a power or process that is on the side of good but is limited in its ability to achieve good. This kind of theological shift results naturally from the realization that the fully personal and all-powerful God of the Bible simply cannot be conceived of as having created us in our present state of sin and suffering.

Adam's Fall and Our Fall

As problematic as we may feel it to be, the traditional understanding is the best. God created humankind good, and through the disobedience of the first man we tumbled into our present wretchedness. Theologians have debated at great length the manner in which we can be said to have fallen "in Adam," but the details of the debate are not important here.[10] However we may explain our relationship to Adam, the uncomfortable facts with which we must deal are the following.

First, *we are involved in Adam's punishment.* The punishment of Adam's disobedience was to be death, and death—both physical and spiritual, meaning separation from God—has been the lot of all human beings since. Even infants and babies in the womb, who cannot be thought to have yet committed any sins of their own, are subject to physical death.

It is not going too far to say that the entire human race thus participates in the punishment of Adam for his first act of disobedience to God. And we participate not only in his punishment but also in his guilt; according to Romans 5:12, when Adam sinned we all sinned. He represented all of us, and we are held accountable for his disobedience. We share the guilt of his sin.

Second, Adam's sin has resulted in the corruption of our nature, so that *we arrive in this world as sinners.* "Behold, I was brought forth in iniquity, and in sin did my mother conceive me" (Ps. 51:5). Unless God intervenes to counteract our natural tendency, we live our entire lives in a state of rebellion against God, thereby adding daily to our guilt before Him or, as Paul puts it, "storing up wrath" against ourselves for the day of judgment (Rom. 2:5). Because the natural human being does not know or love God or live for His glory, even our good acts—our "righteous deeds"—are like a filthy garment before Him (Isa. 64:6), and we increase in guilt even as we perform them.

At an experiential level, this does not create a great problem for most Christians. *We know* we are guilty before God; we feel in our hearts that it is right for God to disapprove of our deeds. The difficulty comes when we try to explain how it is that we came to be in this condition in the first place. Surely it is unfair that God brought all of us into this miserable state because of the sin of just one man! Why does God not give each human being the same chance at remaining righteous that He gave to Adam? Why did He so ordain it that you and I should come into the world incapable of pleasing Him by our behavior?

I confess that I have not found a fully satisfying answer to that question, nor do I expect to find it in this life. In the end I fall back on my confidence that "God is light, and in him is no darkness at all" (1 John 1:5). If an all-wise and perfectly benevolent Creator decided to let the future happiness of the human race hang on the behavior of our first ancestor, then we may be sure that this was the right thing to do, however much we may imagine that we could have come up with a better plan. It is, in any event, plain that our sins are indeed ours; we cannot hold God responsible for them, nor, when we are thinking straight, do we have any real desire to. We reproach ourselves for our sins and blame others for theirs. As mysterious as our existence as sinners may be to us, it is inextricably bound up with our humanness that we be treated like the morally responsible beings we are.[11]

Blaise Pascal expressed the matter well when he wrote:

> Without doubt nothing is more shocking to our reason than to say that the sin of the first man has implicated in its guilt men so far from the original sin that they seem incapable of sharing it. . . . Certainly

nothing jolts us more rudely than this doctrine, and yet, but for this mystery, the most incomprehensible of all, we remain incomprehensible to ourselves.[12]

Pascal is absolutely right: The doctrine of the Fall is a hard doctrine to accept, but without it we find it impossible to make moral and intellectual sense of the human condition.

Why Didn't God Stop Adam from Taking the Fruit?

The question of my Chinese students in Taiwan raises one more issue that must be considered briefly before we move on. Even if we grant God's wisdom in binding up the fortunes of the human race with the behavior of Adam, can't we still fault God for allowing Adam to sin? That is, given that God is all-powerful and all-knowing, couldn't He have created Adam and Eve in such a way that they would not fall? To press the issue still further, why, if God hoped they would remain righteous, did He subject them to temptation in the first place? Surely He could have created a garden devoid of forbidden fruit, and kept the serpent out of it!

The answer most commonly given to questions of this sort is that even an all-powerful Creator cannot create a genuinely free being unless He provides the being with the chance to misuse that freedom. If God had (1) given Adam and Eve no opportunity to sin, or (2) given them natures not susceptible to temptation, or (3) intervened the moment their wills started to move in the wrong direction, then He would effectively have undermined His own highest goal in their creation. That goal was the making of creatures who would give their love to Him by deliberate choice. The creation of man was a gamble that God lost.

I find this answer somewhat helpful but incomplete. Yes, it is certainly the case that the redeemed will love God more for having made a deliberate choice to do so. Also, as I will argue later in the book, a universe in which evil has been allowed temporary sway will in the long run be a richer universe than one that has never fallen. Still, the argument under consideration has great problems. It seems to imply that real freedom is incompatible with an inability to sin, which in turn suggests that even in heaven the saints will be capable of falling. However, all of the Christian tradition has denied that possibility; it is agreed that in heaven the redeemed will be "confirmed" in holiness—that is, they will be brought beyond even the possibility of sin. But if that is possible in heaven, then why was it not possible in the garden? How can it be that God is able to keep countless millions of redeemed human beings and unfallen angels in an eternally holy state in heaven without violating their freedom, but He was incapable of doing the same for Adam and Eve in Eden?[13]

There is another problem with saying that God was incapable of creating free beings who would freely and infallibly choose not to sin. Such a doctrine turns the entire story of the human race, including the Incarnation, death, and resurrection of Christ, into a sort of divine "Plan B," God's effort to bring some good out of a creation spinning out of His control. This is not compatible with the Bible's presentation of God as the One who works out all things in conformity with the purpose of His will (Eph. 1) and who makes known the end of all things before their beginning (Isa. 46:10). I do not believe the Bible permits us to say either that the Fall took God by surprise or that He lacked the power to prevent it.

God's Sovereignty over Evil

Indeed, I do not see how we can avoid the conclusion that the Fall was ordained by God to subserve the overall good of His creation. Of course there is difficulty in this view: It comes dangerously close to saying that God is the author of evil. But this is a problem—perhaps we should say a mystery—that runs throughout the Bible. Joseph's brothers sold him into slavery, but Joseph claimed they were just fulfilling God's purpose (Gen. 45:5–7). Pharaoh held the Israelites in bondage, but God hardened Pharaoh's heart (Ex. 9:12). The Assyrians and Babylonians treated God's people and His temple with disdain and cruelty, but the Bible says that God raised them up for that purpose and "whistle[d] for them from the ends of the earth" (Isa. 5:25–30; cf. 45:1–7). Judas, Caiaphas, Pilate, and the Roman soldiers betrayed, tortured, and crucified Jesus; yet they acted according to God's "definite plan and foreknowledge" and did only what His hand had "predestined to take place" (Acts 2:23; 4:28).

In other words, while God cannot sin, nor does He tempt people to sin (James 1:13), in some mysterious fashion He ordains our sins and uses them in the fulfillment of His great plan for the creation.[14] God certainly did not force or entice Adam and Eve to disobey Him. But He did determine to allow them to do so. As we shall see in chapter 9, His decision to do so appears to proceed from His desire to make the fullest possible manifestation of His merciful character toward His redeemed people.

IS GOD HARSH?

Thinking of God as Unjust and Harsh

Perhaps it will seem to some Christians that in speaking so much of human guilt before God I have merely belabored the obvious. There is a reason for doing so, however. We human beings have a tendency to give lip service to the truth that we deserve divine wrath and then immediately turn around and insist on our "rights" before God. It is unjust, we think, if God does not give all people an opportunity to hear of Christ. Further, it is unjust if He punishes unbelievers in hell.

It is unjust if He makes distinctions between people, giving to one person the ability to repent and believe while withholding it from another.

It is unjust, we suppose, if God allows us to suffer all manner of troubles and pains in this life.

Without a deep and heartfelt recognition of our ill desert before God, we also find parts of the Bible incomprehensibly harsh. How could God order the destruction of the Canaanites, including their babies and small children? How could He repay the grumbling of the Israelites in the desert with plague and the opening of the earth? Why should Ananias and Sapphira have died for the telling of a very small lie to the church?

The answer is that no human being is innocent before God, and, thus, no human being deserves His love and mercy. When this fact is finally grasped, one's entire outlook changes. It is no longer strange that God condemned the Canaanites; what is strange is that He allowed the people of Israel to live. It is not strange that we live in a world of suffering and difficulty; what surprises us is that God permits us to remain in His world at all.

Grace

43

The continued existence of sinful creatures like us is itself a sign of God's forbearance. If we deny our guilt before God and the fact that we genuinely deserve punishment from Him, then we will always be offended by His judgments. If we admit that we deserve nothing *but* punishment from Him, we will be amazed by His patience.

Does God Enjoy Punishing People?

But doesn't this still make God out to be very vindictive? I do not think so. The Bible does not present God as delighting in punishing the wicked; on the contrary, we are shown repeatedly that the heart of the Lord is mercy. God desires to be kind to people everywhere; in fact, He is at all times expressing that kindness in manifold ways, even to those who do not know Him. He makes the sun to shine and the rain to fall on the unjust as well as the just (Matt. 5:45); He is "kind in all his works" (Ps. 145:13, 17).

What is in question here, however, is not the character of God but the legal status of fallen humanity before God. And our status is that of criminals, who deserve nothing less than to be punished according to the full extent of the law. God is at liberty to show mercy. But His mercy can be truly understood only against the background of His justice. Until we see this, we will make no progress in our effort to make sense of His dealings with human beings.

Let us put it simply and clearly. According to the Bible, human beings do not deserve good from God; we deserve death and hell. And because that is what we deserve, God would be acting justly if He brought that penalty upon us. If God had not designed any way by which we could be forgiven and saved but had instead determined to deal with the entire human race according to the strictest justice, nobody would have any right to complain against Him. In the next chapter we must look deeply into the severity of God's justice, in order to understand the punishment that is threatened to and will, in fact, be inflicted on those who do not repent and believe.

JUSTICE AND WRATH

First, though, let us consider one more possible objection. Some might dispute the claim that the language applied by the Bible to the standing of fallen men and women before God is mostly *legal* language. Surely the Bible speaks far more personally when it describes God as "wrathful," bent on vengeance, or angry at the wicked all day long. And this may make us feel that the God of the Bible is less interested in justice than in avenging Himself on His personal enemies. This God seems temperamental, vindictive, and cruel. There are many who feel that the Bible is an archaic and frightening document that can no longer serve to teach modern people the meaning of justice.

Enemies of God's Law and of God Himself

The answer is found in recognizing that those who are the enemies of God are the enemies of His Law; and those who hate His Law are also those who hate God Himself. When the Bible speaks of human guilt and divine justice, it is viewing the matter from the perspective of God as the Lawgiver. When the Bible speaks of God's wrath, it is viewing the same problem—the human rejection of God's will—from the perspective of God as prosecutor or even as victim. In human law the lawgiver and the prosecutor are not generally the same person, nor is it normal for the lawgiver to be the person who has been harmed by a particular crime. But in the case of God, the Lawgiver, the prosecutor of the guilty, and the ultimate object of the sins of the guilty are all one and the same.

God personally determined the rules for human life. God personally is offended and dishonored when those rules are broken. God personally intends to vindicate His Law and His person by avenging Himself on those who have sinned.

In human legal systems, we would attempt at all costs to avoid such a confusion of roles, due to our human inability to be fair and objective about matters concerning our own dignity. If another person harms me, it is not at all wise for the court to allow me to try and convict that person on my own authority; I would be far too likely to act out of motives falling short of a true love of justice. God, however, is incapable of error or sin. If He is indignant toward human sin, it is because indignation—and the punishment to which it leads—is the appropriate and just response to that sin. God's Law, His response to violations of His Law, and His judicial treatment of those who violate His Law, are all in perfect accord with His own nature, a nature in which there is all light and no darkness, in which there exist both perfect knowledge and perfect justice.

In God, in other words, are combined the perfect legislator, the perfect prosecutor, and the perfect crime victim, which means that God's wrath and indignation will always be utterly just, because they will be in perfect proportion to the heinousness of sin.

Wrath That Rises from God's Trampled Law

Nevertheless, of the two concepts, wrath and justice, I suggest we do well to think of justice as the more primary. That is to say, God is angry because of the breaking of His Law.

Putting matters this way better prepares us to understand the cross of Christ. In the atoning death of Jesus we see God—who from one point of view may be said to be angry with sinners or even to hate them—acting decisively to save and forgive them. Their violations of His Law enrage Him, but behind that rage there is a love toward the people themselves. It would be a little strange to say that God simultaneously hates and loves people, but it is not strange at all to say that He loves people yet hates their lawbreaking.

The value of keeping justice as the more primary issue is that it puts the focus on the sinner's guilt rather than on God's anger toward the sinner.

Moreover, the Atonement is presented in the Bible primarily in legal terms. Look once more at Isaiah 53:5–6:

> But he was wounded for our transgressions; he was crushed for our iniquities; upon him was the chastisement that brought us peace, and with his stripes we are healed. All we like sheep have gone astray; we have turned every one to his own way; and the Lord has laid on him the iniquity of us all.

Or again, at Romans 3:25–26:

> God put forward [Christ Jesus] as a propitiation by his blood, to be received by faith. This was to show God's righteousness, because in his divine forbearance he had passed over former sins. It was to show his righteousness at the present time, so that he might be just and the justifier of the one who has faith in Jesus.

The emphasis in both of these passages is on Christ's death as a satisfaction of penal justice. Christ died for our sins. He died to vindicate divine justice. He died to take on Himself the punishment that justly belonged to us. We shall have more to say on this topic in chapter 7.

Father, You have shown me clearly that all human beings are guilty before You, and so You are obligated to none. If You save us, it is solely by Your mercy, and not because any demands of justice constrain You. Yet why is it that almost as often as I review these facts, I find my heart rising up in rebellion against them? Why do I still find it hard to be at peace with these truths that are so central to the Christian faith? Why does my heart continue to assert that You are at fault for allowing me to be born into a world of sin, incapable of not sinning, and then holding me accountable for my sin?

Please subdue my rebellious, prideful heart. Make me willing to accept the truth that my salvation is by grace alone and that You would have done no damage to Your upright and holy character had You chosen to leave me in my guilt. And grant that those who read this book may recognize Your goodness in sending Christ, who alone can make propitiation for their sins. May they run to Him for deliverance from their sins. In Jesus' name, amen.

NOTES

1. George MacDonald, *Creation in Christ,* ed. Rolland Hein (Wheaton, Ill.: Shaw, 1976), 69.

2. Ibid., 71.

3. Ibid., 80–81.

4. We are often told that it is Jesus who has taught us to view God as the Father of all human beings, but as D. A. Carson has pointed out, "The 'fatherhood of God' theme as applied to all human beings everywhere, so much a staple of classic liberal theology, is not supported by a single text from the canonical Gospels"; D. A. Carson, *The Gagging of God* (Grand Rapids: Zondervan, 1996), 302.

5. Jonathan Edwards, *The Salvation of All Men Strictly Examined; and the Endless Punishment of Those who Die Impenitent, Argued and Defended Against the Objections and Reasonings of the Late Rev. Doctor Chauncy, of Boston, in His Book Entitled "The Salvation of All Men," Etc.,* 2nd ed. (Boston: Ewer & Bedlington, 1824), 74.

6. In fact, unless a punishment is just in and of itself, its imposition solely for the purposes of either deterrence or reformation is an act of injustice. See C. S. Lewis, *The Problem of Pain* (New York: Macmillan, 1962), 94.

7. See, for example, John Hick, *Evil and the God of Love* (New York: Macmillan, 1966), chapter 8.

8. For a critical review of modern views of human prehistory, see Sigrid Hartwig-Scherer, "Apes or Ancestors? Interpretations of the Hominid Fossil Record Within Evolutionary & Basic Type Biology," in William A. Dembski, ed., *Mere Creation: Science, Faith & Intelligent Design* (Downers Grove, Ill.: Intervarsity, 1998), 212–35. A more thorough discussion of the reasons for holding to a biblical view of human origins can be found in R. C. Sproul, *Chosen By God* (Wheaton, Ill.: Tyndale, 1986), 79–84.

9. While a commitment to the Scriptures as the ultimate authority for knowledge of God is commonplace among evangelicals, in the current overall theological atmosphere it calls for some defense. I adhere to the understanding of Scripture's teaching about itself that was expressed so eloquently by B. B. Warfield in his *The Inspiration and Authority of the Bible*. It seems crystal clear that Jesus and His disciples believed and taught that the Bible is to be read as the written Word of God. We have no reason to trust any other doctrines taught by Christ and His apostles if we find ourselves unwilling to trust this one. Second, while an attempt to understand the backgrounds and literary prehistory of the biblical books is legitimate, much "higher criticism" has moved off into a realm of complete subjectivity, in which claims are made that cannot possibly be substantiated and in which the assertions of each generation of scholars are refuted by their own students. Finally, it seems plain to me that if the Bible is *not* inspired and authoritative, then we should be honest enough to admit that we have no sure knowledge of God whatsoever. All contemporary liberal theology denies this, but the complete fragmentation of the field of theology is proof that the assertion is true.

10. A good introduction to the topic is John Murray's *The Imputation of Adam's Sin* (Grand Rapids: Eerdmans, 1959). A less technical discussion can be found in Sproul, *Chosen By God,* 84–99.

11. As John Stott wrote, "Our responsibility before God is an inalienable aspect of our human dignity. Its final expression will be on the day of judgment. Nobody will be sentenced without trial. All people, great and small, irrespective of their social class, will stand before God's throne, not crushed or browbeaten, but given this final token of respect for human responsibility, as each gives an account of what he or she has done." John Stott, *The Cross of Christ* (Downers Grove, Ill: InterVarsity, 1986), 95–96.

12. Blaise Pascal, *Pensées* 1.7.31 (London: Penguin, 1995), 35–36.

13. In "Miscellaneous Remarks Concerning the Divine Decrees, Etc.," Jonathan Edwards wrote, "Objectors to the doctrine of election may say, God cannot always preserve men from sinning, unless he destroys their liberty. But will they deny that an omnipotent, an infinitely wise God, could possibly invent and set before men such strong motives to obedience, and keep them before them in such a manner, as should influence them to continue in their obedience, as the elect angels have done, without destroying their liberty? God will order it so that the saints and angels in heaven never will sin, and does it therefore follow that their liberty is destroyed, and that they are not free, but forced in their actions?" Jonathan Edwards, *The Works of Jonathan Edwards,* vol. 2, rev. Edward Hickman (1834; repr., Edinburgh: Banner of Truth, 1986), 541.

14. I do not think this truth has ever been better summarized than in the third chapter of the Westminster Confession: "God from all eternity, did, by the most wise and holy counsel of His own will, freely, and unchangeably ordain whatsoever comes to pass: yet so, as thereby neither is God the author of sin, nor is violence offered to the will of the creatures, nor is the liberty of contingency of second causes taken away, but rather established." *Westminster Confession of Faith* (Glasgow: Free Presbyterian, 1973), chap. 3, art. 1.

2

FOREVER
AND EVER

*It is a fearful thing
to fall into the hands of the living God.*

+HEBREWS 10:31

WHETHER YOU'RE FIVE OR FIFTY-FIVE, some medicine is hard to take. Pharmaceutical companies may sugarcoat it, dye it red, or give it a fruity flavor, but it doesn't matter. The medicine says we are sick, and we cannot deny it. The truth that fallen human beings deserve from God not blessing but punishment is itself a highly bitter pill to take, and many refuse to swallow it. But for those who are willing to accept this truth on the authority of Scripture and who are also willing to persevere in the effort to understand God's justice, the swallowing of bitter medicine has not ended but just begun.

Indeed, the next biblical teaching to be faced is the doctrine that the punishment God allots to the finally impenitent—that is, to those who do not in this life repent and trust in Christ—is both terrible in its intensity and everlasting in its duration.

The thought of eternal misery staggers the imagination. When we experience physical or emotional pain, five minutes can seem endless. A severe bout of nausea can make us wish to die. When we imagine men or women undergoing torture for their faith or their political views, we wonder how they can endure for more than a few hours. The idea that we might one day face pain that is literally endless—pain that after a million million years will be no closer to its termination than at its outset—is an idea that very nearly overloads the mind. And if we are people of even moderate compassion, it is no less troubling to us to think of others undergoing such suffering than to imagine facing it ourselves.

Perhaps the worst thought of all is that someone we love—a beloved grandparent, a brother or sister with whom we have grown up, a parent, spouse, child, or dear friend—might wind up in hell, or might be there already.

TRYING TO WRIGGLE FREE

Small wonder that Christians through the centuries have made every conceivable effort to wriggle free of the doctrine of eternal punishment. Small wonder that the doctrine continues to produce indignant denials on the part of many. Its acceptance requires a mighty act of humiliation, in which we put aside our penchant for telling God what is just and right and instead meekly learn about true justice from His Word.

But we are moving too fast. I assume that the reader, like me and like most Christians, desires to find an alternative to the traditional doctrine of hell. I furthermore believe that this desire is normal and reasonable. It is possible that if we were unfallen, we would immediately and intuitively perceive the justice of eternal punishment for sinners. In our present state, however, it is only to be expected that we will chafe under this doctrine until we have been shown clearly that it is true. How, we ask, can eternal punishment be consistent with the love and mercy of God? How can suffering that is infinite in duration ever be a just recompense for the finite number of sins committed by an individual in his or her lifetime? How can redeemed human beings—let alone God Himself—ever be truly and completely happy in heaven as long as there are others who remain in agony?

These are not unreasonable questions. They deserve thoughtful answers. Let us, then, explore the teaching of the Bible on the subject of hell. We will begin by looking at the alternatives to eternal punishment and showing why they are untenable (chapter 2) and conclude with the nature of such punishment (chapter 3).

THE PROSPECT OF UNIVERSAL SALVATION: UNIVERSALISM

We start with universalism, which is the belief that in the end, all human beings will be saved. Probably the earliest major exponent of universalism was the great Alexandrian theologian Origen, who lived in the third century A.D. According to Origen, the sufferings of hell are remedial in character and will result in the eventual salvation of all human beings and even all fallen angels: "For all wicked men, and for [demons], too, punishment has an end, and both wicked men and [demons] shall be restored to their former rank."[1] Origen's ideas seem to owe more to Platonic philosophy than to Scripture, however, and they were eventually declared heretical. Universalism did not play a major role in Christian thought until the nineteenth century, by which time the European Enlightenment had persuaded numbers of thinkers to place greater confidence in their own reason than in supernatural revelation.

In the twentieth century, universalism became the accepted position of the overwhelming majority of liberal theologians of all denominations, and the traditional belief in hell came to be viewed as outmoded and barbaric. Among Christians holding a high view of Scripture, universalism has never enjoyed great favor, but there have nevertheless been those who, like Origen and like George MacDonald, have attempted to reconcile belief in universal salvation with biblical faith.

How do universalists defend their beliefs? Jesus says that at the time He will send one group of people (the "sheep") into eternal life, He will also send another group (the "goats") into "eternal fire prepared for the devil and his angels" (Matt. 25:41). Paul writes that those who do not know God and do not obey the gospel "will suffer the punishment of eternal destruction, away from the presence of the Lord and from the glory of his might" (2 Thess. 1:9). How can such texts ever be reconciled with the hope that in the end all will be saved?

Universalism and the Authority of the Bible

For many universalists—probably the majority—the answer is that those texts *cannot* be reconciled with universalism; however, universalists conclude the texts themselves are wrong. Biblical passages that speak of eternal punishment do not represent the true Christian faith; they are holdovers from various ancient sub-Christian belief systems and are not to be treated as authoritative.[2]

Such a cavalier attitude toward Scripture may be shocking to evangelical Christians, but it is the rule rather than the exception in many theological circles. We are assured that human reason suffices to tell us that punishment that is everlasting and has no reformative value is simply cruel. If the Bible takes another view of the matter, well, so much the worse for the Bible.

For many theologians, universalism is nothing less than a necessary deduction from the love of God. If God is love, then it must be the case that He will, by hook or by crook, see to it that all are saved. Damnation is ruled out by the very concept of divine goodness. We may safely ignore biblical passages that appear to teach it.[3]

The fundamental error in this variety of universalism (apart from its fatal unwillingness to accord the Bible its proper authority) is that it does not take into account the issues we discussed in the first chapter. The great problem created by the clash between God's holiness and man's sin—a problem that comprises, far and away, the single greatest concern of the entire Bible—is peremptorily swept away; the assumption is made and never questioned that God is adequately and fully represented by the symbol of a human parent and is never to be understood as lawgiver or judge. In this way, punitive justice is removed from the picture altogether.

To those who think this way, the truth of their reasoning seems self-evident. God is loving; therefore, He will not punish at all or will punish only to reform.

Yet this is not self-evident. Why should we assume that the Creator is as nonchalant about our sins as we are? On what basis do we establish our belief that He has no interest in requiting sin with strict, punitive justice? How, other than through sheer arrogance, do we conclude that our ideas of God's love are more refined than those of Moses, Isaiah, Jesus, and Paul?

The only honest response is that this form of universalism—and, indeed, this entire approach to the study of God—is based entirely upon self-centered arrogance. It is in fact simple idolatry, because it amounts to a decision not to submit our minds and hearts to the true God but rather to create a god in our own image. Theologians who eliminate significant doctrines of Scripture because they do not fit their preconceived notions of God are always operating subjectively, and we may safely, though sadly, say of them, as Jesus said of the Pharisees: "Let them alone; they are blind guides"(Matt. 15:14).[4]

Biblical Universalism?

Yet there are others—and George MacDonald is a good representative of them—who try to reconcile universalism with a high view of the Bible's authority. How do they do this? Generally, by accepting the Bible's descriptions of hell as a place of torment but insisting that no person's stay there will be eternal. God will punish the wicked, yes, but He will do so to the end that they may see the error of their ways and repent. And because God is both all-wise and all-powerful, He will surely be able to give to each sinner the right mixture of punishment and gentle invitation to effect that person's repentance.

It is precisely this combination of a serious belief in hell with a hope in universal salvation that initially made the writings of George MacDonald so attractive to me. MacDonald sees hell as a place of very real suffering, a place where God "will hold his children in the consuming fire of His distance until they pay the last penny, until they drop the purse of selfishness with all the dross that is in it, and rush home to the Father and the Son. . . . I believe that no hell will be lacking which would help the just mercy of God to redeem His children"; MacDonald is confident that God's aim to redeem cannot ultimately fail: "Not the power of sin itself can close all the channels between creating and created."[5]

This is a stirring vision, a vision of a God whose sole desire is to win the hearts of all of His erring creatures and whose wisdom and power virtually guarantee His ultimate success. For me as a young Christian, MacDonald's writings were enormously appealing because they seemed to show a way to believe in universal salvation without abandoning the teaching of the Bible.

In the end, though, I concluded that MacDonald's views were, in fact, profoundly unbiblical and wrong, and I believe the same must be said of all universalism. Universalism begins with a false logic, and on the basis of that false logic it badly misreads the Bible. Both the bad logic and the bad biblical interpretation must be exposed and clearly understood for what they are.

THE LOGICAL PROBLEMS OF UNIVERSALISM

Fallacy 1: God Uses Judgment Only to Bring Repentance

The logical difficulty lies, first of all, in the assumption that a good God would never inflict punishment that had no hope of effecting the sinner's repentance. As we saw in the previous chapter, this assumption is at odds with both Scripture and our common-sense understanding of justice. The reality is that God punishes sinners because their sins deserve punishment, and the addition of the goal of reformation is not needed to make the punishment just. In relation to the fallen human race as a whole, God stands not as a Father but as a judge, and He is quite prepared to vindicate the dignity of His Law by inflicting punishment on those who have broken it. This does not make God cruel or vindictive; it makes Him just.

Fallacy 2: God Must Plead and Chastise for Repentance

A second fallacy, which we will investigate more fully in part 2, is the assumption that God desires to save every individual human being but is so hindered by His respect for the freedom of the human will that He can only plead and chastise in His effort to effect repentance. According to this logic, for man to be truly free, God must relinquish His own freedom of action; where human liberty begins, God's liberty must end. Consequently, in order to produce children who will love Him freely, God has voluntarily limited His power to change the human heart. In this life He hounds the human soul in an unceasing effort to persuade it to repent, and if that pursuit has not succeeded by the time the person dies, it is simply carried forward into hell.

At this point the universalist confronts a serious problem. If human freedom really does limit divine freedom, then it would seem impossible to state with confidence that all souls will be saved. No matter how great the inducements God may present to the individual soul, that soul always retains the power to say no. This is the reason C. S. Lewis, for all his admiration for George MacDonald, did not adopt MacDonald's universalism. As Lewis puts it in *The Problem of Pain*, "The Divine labour to redeem the world cannot be certain of succeeding as regards every individual soul. Some will not be redeemed." Or again,

> I would pay any price to be able to say truthfully "All will be saved." But my reason retorts, "Without their will, or with it?" If I say "Without their will" I at once perceive a contradiction; how can the supreme voluntary act of self-surrender be involuntary? If I say "With their will," my reason replies, "How if they *will not* give in?"[6]

I believe that Lewis has set up a false choice. It is, I suggest, untrue to Scripture to suggest that God's will and ours are related in such a way that God's concern for our freedom winds up tying His hands. I will attempt later to show why this is the case. For the time being, however, it is sufficient to say that Lewis, MacDonald, and most universalists share the assumption that God cannot directly change the human will without violating it, and that He is therefore limited by the freedom with which He has endowed His creatures. And this means that even if He has infinite time in hell in which to harass, chastise, and cajole sinful human beings, no one can ever be confident that all will finally yield to Him and accept salvation.

Universalists like MacDonald want to have it all. They insist on the sovereign freedom of the human will, but they also insist that ultimately every human being will submit to God. Their hope is that since God has unlimited time and unlimited wisdom, surely He will find a way to convince every soul to repent. We may well sympathize with such a hope, but we must insist that it can never be more than a hope. Logically speaking, confidence in universal salvation is canceled by the assertion that to be human is to have the power to reject God's grace.

The Scriptural Teaching of Condemnation and Destruction

The greater difficulty with universalism, however, lies in its mistreatment of the Bible. The biblical texts that deal with hell simply do not permit a universalist interpretation. According to Scripture, the impenitent will be destroyed (Matt. 7:13; Rom. 9:22; Phil. 3:18–19; 1 Thess. 5:3; 2 Peter 2:3), condemned (Matt. 23:33; John 5:29), thrown into the fiery furnace (Matt. 13:42), cast into the lake of fire (Rev. 20:14; 21:8), consumed (Isa. 33:14; Heb. 10:26–27), devoured (Rev. 20:9), and consigned to outer darkness (Matt. 8:12; 22:13; 25:30; Jude 13).

None of these terms suggests or even allows the interpretation that God's design in hell is the reformation of the sinner. Their clear implication is that the separation between the redeemed and the condemned is a final one. This same truth is implied in Jesus' story of Lazarus and the rich man, where we learn that traffic between hell and heaven is not permitted (Luke 16:26).[7] It is also taught in the many texts in which punishment and mercy are contrasted with one another. "O Lord God Almighty, the God of Israel, rouse yourself to punish all the nations; show no mercy to wicked traitors" (Ps. 59:5 NIV). If punishment were for the purpose of reformation, then it would be an expression of mercy. But that would mean that punishment and mercy could never be placed in opposition to one another as they are in this passage.

The Biblical Arguments for Universalism

The Response by MacDonald: Matthew 5:26

Despite these passages, some universalists look at certain, limited passages to suggest the condemned may eventually be released from judgment. MacDonald builds his confidence in the reformatory power of hell on a single verse, Jesus' statement in Matthew 5:26 that the one who fails to settle his debts with his adversary may be thrown into prison, there to remain until he has "paid the last penny." From this verse MacDonald draws the conclusion that those who are thrown into hell will stay there until they have fully repented of their sins.[8]

Unfortunately for this interpretation, it is far from certain that hell is in view at all in this passage, and it is quite certain that the nature of hell is not Jesus' topic. As New Testament scholar D. A. Carson has written of the verse, "It would be making the metaphor run on all fours to deduce that Jesus is teaching that the heavenly court will condemn guilty people to 'prison' (hell?) only until they've paid their debts."[9] Instead, Jesus is concerned to teach His hearers that they must not postpone acts of personal reconciliation, lest by delaying they anger their adversaries still further.

It is true that in the broader context of Matthew 5:22–26 Jesus is raising the issue of the ultimate spiritual consequences of unresolved anger, but it is not at all clear that the "prison" of verse 25 is to be taken as representing hell. And if indeed the prison does represent hell, it remains highly doubtful whether it is possible for a person in hell ever to pay the debt he owes to God. In fact, Edwards is able to use the same verse as the basis of an argument for everlasting punishment![10] It is perverse for MacDonald to build his entire doctrine of hell on a verse that is not primarily intended to teach on the topic while ignoring innumerable verses that do teach about hell and contradict his doctrine.

The Response by Pannenberg: 1 Corinthians 3:12–15

More recently, the influential German theologian Wolfhart Pannenberg has fallen into the same error as MacDonald, constructing a theory of hell on a single passage of Scripture. In Pannenberg's case, the passage is 1 Corinthians 3:12–15, in which Paul wrote that on the day of Christ the works of believers will be tested by fire. The person who has built upon the foundation of Jesus Christ with precious materials will receive rewards, while the one who has built with wood, hay, and straw will be saved, but only "as one escaping through the flames" (v. 15 NIV). It seems clear that Paul was describing only believers (those who build on the foundation of Jesus Christ), and that his topic was eternal rewards. We are saved solely by grace received through faith, but the quality of our experience in eternity will depend upon the quality of our service to God here and now. Yet Pannenberg manages to find in this text a full-blown doctrine of purgatory.

Pannenberg sees the fire of 1 Corinthians 3:13 as referring to purification, and he then concludes that this must be the meaning of

allegorizing

59

the image whenever the New Testament speaks of fire in relation to judgment. And since the fire of judgment is intended only to purify, final damnation is no more than a theoretical possibility for the very few:

> In view of the plain NT statements on the matter we certainly cannot rule out the possibility of the eternal damnation of some. In certain cases nothing may remain when the fire of the divine glory has purged away all that is incompatible with God's presence. But this possibility is not a constitutive part of the thought of divine judgment in terms of the purifying fire of 1 Cor. 3:10–15. It is rather a borderline case, and one against which Christians, as Paul tells us, are protected by their fellowship of faith with Jesus Christ, and against which also all those of other peoples and cultures are protected who are unwittingly close to the kingdom of God in terms of the Beatitudes of Jesus or the parable of the sheep and the goats (Matt. 25:31–46).[11]

Pannenberg is an extraordinarily gifted scholar, but his recklessness here is breathtaking. The passage in 1 Corinthians 3 does not contain a doctrine of purgatory; it is concerned only with the doctrine of heavenly rewards for believers. The Beatitudes describe the kind of character Jesus expects of His disciples; they say nothing about the spiritual status of the non-Christian. And as for the parable of the sheep and the goats, there is nothing in the context of Matthew 25 to suggest that the parable envisions the salvation of persons who have not heard of Christ. The most reasonable interpretation of the passage is that the "sheep" are those who have shown their love for Christ by ministering to others. The parable is intended to teach that faith without works is dead, not that works make faith unnecessary.

Most important, it is utterly inappropriate to subordinate the many passages that deal explicitly with hell to a single text that has an altogether different purpose. As much as I would love to believe that all (or virtually all) will be saved, I find it extremely unsettling that it seems possible to maintain the universalist position only by drawing illegitimate inferences from passages that don't speak of hell while simultaneously ignoring the numerous passages that do.

The Cosmic Work of Christ: Romans 5:18; 11:32, Etc.

Yet another approach to finding a biblical basis for universalism builds on passages that describe the work of Christ in universal or cosmic terms. If one is willing to ignore both the immediate contexts of the passages themselves and the larger context of Scripture as a whole, it is quite easy to press these passages into the service of one's universalist assumptions. One such passage is Romans 5:18, which reads, "Therefore, as one trespass led to condemnation for all men, so one act of righteousness leads to justification and life for all men." If the first half of the sentence is to be taken literally, say the universalists, then so should the second half; that is, if it is literally true that Adam's sin plunged the entire human race into condemnation, then on the basis of Paul's statement it must also be true that Christ's obedience literally brings salvation to the entire human race.

This is an illegitimate conclusion. In the first place, Paul elsewhere (for example, 2 Thess. 1:8–9) explicitly teaches that not all will be saved. In the second place, the meaning of Paul's statement is that just as all who are fallen are fallen because of their union with Adam, so also all who are justified are justified because of their union with Christ. Human fallenness results from the sin of Adam; human salvation results from the obedience of Christ. It would be untrue to the argument of the first five chapters of Romans, which have taught that the whole world stands under condemnation and that only those who turn to Christ in faith are reconciled to God, to have Paul suddenly asserting universal salvation.[12]

It is similarly mistaken to draw universalistic implications from Romans 11:32: "For God has consigned all to disobedience, that he may have mercy on all." Again we face the insuperable problem that to read the verse as indicating universal salvation is to make Paul inconsistent with his own teaching elsewhere. Furthermore, the context of Romans 9–11 strongly implies that Paul's meaning is that God's mercy is not limited by the distinction between Jew and Gentile. God has bound all persons over to disobedience in order that He may have mercy on all who, regardless of their racial origin, place their faith in Christ.

The same problems arise when we consider other texts often cited by universalists: Colossians 1:19–20; John 10:16; John 12:32; and

1 John 2:2. It is certainly true that these verses teach that the work of Christ has universal implications and will result in the salvation of men and women of all nations. It is also true that Colossians 1:19–20 teaches that it is on the basis of Christ's death that God will bring the universe under the rule of Christ. But it is not evident from these passages that each and every individual will be saved; and in view of the New Testament's repeated insistence that hell is a real place that will have real inhabitants, it is perverse to make these passages teach universal salvation. The same gospel of John in which Jesus promised to "draw all people" to Himself (12:32) also contains His declaration that those who do not believe in Christ stand "condemned already" because they have not believed in His name (3:18). In that gospel Jesus added that such people, far from being saved, will "die in [their] sins" (8:24).

We must say it again: A doctrine that can be maintained only by silencing the many passages that speak of the impenitent as being destroyed, consumed, cast into hell, consigned to darkness, or thrown into the lake of fire can never claim the wholehearted allegiance of biblically oriented Christians.

A FINAL ARGUMENT FOR UNIVERSALISM

But Can't We at Least Hope?

Still one more variety of universalism must be considered. The Roman Catholic theologian Hans Urs von Balthasar has argued that while we may not dogmatically insist that all will be saved, we are nevertheless entitled to *hope* that salvation will be universal.[13] How can this be?

Von Balthasar says that in view of the biblical statement that God "desires all people to be saved" (1 Tim. 2:4), the New Testament prophecies of final judgment should be understood as threats that will be fulfilled if, and only if, there are those who do not finally turn from evil. Just as God promised to destroy Nineveh but then changed His mind when the city repented (Jonah 1:1–2; 3:10), so in the New Testament He threatens judgment against the wicked but always with the unspoken provision that if people repent, the condemnation will be averted. Thus while we can say with certainty that *if* anybody refuses ultimately to repent, he or she will be cast into hell, what we cannot say is whether there will be any such person.

I do not enjoy saying no to the hope of universal salvation. I will be overjoyed to learn, at the time of judgment, that von Balthasar and other universalists were right after all. But I confess that I do not find this argument remotely persuasive, for two reasons. First, von Balthasar's doctrine works only if we assume that God provides people with postmortem opportunities to hear the gospel and repent of their sins. We know very well that not all people repent in this life, so in order for it to be possible for all to be saved, God must provide further chances beyond death.

In assuming that this is the case, von Balthasar is following the lead of a vast number of theologians, including some who may be considered evangelical. And I would have to agree that there is no text of Scripture that clearly and unambiguously states that all hope ends with death. But I would also insist that within the canonical Scriptures there is not a single text that seems aimed at encouraging such a belief, while there are many passages that tell strongly against it. Hebrews 9:27 implies that what follows death is not further opportunity to repent, but judgment. The parable of Lazarus and the rich man (Luke 16), which could have provided Jesus with a wonderful opportunity to teach about postmortem evangelism, is instead told in such a way as to discourage such hope. The repeated refrain of the New Testament is that the final judgment will be based upon our deeds in this life, with no suggestion that either actions or decisions made beyond death will have any power to change our fate. Von Balthasar's "hope" that all will be saved is based upon an assumption that can by no means be established by Scripture.

Are God's Threats Conditional?

Second, and worse, while we must certainly grant (particularly on the basis of the book of Jonah and similar portions of Scripture) that God has a right to make threats that are conditional, and that He is under no obligation to make known to us the conditions under which the threatened judgment may be averted, to read all of the Bible's statements about the future of the impenitent in this way is forced and unnatural. Jesus says that at His return He will separate the nations into two groups, sending one group into eternal life and the other into eternal death (Matt. 25:31–46). Paul says that on the day of Christ the disobedient will be punished with everlasting destruction and excluded from the presence of the Lord (2 Thess. 1:8–9). Peter describes some people as "destined" for disobedience, and in Romans Paul speaks of them as "vessels of wrath prepared for destruction" (1 Peter 2:8; Rom. 9:22). I confess that it is very hard for me to doubt that Jesus, Paul, and Peter believed that some people will indeed be lost.

And these are not the only texts. Jesus said it would be better for Judas if he had never been born (Matt. 26:24); how can this statement be reconciled with Judas's eventual salvation? And what of the graphic depiction of judgment in Revelation 20:15, where those whose names are not written in the Book of Life are thrown into the lake of fire; can we really take this as a mere conditional threat? And what of the Lord's observation that the road that leads to destruction is broad and many enter by it (Matt. 7:13)?

One way to evaluate this question is to ask ourselves how God might have expressed Himself differently if He had wanted us to believe that there will, in fact, be some who are lost. What more could God possibly say—beyond what He has said already—to persuade von Balthasar that there is indeed a hell and that it is populated? I just can't see that we have any grounds for doubting that the texts that speak of the ultimate destruction of the lost are intended to teach us something real and certain about the eternal future.

In the end, what von Balthasar's proposal comes down to is this: If we make the (biblically unwarranted) assumption that God offers people the opportunity to repent beyond the grave, and if we add the further (arbitrary and unnatural) assumption that texts that appear to tell us something about the future in fact tell us only what the future *could* be, then we have a basis for believing that perhaps all people will be saved. This may satisfy von Balthasar, but it certainly does not satisfy me. Universalism, even in the attenuated form proposed by von Balthasar, requires us to take too many liberties with the Bible to be credible.

THE PROSPECT OF AN END TO ONE'S SOUL: ANNIHILATIONISM

If universalism is to be rejected, might it not still be possible to avoid the doctrine of everlasting punishment by postulating that the meaning of texts that speak of the wicked being destroyed, consumed, or cast into fire is that they will at some point simply cease to exist? Maybe we can argue that God annihilates those who refuse to repent, or even that in some way, through their rejection of truth and grace, they annihilate themselves. Or to put the matter just a little differently, perhaps we can say that immortality is conditional upon repentance and faith, and that those who refuse to believe will just pass into nonexistence, either immediately upon death or after a time of punishment. Perhaps in the end, all that will remain of the wicked is insentient smoke and ash.

Such a thought is a good deal less pleasing than the prospect of universal salvation, but at least it seems to respect man's right to refuse God. It also protects us from the horrifying thought that a portion of the human race will suffer never-ending, conscious torment. So it is not surprising that many writers have worked hard to make a biblical and rational case for annihilationism. Recent proponents of annihilationism include the evangelical scholars John Stott, John W. Wenham, and Clark Pinnock.

Moral Arguments for Annihilationism

How do annihilationists build their case? As with universalism, the starting point is often a moral consideration rather than a biblical one: Annihilationism is implied by the love of God, who surely would not keep an impenitent creature in existence for the sole purpose of torturing it. "If God be defeated," writes George MacDonald, "He must destroy, that is, He must withdraw life. How can He go on sending forth His life into irreclaimable souls, to keep sin alive in them throughout the ages of eternity?"[14] MacDonald is convinced that God *cannot* be defeated by His creatures. In the end, he says, all will repent and be saved. But other writers have taken seriously the possibility that God may be unable to save all people, and they have then followed the same logical path as MacDonald to the conclusion that those who are not saved must be destroyed. For them, the annihilation of the wicked is a straightforward deduction from the goodness of God.

But of course, this is an assertion without supporting evidence. That the endless punishment of the wicked could serve no good purpose is a claim repeatedly made by annihilationists but never proved by them. As we saw in chapter 1, God's purpose in punishing the wicked is not to reform them but to vindicate the dignity of His Law. That means that God does not consider their punishment a defeat but a victory, a triumphant expression of His holiness. Moreover, it seems to be the teaching of Scripture that the eternity of hell does not make the punishment of the lost cruel and unusual but merely just. Both Scripture and reason give us strong cause for doubting the logic that states that the only just way for God to deal with the impenitent is to destroy them.

A second moral argument for annihilationism is that the endless punishment of the wicked is incompatible with the happiness of the redeemed in heaven. As long as one soul is in agony, the law of love will prevent all other souls from experiencing fullness of joy. Even God Himself cannot be truly happy as long as any of His creatures are miserable. Therefore God must deal with the finally impenitent as a veterinarian deals with animals that cannot be healed, mercifully ending their existence. Only then, when all misery and sin have been done away with once and for all, will the inhabitants of heaven be able to freely rejoice.[15]

This is an argument with very deep emotional appeal. How indeed could I rejoice in my salvation if I knew that my parent, my child, or my friend remained in torment? Would not the continued torment of the lost in hell turn heaven itself into a place of grief and spiritual agony?

Well, maybe so and maybe not. The hard truth is that when the Bible portrays the response of the redeemed to the sufferings of the lost, it does not picture them as choked with sorrow. On the contrary, the impression given by Scripture is that the punishment of the wicked will be a source of joy and satisfaction to those who have been saved, both because it will heighten their gratitude for their own salvation and because it will represent God's triumph over human iniquity. Revelation 6:9–10 portrays the souls of the martyrs crying out for God to avenge their blood. In Revelation 19:1–3 the redeemed give God praise for doing just that—judging the great prostitute and avenging on her the blood of His servants. Revelation 14:9–11 is particularly interesting:

And another angel, a third, followed them, saying with a loud voice, "If anyone worships the beast and its image and receives a mark on his forehead or on his hand, he also will drink the wine of God's wrath, poured full strength into the cup of his anger, and he will be tormented with fire and sulfur in the presence of the holy angels and in the presence of the Lamb. And the smoke of their torment goes up forever and ever, and they have no rest, day or night, these worshipers of the beast and its image, and whoever receives the mark of its name." (emphasis added)

From these passages we may make three observations. First, it appears that the suffering of the wicked is never-ending: "And the smoke of their torment goes up forever and ever, and they have no rest, day or night." It is not clear that Revelation 14:11 can be reconciled with annihilationism. Second, the torment of those who have worshiped the Beast will take place in full view of the holy angels and the Lamb. Although the saints are not mentioned, we are told that the sight of the punishment of the wicked is not incompatible with Christ's joy or that of the angels. If that is so, then it would seem to follow that it is also not incompatible with the joy of Christ's people. Third, the impression given by all three passages is that the condemnation of the wicked will be a source of satisfaction, not sorrow, to the redeemed. The annihilationists' claim that God and His people cannot be happy while the wicked suffer their just punishment appeals to our sentiments, but it appears to be flatly contradicted by Scripture. It fails to take into account that the saints in glory rejoice in *all* of God's works, including those in which He displays His holy hatred of evil.

The "Destruction" of the Wicked

If the moral arguments are not sufficient to establish the annihilationist case, what about arguments based on Scripture? Here there are two main approaches. Both are initially plausible, but both finally fail to persuade. First, there is the argument from the terminology of destruction. Jesus speaks of a broad road that leads to "destruction," which He contrasts with a narrow road leading to "life" (Matt. 7:13–14). Paul says that those who disobey the gospel will be punished with "eternal destruction" (2 Thess. 1:9). John writes that God so loved the world that he gave his only Son, that whoever believes in him may not "perish."

67

In these texts and in several others (John 10:28; 17:12; Rom. 2:12; 9:22; Phil. 1:28; 3:19; 1 Thess. 5:3; Heb. 10:39; James 4:12; 2 Peter 3:7, 9) it seems at first glance that the punishment with which the wicked are threatened is annihilation. "It would seem strange," writes John Stott, "if people who are said to suffer destruction are in fact not destroyed."[16]

But there are two difficulties with this argument. The first is that the word-group translated in the Bible by the words *destroy* or *destruction* has a range of meanings in Scripture. Its use does not always imply that the thing "destroyed" no longer ceases to be. It is used to refer to the "lost" coin and "lost" son of Luke 15, to the "ruined" wineskin of Matthew 9:17 (NIV), and to the "waste" of the ointment used to anoint Jesus in Matthew 26:8.[17] In none of these cases are we to suppose that the object or person in question is being annihilated, but rather that it is—in one sense or another—ruined, lost, or unusable. This means that before we conclude that the "destruction" of the impenitent means their annihilation, we will have to consider the possibility that it instead denotes the ruined quality of their continued existence.

And this is precisely what the word seems to mean when it is used of the final fate of the "Beast" in the book of Revelation. In Revelation 17:8, 11 we read that the Beast will go to his "destruction." But in Revelation 20:10 we learn that the Beast, together with the devil and the False Prophet, "will be tormented day and night forever and ever." Some have suggested that the "Beast" is not an individual but rather a symbol for the world's resistance to God. But it is hard to see how a mere symbol can suffer torment. Furthermore, most evangelical Christians understand the devil to be not a symbol but a being, and Revelation 20:10 describes *his* fate as consisting of eternal torment.

It appears, then, that at least in the case of the devil, the Beast, and the False Prophet, "destruction" does not mean annihilation but everlasting punishment. And if that is what the word means when applied to these beings, there is no exegetical basis for saying that it must mean something else when applied to humans.

The second difficulty is that destruction is only one of several images used to describe the fate of the damned, and some of the others are difficult, if not impossible, to reconcile with annihilationism. In several places Jesus described hell as a place of darkness or of weeping and gnashing of teeth (Luke 13:25–30; Matt. 22:13; 25:30). In 2 Thessalonians 1:9 Paul portrayed the lost as suffering "eternal destruction," but in the very next phrase he wrote that they would be "away from the presence of the Lord and from the glory of his might." The Scriptures speak of those who will rise to "shame and everlasting contempt" and says that they will experience no rest (Dan. 12:2; Rev. 14:11).

In these passages the continued existence of the lost appears to be assumed, for how else could they experience the suffering, remorse, shame, and restlessness that is the evident meaning of these pictures? A person who no longer exists can neither weep nor gnash his teeth nor recognize his exclusion from the presence of God nor experience contempt.

Annihilationists may answer that the lost are first punished and then destroyed. Indeed, they must give this answer if they are to honor the biblical principle that the punishment of the wicked is in proportion to their sins, for if God simply annihilated the lost without punishing them, He would be treating all of them exactly alike. But where does Scripture suggest such a sequence? And how can this sequence—punishment followed by annihilation—be reconciled with the annihilationist claim that eternal punishment is annihilation?

A much more probable interpretation is that "destruction," "weeping and gnashing of teeth," and exclusion from God's presence are complementary descriptions of the same terrible reality. The same must be said of the phrase "eternal punishment" (Matt. 25:46), which we find in Jesus' description of the fate of the "goats" in Matthew 25:31–46. The clearest hint to the meaning of this phrase is given a few verses earlier, where Jesus condemns those on His left to the "eternal fire prepared for the devil and his angels" (v. 41). If it is the fate of the devil to be tormented day and night forever (Rev. 20:10), then it seems plain that this is also what Jesus means when He speaks of the "eternal punishment" of condemned human beings.[18] "Destruction," then, refers to the ruined, miserable state of the lost, not to the cessation of their existence.

Is Fire a Symbol of Annihilation?

A second argument for annihilation proceeds from the frequent use of fire, blazing fire, a lake of fire, or a lake of burning sulfur as images for hell. As we have seen, universalists like George MacDonald and near-universalists like Wolfhart Pannenberg like to see fire as a symbol of spiritual purification. Annihilationists prefer to view it as a symbol of annihilation, and they point out that the natural tendency of fire is to consume its fuel, not to torture it indefinitely. Annihilationists ask whether the smoke that rises forever and ever (Rev. 14:11) may not be simply an everlasting reminder of the torment of souls who suffered for a time as they were being "burned" into nonexistence.

Once again, we must admit that there are verses that could readily be taken in this sense. Several passages compare the wicked to trees (Matt. 3:10), chaff (Matt. 3:12; Luke 3:17), or branches (John 15:6), the fate of which is to be thrown into fire and burned. The writer to the Hebrews speaks of raging fire that will "consume" the enemies of God (Heb. 10:26–27). If these passages were the only descriptions we had of hell, we would very naturally assume that it is the fate of the lost to be destroyed in much the same way that fire in this world destroys its fuel.

Again, though, we stumble over the fact that it is stated specifically of the devil, the Beast, and the False Prophet that they are to be "tormented day and night forever and ever" in the lake of burning sulfur (Rev. 20:10). And this same lake of fire is the destination of all those human beings whose names are not written in the Book of Life (v. 15). It seems rather plain that the "lake of fire" is neither a place of purification nor one where the lost cease to exist, but rather a place where they suffer endless misery, where "the smoke of their torment goes up forever and ever" and where they have "no rest, day or night" (Rev. 14:11). Here, the imagery of fire is apparently used to indicate neither their purification nor their annihilation but rather the intensity of their suffering. Jonathan Edwards justly insists that annihilation is what the wicked will yearn for but will never receive.[19] The complaint of the rich man to Abraham was, "I am in anguish in this flame" (Luke 16:24).

HELL AND THE IMMORTALITY OF THE SOUL

Two other ideas that are closely related to annihilationism need to be dealt with quickly. The first is the proposal that the traditional idea of hell as everlasting punishment owes more to the Greek doctrine of the immortality of the soul than it does to the teaching of the Bible. It is argued by some that it is more true to the biblical view of man to say that the natural fate of dying human beings, apart from the gift of eternal life in Jesus Christ, is to simply cease to exist. The soul's immortality is not natural but conditional: If we repent and trust in Christ we will live forever; otherwise, after death we will experience annihilation.[20]

This argument is, in the words of Robert A. Peterson, "vastly overrated."[21] It is true that only God is immortal in the fullest sense of the word, since only He has neither beginning nor end. It is also true that the focus of the Bible, unlike Greek philosophy, is not on the "survival of the soul" but rather on the eventual resurrection of the body and the restoration of the dead to a life that is fully physical. And it is certainly true that human existence both now and eternally is completely dependent on the will and power of God. But it goes against many passages of Scripture to suggest that physical death ends the existence of all except those who have believed in Christ.

That human beings have souls that survive the death of the body is established by Jesus' words to the thief on the cross (Luke 23:43), by Paul's expectation that upon his death he would be "with Christ" (Phil. 1:23), by his discussion in 2 Corinthians 5:1–5 of death's power to "unclothe" us (v. 4) of our bodies, and by the statement about Judas that he abandoned his ministry "to go where he belongs" (Acts 1:25 NIV). It is affirmed by Jesus' parable of Lazarus and the rich man (Luke 16:19–31), in which both the righteous man and the wicked one continue to exist beyond physical death, as well as by the many verses pertaining to the ultimate judgment of all people (e.g., Rev. 20:12). No Christian theologian needed to consult the Greek philosophers to arrive at the conclusion that human souls survive death; this is a thoroughly biblical idea.

The second idea is a subtler one: Although God does not annihilate the wicked, in effect they annihilate themselves. Because of the corrosive power of sin, they gradually decay into something subhuman and impersonal. B. B. Warfield mentions several varieties of this belief in his study of annihilationism,[22] and I believe we see something similar in C. S. Lewis's conjecture that "a damned soul is nearly nothing: it is shrunk, shut up in itself."[23] With this idea we need not necessarily disagree, unless (as I fear is often the case) it is put forward as a means of reducing the horror of hell or of suggesting that the lost do not suffer consciously. If that is the intent, however, then

I think we must remind ourselves that hell is consistently portrayed in the Bible as a place of weeping, wailing, gnashing of teeth, and torment. The rich man in the parable of Lazarus experienced torment in hades. As noted earlier, Jesus said of Judas that it would have been better for him had he never been born, an idea that seems compatible only with everlasting punishment.

CAN WE BANISH HELL?

As much as we would like to banish the very idea of hell, the Bible just does not permit us to do so. We cannot argue that all will be saved, or that the lost will cease to exist, or even that they will lose their awareness of their misery. Just what their existence will be like after millennia of suffering is a question from which we turn with dismay. No doubt Lewis is pointing to something true when he imagines the damned as withering, decreasing, shriveling. Nevertheless, this is not the main thought of the Bible, which stresses the experience of the lost in terms of grief and pain.

We must, therefore, squarely face up to the reality of everlasting, conscious punishment. In the next chapter we will, with fear and trembling, attempt to probe a little deeper into the nature of that awful, eternal reality.

My gracious, loving Father, the doctrine of eternal punishment shatters me and reduces me to confusion and embarrassment. I have often spoken with disdain of those who at various times of history have been complacent in the face of terrible suffering on the part of their fellow human beings, but what is to be said of someone who can be so little troubled by the thought that millions of his fellow creatures are destined to an eternity of torment? Should this thought not drive me to far greater efforts in prayer, evangelism, and service? Surely the truth, Father, is that this doctrine has penetrated only superficially into my heart and life, such that I have hardly begun to know what it is to take Your wrath with perfect seriousness and to struggle in prayer for and in witness to those who are lost.

That I may draw close to the spirit of Christ, I ask again that You strengthen my mind to understand sound doctrine, humble my proud heart to receive it, and embolden my spirit to proclaim and live it. I would gladly reject the doctrine of hell; but if I may not, then let me so receive it as to

be haunted by it, and so believe it as to be incapable of cravenly withholding
Your truth from those in danger of everlasting loss. In Jesus' name I pray. Amen.

NOTES

1. Origen, *On First Principles,* trans. G. W. Butterworth, (Gloucester, Mass.: Peter Smith, 1973), 146. There is, however, scholarly debate over the precise original meaning of Origen's ideas. See the summaries in Hans Urs von Balthasar, *Dare We Hope "That All Men Be Saved"?* (San Francisco: St. Ignatius, 1988), 58–64, and Frederick W. Norris's chapter, "Universal Salvation in Origen and Maximus" in Nigel M. de S. Cameron, ed., *Universalism and the Doctrine of Hell* (Grand Rapids: Baker, 1992), 35–72.

2. Jürgen Moltmann, for example, asserts that Jewish and early Christian ideas of divine judgment are based upon Iranian dualism and are fundamentally incompatible with Jesus' message of divine grace. See *The Way of Jesus Christ* (Minneapolis: Fortress, 1993), 336–38. The assertion of a non-Jewish origin for the biblical idea of judgment has not been proved, however; and even if it were, a high view of biblical inspiration would compel us to view the Bible's use of that idea as authoritative.

3. Friedrich Schleiermacher, the early nineteenth-century theologian often called "the father of liberal theology," calmly assured his readers that the doctrine of everlasting punishment was based on a misreading of the Bible. Unfortunately, Schleiermacher did not see fit to back up his teaching with exegesis of the passages that have always been understood as teaching the doctrine. Instead, he built his argument for universalism entirely on moral considerations. See *The Christian Faith* (Edinburgh: T & T Clark, 1989), 539–42, 720–22.

4. Or at least this is so with regard to soteriology. I have learned much from liberal theologians in other areas of theology, but I have yet to encounter one whose doctrine of salvation can withstand scrutiny from a biblical perspective. Like Felix in Acts 24, who listened with interest to Paul until he began to speak of righteousness, self-control, and judgment, there are theologians who listen attentively to the Bible on every topic but the most important one.

5. George MacDonald, *Creation in Christ,* ed. Rolland Hein (Wheaton, Ill.: Shaw, 1976), 74–77. MacDonald's confidence that, given enough time, God will succeed in winning the hearts of all the lost is echoed by John Hick, to whom "It seems morally (though still not logically) impossible that the infinite resourcefulness of infinite love working in unlimited time should be eternally frustrated, and the creature reject its own good, presented in an endless range of ways." John Hick, *Evil and the God of Love* (London: Macmillan, 1966), 379–80.

6. C. S. Lewis, *The Problem of Pain* (New York: Macmillan, 1962), 118–19.

7. It is sometimes objected that the story of Lazarus gives us information only about the intermediate state of souls after death, not about their final assignment to heaven or hell. This may be so, but the question must then be asked why we should suppose movement between the two spiritual destinations to be possible after the Judgment when it was not possible earlier. In the absence of any scriptural support for the idea that the damned can be released from hell, the story

of Lazarus should be understood as teaching that death ends all opportunity for repentance and salvation.

8. See his sermon "The Last Penny" in MacDonald, *Creation in Christ,* 167–76.

9. D. A. Carson, *The Sermon on the Mount* (Grand Rapids: Baker, 1978), 43.

10. Jonathan Edwards, "The Eternity of Hell Torments," in *The Works of Jonathan Edwards,* vol. 2, rev. Edward Hickman (1834; repr., Edinburgh: Banner of Truth, 1986), 86. Edwards's argument is that sin is an infinite evil, and therefore the sinner's debt can never be offset by a finite punishment.

11. Wolfhart Pannenberg, *Systematic Theology,* vol. 3 (Grand Rapids: Eerdmans, 1998), 620.

12. "What the apostle is interested in showing is not the numerical extent of those who are justified as identical with the numerical extent of those condemned but the parallel that obtains between the way of condemnation and the way of justification. It is the *modus operandi* that is in view. All who are condemned, and this includes the whole human race, are condemned because of the one trespass of Adam; all who are justified are justified because of the righteousness of Christ." John Murray in *The Epistle to the Romans* (Grand Rapids: Eerdmans, 1968), 203.

13. Hans Urs von Balthasar, *Dare We Hope?,* 1–28. Richard John Neuhaus has followed Balthasar's approach in his *Death on a Friday Afternoon* (New York: Basic Books, 2000) and in his article "Will All Be Saved?" in *First Things* 115 (August/September 2001): 77–80.

14. MacDonald, *Creation in Christ,* 74.

15. Friedrich Schleiermacher used this same consideration as a proof of universalism: Heaven is a place of perfect happiness, but perfect happiness is impossible if any are lost; therefore, all must be saved (see *The Christian Faith,* sec. 163, 720–22).

16. David L. Edwards and John Stott, *Evangelical Essentials: A Liberal-Evangelical Dialogue* (Downers Grove, Ill.: InterVarsity, 1988), 315–16.

17. See D. A. Carson, *The Gagging of God* (Grand Rapids: Zondervan, 1996), 522.

18. See Robert A. Peterson, *Hell on Trial: The Case for Eternal Punishment* (Phillipsburg, N. J.: P & R Publishing, 1995), 165.

19. John Gerstner, *Heaven and Hell: Jonathan Edwards on the Afterlife* (Grand Rapids: Baker, 1980), 75. Edwards's own refutation of annihilationism can be read in his sermon, "The Eternity of Hell Torments," in *Works,* vol. 2, 83–89.

20. See, for example, Clark Pinnock's chapter in William Crockett, ed., *Four Views on Hell* (Grand Rapids: Zondervan, 1992), 135–66, and Edward William Fudge's chapters in Fudge and Robert A. Peterson, *Two Views of Hell* (Downers Grove, Ill.: InterVarsity, 2000).

21. Peterson, *Hell on Trial,* 177.

22. Benjamin B. Warfield, "Annihilationism," in *Studies in Theology* (1932; repr., Grand Rapids: Baker, 2000), 456–7.

23. C. S. Lewis, *The Great Divorce* (New York: Simon & Schuster, 1996), 120.

3

THE LIGHT OF ISRAEL WILL BECOME A FIRE

The light of Israel will become a fire, and his Holy One a flame, and it will burn and devour his thorns and briers in one day.

+ISAIAH 10:17

HELL IS NOT A PLEASANT or popular topic. In fact, it is likely the least popular of all topics. Anthologers of American literature may continue to reproduce Jonathan Edwards's "Sinners in the Hands of an Angry God," but certainly not because they agree with his doctrine or even believe his theme is worth talking about. The sermon has historical interest, and perhaps it gives us a gratifying reminder of how much more enlightened we are than were our colonial forebears. But eternal punishment is hardly to be regarded as a proper topic for polite conversation.

Almost without exception, modern people are wholehearted followers of some version of what William James called "the religion of healthy-mindedness." We think, speak, and sing of only happy themes. We go to great lengths to avoid thinking of death, and in this we are rather successful. We are more successful still in avoiding all thought of judgment.

POSITIVE MESSAGES ONLY, PLEASE

Sad to say, this avoidance of the doctrine of hell is nearly as common in the church and among pastors as in the wider society. We Christians gather to praise God for His grace and forgiveness, but generally without taking time to think of what our position would be if God were not gracious and forgiving. Those of us who are pastors strive to be, above all else, warm, likable, affirming, and cheerful. Our pulpit ministries consist largely of encouraging messages on how to succeed in life; the great aim of the preacher is to be always "uplifting" and at all costs to avoid leaving people feeling troubled or fearful. Our models are "motivational speakers" who have mastered the art of conveying only encouraging truths and of doing so with a maximum of humor and, often, a minimum of serious thought.

I remember attending a worship service in a very large church famous for its "seeker-sensitive" philosophy. As I sat and listened to the determinedly upbeat music, watched the preacher present his message without once losing the smile from his face, and noted that at no point in the service were we invited to confess our sins to God or ask His forgiveness, I found myself wondering what would happen if Martin Luther, John Calvin, or Jonathan Edwards were to come back to life and walk into the sanctuary. My conclusion was that none of those past worthies would be able to make heads or tails of the worship service, and that if by some mistake one of them were allowed to address the congregation, the people would make neither heads nor tails of his sermon.

American Christianity is so deeply affected by the mentality of marketing that it is difficult to discover any meaningful connection between modern evangelicalism and the urgent concern of Paul to clear himself "of the blood of all men," to warn them night and day with tears, that he might "by all possible means . . . save some" (Acts 20:26–27 NIV; 1 Cor. 9:22 NIV; cf. Phil. 3:18).[1] I'm afraid we modern preachers are far more concerned to clear ourselves of the charge of being overly serious.

THE VITAL DOCTRINE OF DIVINE PUNISHMENT

This is all very wrongheaded and foolish, not to mention disobedient. The pastor who won't address the subject of divine wrath is about as useful to the human race as the physician who won't inflict the discomfort of an inoculation. Our failure to think and speak about eternity impoverishes us. Christians as diverse as Dante and Milton, Ignatius of Loyola and Jonathan Edwards of Stockbridge have agreed that belief in and reflection on the biblical doctrine of hell is essential to both Christian spirituality and Christian mission. Thinking about hell heightens our awe of God. It drives us to seek His mercy. It deepens our gratitude for His salvation. It stimulates us to obey His command to take the gospel to all people.

Not surprisingly, our current unspoken taboo against this subject has just the opposite effect: It diminishes God, leaves uncut the nerve of our self-righteousness, and undermines concern for the lost.

This neglect of the topic of hell is, moreover, self-reinforcing. Because we do not think about hell, we feel no anguish over it; and because the peril of the lost has no emotional impact upon us, we see no reason to talk, teach, or preach about eternal punishment. For our secular contemporaries the effects are similar: The silence of the church on the topic of judgment encourages them to ever-greater permissiveness, and the resulting hardness of heart closes their minds all the more to the reality that they will one day be held accountable for their actions. Hell is unreal to modern people because it feels unreal; but it feels unreal because it has been many decades since the church was willing to speak vigorously of its reality.

JESUS ON ETERNAL PUNISHMENT

How different all this is from the example of Jesus! It has been rightly said that we owe the doctrine of eternal punishment primarily to Jesus; certainly He spoke more of hell than any other biblical writer or speaker.[2] He also seems to speak more frequently of hell than of heaven. Like Jonathan Edwards, but quite unlike most modern evangelists, Jesus was not in the least ashamed to introduce the fear of hell as an incentive to repentance and faith:

I told you that you would die in your sins, for unless you believe that I am he you will die in your sins. (John 8:24)

And do not fear those who kill the body but cannot kill the soul. Rather fear him who can destroy both soul and body in hell. (Matthew 10:28)

And if your hand causes you to sin, cut it off. It is better for you to enter life crippled than with two hands to go to hell, to the unquenchable fire. (Mark 9:43)

Enter by the narrow gate. For the gate is wide and the way is easy that leads to destruction, and those who enter by it are many. (Matthew 7:13)

For God did not send his Son into the world to condemn the world, but in order that the world might be saved through him. Whoever believes in him is not condemned, but whoever does not believe is condemned already, because he has not believed in the name of the only Son of God. (John 3:17–18)

Our modern squeamishness about this doctrine puts us out of touch with the Lord of the church. To put it bluntly, it is hypocritical for us to call ourselves disciples of Jesus if we are unwilling to face the doctrine of hell. To reject or ignore His teaching, or to join modernity in its conceited and ignorant belief that we have outgrown it, is in reality to reject Jesus' authority over the church and over our own lives.

Indeed, in our current culture we desperately need preachers who have the courage to speak frequently and seriously about judgment. We are afraid of being taunted that we are just trying to scare people. But perhaps people need to be scared; Jesus certainly seems to have thought so. And perhaps we preachers ourselves need to be scared—by the biblical insistence that the one who fails to warn a sinner of the consequences of his sin becomes accountable for his blood (see Ezek. 33:6).

HELL: PART OF THE MESSAGE

Certainly we must not only preach judgment; we are to set forth Christ in all of His beauty, gentleness, and grandeur, and to emphasize

His invitation to all to repent and believe. We are also to speak of the implications of the gospel for every realm of human life. We must strive to present what Paul called "the whole counsel of God" (Acts 20:27). But if we exclude from our presentation the consequences of the refusal to repent and believe,[3] then we are failing to follow the example of Jesus and are heightening our own guilt before God (see James 3:1).

But just what is it that we are to think or say about hell? It is agreed on almost all sides that the biblical descriptions of hell are at least in some measure metaphorical rather than literal. It is difficult to see how one and the same reality could simultaneously and literally be described as "eternal fire" and a place of "utter darkness" (Jude 7, 13), since fire normally produces light, which dispels darkness. Again, as we saw in the last chapter, unless we are willing to pit Scripture against Scripture, the texts that speak of hell as a place of destruction must be understood as using the idea of destruction as a metaphor for a ruined but continued existence.

What are we to make of all this? How can we think constructively about a reality which we have not seen and which is described to us in largely figurative language?

BOTH SELF-PUNISHMENT AND DIVINE PUNISHMENT

One twentieth-century author who was not afraid to write about hell was C. S. Lewis. His book *The Great Divorce* is an imaginative and powerful refutation of the common notion that all people desire heaven. In the course of a fantastic visit to heaven he watches numerous people deciding that hell is the place for them. One man is too proud to enter heaven in the presence of a former murderer. A modernist theologian thinks that hell offers a greater scope for the exercise of his intellectual creativity. Other inhabitants of hell, offered the opportunity to relocate to heaven, cannot give up their greed, their unhappiness with God's management of the universe, or their concern for the opinions of others. In each case, the choice to reject joy is made by the person himself or herself.

Lewis's portraits are convincingly drawn and help us to grasp the truth that all who are lost will have only themselves to blame for their damnation. J. I. Packer expresses this same doctrine when he writes that:

we choose

God's wrath in the Bible is something which men choose for themselves. Before hell is an experience inflicted by God, it is a state for which man himself opts, by retreating from the light which God shines in his heart to lead him to Himself. . . . In the last analysis, all that God does subsequently in judicial action towards the unbeliever, whether in this life or beyond it, is to show him, and lead him into, the full implications of the choice he has made.[4]

A Person's Choice

This is a very biblical and important truth, and one that every person who speaks about divine judgment needs to understand. We must not think of hell as a punishment arbitrarily imposed by God. We must learn to see it as the natural outgrowth of the person's own choices and of his or her inborn distaste for God. Paul tells us in Romans 8:7 that "the mind that is set on the flesh is hostile to God, for it does not submit to God's law; indeed, it cannot." What this means in practice is that left to themselves, human beings inevitably reject God's authority over their lives, even if the result is that they must ultimately miss His greatest blessings. Indeed, they are not capable of seeing His blessings as blessings. A heaven characterized by praise of God and complete devotion to His will cannot possibly appeal to the person who still wishes to live life on her own terms, without God's interference.

Because this is so, I believe that Lewis's *The Great Divorce* deserves careful and repeated study. We need to learn to recognize in ourselves and in others those choices that lead to damnation. Preachers, especially, need to have the courage to show their hearers that anytime they reject either the authority or the mercy of God they are in effect choosing to live in hell rather than heaven; and that if that pattern of choosing is not changed, it will lead eventually to a damnation for which the person will have only himself to blame. Hell is self-punishment, the natural outgrowth of the decision not to acknowledge God and receive His grace.

Not Self-Punishment Alone

Nevertheless, this is only one side of the truth, and we must be careful that we do not overemphasize it. As much as I have benefited from

Lewis's views on heaven and hell, I find them troubling in some ways. In *The Great Divorce* hell is presented less as a place of punishment than as a place where God simply leaves people alone. Perhaps it would be more accurate to say that in Lewis's view, God's determination to leave people to their own sins *is* their punishment. As he writes, "There are only two kinds of people in the end: those who say to God, 'Thy will be done,' and those to whom God says, in the end, 'Thy will be done.'"[5] In the first case the person is choosing everlasting joy; in the second, God is respecting his or her freedom to be unhappy.

While there is much truth in this presentation, it does not do full justice to the biblical teaching. When the New Testament speaks of judgment, it places less emphasis on the role of human choice than on God's role as the holy and righteous judge. Consider a few of Jesus' statements about hell in the gospel of Matthew, and pay particular attention to the verbs I have emphasized:

Every tree that does not bear good fruit is cut down and thrown *into the fire.* (7:19)

. . . while the sons of the kingdom will be thrown *into the outer darkness. In that place there will be weeping and gnashing of teeth.* (8:12)

"The Son of Man will send his angels, and they will gather *out of his kingdom all causes of sin and all law-breakers, and* throw *them into the fiery furnace. In that place there will be weeping and gnashing of teeth.* (13:41–42)

And if your hand or your foot causes you to sin, cut it off *and* throw it away. *It is better for you to enter life crippled or lame than with two hands or two feet to be* thrown *into the eternal fire.* (18:8)

Then the king said to the attendants, "Bind him hand and foot and cast *him into the outer darkness. In that place there will be weeping and gnashing of teeth."* (22:13)

"'And cast *the worthless servant into the outer darkness. In that place there will be weeping and gnashing of teeth.'"* (25:30)

What we need to notice in these statements is that Jesus is not the least bit nervous about portraying God, the angels, or Himself as taking a very active role in consigning the wicked to hell. The image is not that of a God who sadly stands by, helplessly shaking His head with grief as His creatures insist upon damning themselves. On the contrary, God actively condemns the wicked to everlasting punishment. He throws them into hell.

Not only is this so, but in Luke 13:24–28 Jesus pictures the wicked as wanting to enter the kingdom but being unable to:

> *Strive to enter through the narrow door. For many, I tell you, will seek to enter and will not be able. When once the master of the house has risen and shut the door, and you begin to stand outside and to knock at the door, saying, "Lord, open to us," then he will answer you, "I do not know where you come from." Then you will begin to say, "We ate and drank in your presence, and you taught in our streets." But he will say, "I tell you, I do not know where you come from. Depart from me, all you workers of evil!" In that place there will be weeping and gnashing of teeth, when you see Abraham and Isaac and Jacob and all the prophets in the kingdom of God but you yourselves cast out."*

Certainly it is true that all who are condemned have only themselves to blame for their destruction. They have chosen to sin; they have chosen to turn away from whatever degree of light they have been given; they may well have ignored or scorned God's offer of mercy in the gospel. The emphasis, on the voluntary nature of damnation is a biblical emphasis, and it has its place. But it must not be allowed to cancel out the equally biblical emphasis on hell as a place where the wicked are actively punished by God. It is true that they have turned their backs on God. It is true that they would experience no joy in heaven. But it is not true that in hell they are simply left to themselves, nor is it true that God is a helpless observer of their damnation. God sends them to hell, and He does so in order that He may punish them.

Balancing Two Truths About Hell

These two truths—that human beings both choose hell and are cast there by a wrathful God—are not easy to keep in proper balance. I suggest, though, that of the two the second truth is the one that needs to be emphasized today. Hell is a place of punishment, a place of misery, a place from which the lost wish desperately to escape. They may be said to have chosen hell in the sense that they have rejected God's authority and grace, but they have not chosen the torment they experience there. In hell they are not just left to their own devices; instead, they are forced, moment by moment, to face the consequences of their own sin. It is true enough that if they were offered heaven they would still reject it, because in their hearts they hate God. But if heaven is unattractive to them, so is hell. God does not leave them to nurture their grudges and hatreds and conceits in peace. He punishes them for those sins. As we live our lives on this earth and make our moral and spiritual choices, we are not merely to fear our own bad decisions. We are to fear God, the One who, after the killing of the body, has the power to throw us into hell (Luke 12:5).

Indeed, for a preacher, these two truths should be complementary emphases that help the sinner to recognize the perilous position in which he stands. The sinner must first be shown that his own choices are hellish choices, that day by day he is becoming a creature more suited to hell than to heaven. But then, because in his pride and vanity he may decide that he would rather be damned on his own terms than to submit to God's, he must also be shown that God plans to repay his rebellion with unending, pitiless punishment.

THE PRESENCE AND ABSENCE OF GOD

This leads us to the question of God's role in eternal punishment. In 2 Thessalonians 1:9 Paul writes that those who do not believe the gospel will be punished with eternal destruction "away from the presence of the Lord and from the glory of his might." On the basis of this text it is often said that what characterizes hell is the absence of God. Probably nobody who makes such a statement intends to deny the doctrine of God's omnipresence. God is not subject to the limitations of space. Obviously He is in some sense present in hell. But what is often meant when people speak of God's absence from hell is that God withdraws Himself from that place; He shields His eyes from the misery of the lost. He ordains their misery, yet He does not wish to be present to witness it.

For many people, the idea that God is absent from hell serves both to highlight the misery of the lost and to safeguard the character of God from the charge that He takes delight in human torment.

These are difficult matters. The Bible does indeed insist that God takes no pleasure in the death of the wicked, but rather in their repentance (Ezek. 18:23). Nevertheless, while we surely are not to believe that God rejoices in the suffering of the wicked for its own sake, we must believe that He rejoices in their punishment as an expression of His justice. And the vast number of texts that speak of God as directly involved in punishing the wicked require us to think of Him as very much present in hell. God does not merely send fire upon the lost; He Himself is the consuming fire with which they must dwell eternally (Heb. 12:29; Isa. 33:14). He does not merely consign them to punishment; He punishes them.

If this is so, then what are we to make of 2 Thessalonians 1:9, which speaks of those who do not believe as being banished from God's presence? We are to understand from this that they are banished from His blessings and from all enjoyment of His glory. God eternally smiles upon the redeemed, but He eternally frowns upon the wicked. He is the witness and the cause of their misery, but He is not moved by it. He does not relent or sympathize. He never swerves from His intention to glorify His justice through their punishment.

Another way of expressing this is to say that God is the eternal, implacable enemy of the lost. In this life they showed their enmity to Him by their disobedience to His Law and their hostility to His grace; now they must experience the consequences of their choices in the form of unrelenting wrath. On the Day of Judgment, says Paul, "there will be wrath and fury" for those who reject the truth and follow evil (Rom. 2:8). The writer of the Revelation sees the mighty of the earth hiding in caves and under rocks and calling out to the mountains, "Fall on us and hide us from the face of him who is seated on the throne, and from the wrath of the Lamb, for the great day of their wrath has come, and who can stand?" (Rev. 6:16–17). The author of Psalm 21 foresaw a time when God would lay hold of all His enemies and swallow them up in His wrath (vv. 8–9). And Moses, in Psalm 90:11, shrank from the thought of God's indignation toward the wicked: "Who considers the power of your anger, and your wrath according to the fear of you?"

Notice that the Bible does not support the popular idea of hell as a place where the lost are tormented by gleeful devils. The New Testament makes it clear that the devils themselves will be in torment (Matt. 8:29; Luke 8:31), but it never directly suggests that they will play a role in punishing lost men and women. Even Jonathan Edwards, who normally hewed very closely to the actual statements of Scripture, seems to me to have overstepped in his assumption that many of the torments in hell will be administered by demons or by other lost human beings.[6] We cannot say that this is impossible. It may well be that the damned are allowed to torment one another. But the Bible never presents this idea to us as a doctrine to be believed. Sartre was wrong; hell is not "other people." Nor is hell the abandonment of human beings to a demonic power that is not itself subject to suffering. What is truly terrible about hell is that there God Himself is the tormenter of the damned. There God, the "Light of Israel," becomes a consuming flame (Isa. 10:17) to destroy all who have opposed Him.

THE IMAGERY OF HELL

But what is the nature of this flame? As already noted, there is an apparent contradiction between the hellish pictures of a lake of fire and utter darkness. It seems plain that we cannot take these pictures completely literally. On the other hand, it also seems plain that we are not at liberty to drain them of their horror by pronouncing them merely metaphorical. Metaphorical they may be, but they are clearly intended to point us to a terrible reality.[7]

It is likely that in our present state we are not capable of really understanding either heaven or hell. Nevertheless, we ought to follow up the clues we have been given. In the case of heaven, the fact that the redeemed will have resurrected bodies suggests that their life will have a physical dimension to it, however different that experience of physicality may be from what we know here and now.

Again, the various pictures of heaven in the Revelation—a city with high walls, streets paved with gold, life-giving fruit trees, the absence of sun and moon—are intended to teach that in that place the redeemed experience complete security, abundance, renewal, and the constant and immediate presence of God. The pictures may not be literal, but they are full of meaning.

The Lake of Fire

In the case of hell, the image of a lake of fire appears designed to convey the idea of suffering that is unbearable in its intensity. "The sinners in Zion are afraid; trembling has seized the godless: 'Who among us can dwell with the consuming fire? Who among us can dwell with everlasting burnings?'" (Isa. 33:14). Isaiah's use of the imagery of fire and the New Testament texts that describe hell as a place of blazing fire appear to coincide. All of us know how painful a burn is; these texts invite us to extrapolate from our experiences of being burned to the idea of a place where one's entire body endlessly suffers the excruciating pain of contact with fire. Such pain is almost unimaginable, and when one thinks of suffering it forever, without respite and without hope, the idea is almost too terrible to contemplate.

The image of fire seems designed to tell us that the misery of hell is intense, and the picture of a lake of fire into which people are thrown tells us that that misery will envelope the damned. It will be unbearable and inescapable.

Will that misery be physical, spiritual, or both? The fact that the lake of fire is a place of everlasting torment for Satan, who has no physical body and is presumably impervious to physical fire, suggests that we should not be too quick to think of hell's torment as primarily physical. Even in this life we experience pains that can be described as spiritual, emotional, or mental. Among these are sorrow, regret, fear, unfulfilled desire, a consciousness of God's disfavor, and hopelessness. It is not difficult to imagine that in hell these pains are vastly greater than our worst experience of them in this life, and that they are made all the worse by the fact that they grow endlessly stronger and stronger. One can imagine (though one certainly does not like to) that the damned are engulfed in sorrow, rage, and horror, and that the "fire" with which they must dwell burns them from within as well as from without.

Still, the fact that the wicked as well as the righteous will participate in the resurrection (Dan. 12:2; John 5:28–29; Acts 24:15; Rev. 20:5) suggests that the punishment of the wicked must have a physical aspect to it as well. If we conclude that the righteous will experience physical pleasures in heaven, it seems to follow that the damned will experience physical pains in hell. I believe we must speak cautiously, since the truth is that we know very little of the nature of the resurrection body (1 Cor. 15:35–44). But the Bible does portray the lost as having bodies. It therefore seems most likely that the punishments of hell involve the whole person and consist of pains both physical and emotional.

Outer Darkness

What of the image of hell as "outer darkness" (Matt. 8:12; 22:13; 25:30) or "blackest darkness" (Jude 13 NIV)? This emphasizes not pain but desolation. To be in darkness is to be abandoned, disoriented, fearful, and lost. The image suggests the total absence of divine blessing and the consciousness that one is not the object of divine mercy and never will be. When Jesus uses the image of darkness to refer to hell, He always describes it as a place where there will be "weeping and gnashing of teeth," which further implies both misery and despair.

Hell, then, is a hopeless place, devoid of the light of love or joy. It does not seem possible that it is a place from which the light of truth has completely fled; at the least, the damned are forced to face the truth of their own sinfulness and of God's anger toward them. But that may well be the only truth they know, and that their minds twist this way and that in the effort not to know the things they know. Whether it is a place of physical darkness seems unclear; the image appears to have a primarily spiritual significance. But it is a place that produces in its inhabitants the same experience of terrified desolation that we feel when we find ourselves alone in total darkness.

Gehenna

One other image should be considered. The most common New Testament word for hell is *gehenna,* which scholars agree is derived from the Hebrew name *ge-hinnom,* or Hinnom Valley. The Hinnom Valley is located southwest of Jerusalem. At one stage in Israelite history it witnessed the sacrifice of children to the Ammonite god Molech (2 Kings 23:10; Jer. 7:31; 32:35), and Jeremiah promised that it would one day be known as the "Valley of Slaughter" (Jer. 7:32; 19:5–6). In time the valley became a kind of dump where people used sulfur to burn their garbage and offal. When Jesus spoke of hell as a place where "their worm does not die, and the fire is not quenched" (Mark 9:48),

He was thus evoking the image of an accursed, smoky, evil-smelling incineration dump crawling with maggots.

From this image we can infer that hell is to be regarded as a place where God casts aside the lost as we cast aside trash or waste. Garbage is useless; it is fit only to be consigned to the fire and the worm, and once discarded it is not again retrieved.

Hell is thus a place of final and irretrievable loss, and the damned are viewed by God with utter distaste and with a determination to abandon them forever.

All of these images—a lake of fire, a blazing furnace, a place of utter darkness, an incineration dump—have an absolute quality about them, in that it is difficult to imagine gradations of suffering for those tormented in these ways. Being cast into a lake of burning sulfur would produce agony in every nerve ending; being banished to blackest darkness would isolate and terrify every soul so treated. Yet the Bible makes it clear that judgment is according to our deeds (2 Cor. 5:10), and Jesus teaches that punishment will be meted out in accordance with the degree of one's knowledge of the will of God (Luke 12:47–48; Matt. 11:22–24; see also Rom. 2:12).

This provides another good reason for us to interpret the images of hell as primarily metaphorical rather than literal. Hell will be terrible for all who end up there, but it will be more or less terrible depending on the kind of lives they have lived in this world. God's judgment will be just, and His punishments will be perfectly proportionate to our sins. According to Edwards, "The damned in hell would give the world to have the number of their sins one less."[8]

WHY ETERNAL PUNISHMENT?

The single most difficult aspect of the doctrine of judgment is an eternal hell. This staggers the imagination and produces rebellion in our hearts. To think of people suffering insupportable pain for a few moments, days, or years is bad enough, but how terrible to imagine suffering that literally never ends! As we saw in the previous chapter, we have good reason to believe that this is the meaning of the biblical statements about hell. It would be helpful, though, if we could arrive at some understanding of the rationale for eternal punishment.

How can it be just for God to requite the finite number of sins we can commit in this life with a punishment that is never ending? The Bible does not provide an answer to this question, but I am aware of three main lines of reasoning that have been offered to resolve the difficulty.

An Infinite Series of Sins?

The first suggestion is that the lost are punished not only for the sins they committed in this life but also for their ongoing rebellion in hell, and since they never cease to sin, they are never able to pay for their sins through their punishment. Each new measure of suffering produces new expressions of defiance, and these new sins must themselves be punished; and so on ad infinitum. On this view the lost are, so to speak, unable to catch up with their guilt.

There is surely some degree of truth in this idea. It is certain that the damned continue to sin, and it is rational to suppose that their sins add to their punishment. But there is also a problem with this view. Scripture seems to regard eternal punishment as the proper recompense for sins committed in this life, without any consideration of the guilt of sins committed in the life to come. "For we must all appear before the judgment seat of Christ, so that each one may receive what is due for what he has done in the body, whether good or evil" (2 Cor. 5:10). We could, of course, argue that an eternity of sinning, with consequent punishment, is itself the punishment of the sins of this life; that is, that God condemns the wicked to remain wicked and to suffer the consequences of their wickedness forever. But it seems to me that we are on firmer ground if we seek a rationale for everlasting punishment that does not require us to imagine an infinite series of sins.

The Eternality of Guilt?

The second suggestion, laid out by W. G. T. Shedd in his book *The Doctrine of Endless Punishment,* is that punishment lasts forever because guilt lasts forever.[9] Shedd explains:

The endlessness of future punishment, then, is implied in the endlessness of guilt and condemnation. When a crime is condemned, it is absurd to ask, "How long is it condemned?" . . . All suffering in the next life, therefore, of which the sufficient and justifying reason is guilt, must continue as long as the reason continues; and the reason is everlasting. If it be righteous to-day, in God's retributive justice, to smite the transgressor because he violated the law yesterday, it is righteous to do the same thing to-morrow, and the next day, and so on ad infinitum; because the case ad infinitum remains unaltered. The guilt incurred yesterday is a standing and endless fact. What, therefore, guilt legitimates this instant, it legitimates every instant, and forever.[10]

Shedd realizes that this argument seems contrary to human jurisprudence, in which a criminal is punished for a finite length of time for his crimes and then declared to have paid his debt to society. This practice causes us to suppose that at the end of the time of punishment, the guilt is expunged. But Shedd insists that human justice differs from divine justice in two important ways. First, human courts see only a part of the criminal's guilt; they consider the crime's damage to society but ignore its affront to the honor and majesty of God. God, on the other hand, sees every facet of the individual's guilt. Second, human courts rightly aim not only at the punishment of guilt but also at the protection of society and the deterrence of further crime. In contrast, the divine justice of the Last Judgment has no reformatory or protective element; it is retributive only, designed to vindicate God's Law and inflict on the person the punishment his sins deserve. For both of these reasons, it is appropriate for human courts to give limited sentences, even though those sentences do not, in fact, remove guilt.

Shedd's argument is impressive. He argues that while it is right and proper for human courts to punish misbehavior with finite punishments, this very practice obscures for us the reality of the permanence of guilt. The criminal who has been imprisoned for three years for a bank robbery is no less guilty at the end of the sentence than he was at its beginning, even though it is not in either his or society's best interest to continue his punishment. Neither the length of his sentence nor the greatness of his suffering actually works to remit or diminish his guilt. And since God, beyond the Last Judgment, is no longer concerned with either the rehabilitation of the sinner or the protection of society, He will view the criminal's guilt as permanent and will punish that guilt for as long as it lasts, which is to say forever.

If Shedd's argument is sound, then the first suggestion considered above—that the endlessness of punishment is the result of the endless commission of sin in the world to come—is shown to be mistaken in that it presupposes that a person who did not continue to sin in hell would eventually, through his suffering, pay back to God what he owed Him for his sin. Shedd's argument seems to establish the justice of eternal punishment for finite sin.

On the other hand, Shedd's view also entails some difficulties. First, in saying that one reason why punishments inflicted by a human court are finite in length is that human courts see only a portion of the criminal's guilt, Shedd seems to call into question his earlier insistence that all guilt, by its very nature, is everlasting. Shedd wants to supplement the idea of the unending nature of guilt with the further consideration that sin is an offense against the Supreme Being. But if guilt is inherently unending, then all crimes—no matter how large or small or against whom committed—are automatically worthy of eternal punishment. No matter that the human court sees only a portion of the criminal's guilt; that portion in itself deserves endless punishment. It seems as though Shedd himself is not fully satisfied with the idea that guilt is endless, however, and so he goes on to augment it with an additional explanation not really compatible with the first one.

A greater problem with Shedd's view is that if punishment has no tendency whatsoever to expiate guilt, then it becomes very difficult for us to understand why Jesus' death had power to achieve atonement for sins. If punishment is not an offset for sin, how is God able to remit our sins on the basis of His punishment of His Son on the cross? The logical implication of Shedd's idea that guilt is inherently eternal would appear to be that even the death of the guiltless Christ cannot suffice to take our guilt from us.

The Infinite Evil of Sin

The third—and in my view the strongest—explanation of hell's eternity is one first used by the medieval theologian Anselm of Canterbury and most clearly expressed by Jonathan Edwards. This is the argument that because God is a Being of infinite worth, to whom we owe an infinite obligation, sin against God is an infinite evil requiring an infinite punishment. And since the punishments of hell cannot be infinite in intensity, as that would violate the principle that the lost are punished according to their deeds, it must be the case that hell is infinite in duration. Edwards puts it this way:

> Our obligation to love, honour, and obey any being, is in proportion to his loveliness, honourableness, and authority; for that is the very meaning of the words. When we say any one is very lovely, it is the same as to say, that he is one very much to be loved. Or if we say such a one is more honourable than another, the meaning of the words is, that he is one that we are more obliged to honour. If we say any one has great authority over us, it is the same as to say, that he has great right to our subjection and obedience.
>
> But God is a being infinitely lovely, because he hath infinite excellency and beauty. To have infinite excellency and beauty, is the same thing as to have infinite loveliness. He is a being of infinite greatness, majesty, and glory; and therefore he is infinitely honourable. He is infinitely exalted above the greatest potentates of the earth, and highest angels in heaven; and therefore he is infinitely more honourable than they. His authority over us is infinite; and the ground of his right to our obedience is infinitely strong; for he is infinitely worthy to be obeyed himself, and we have an absolute, universal, and infinite dependence upon him.
>
> So that sin against God, being a violation of infinite obligations, must be a crime infinitely heinous, and so deserving infinite punishment. Nothing is more agreeable to the common sense of mankind, than that sins committed against any one, must be proportionably heinous to the dignity of the one being offended and abused. . . . The eternity of the punishment of ungodly men renders it infinite.[11]

From this perspective, the power of the Atonement lies in the infinite value of Jesus Christ: "By reason of the infinite dignity of his person, his sufferings were looked upon as of infinite value, and equivalent to the eternal sufferings of a finite creature."[12]

This argument has come under attack in recent days. Annihilationists Edward Fudge and Clark Pinnock both assail the idea that the heinousness of a crime depends on the dignity of the one against whom it is committed, arguing that it violates the biblical principle that all people are to be treated equally. Fudge believes that Anselm derived his theory from medieval feudalism, in which a serf was deemed of less importance than a lord, and he points out that the making of such distinctions in human worth stands in contradiction to the Law of Moses.[13]

Fudge could be right that feudalism provided Anselm with the background for his thinking on this subject, but in my view neither Fudge nor Pinnock is successful in proving that the theory is wrong. It is a simple reality that we judge the evil of a deed in part on the basis of our assessment of the worth of the being against whom the deed was committed. The wanton killing of a dog is a more serious matter than the wanton killing of a mosquito, and the murder of a human being is a good deal more serious yet. In fact, while all murder is horrible, most people would agree that killing one's own mother is even more terrible than killing a stranger, and the assassination of a head of state is particularly heinous because it is a crime not only against the individual but also against the state itself.

If this is so, then the argument of Anselm and Edwards makes a good deal of sense. It does not seem unreasonable to suggest that because God is infinitely great, no finite punishment can ever counterbalance the evil of sin against Him.

In my view, this approach to the question of "Why eternal punishment?" is superior to the others in three ways. First, unlike the first explanation, it successfully explains why the finite sins of a human lifetime should deserve an eternity of suffering. Edwards would certainly not deny that the damned continue to sin in hell, but he does not need to point to those postmortem sins to justify eternal punishment. Any sin, because it is a sin against an infinitely worthy God, cries out for a punishment that is similarly infinite. In this way, Edwards's explanation seems consistent with the scriptural representation of hell as punishment for the sins committed in this life.

Second, this approach goes further than Shedd's to help us understand the logic of the Atonement, since it allows that punishment is indeed an offset to sin, provided that the magnitude of the punishment (or the dignity of the one punished) corresponds to the heinousness of the offense. Now I have to confess that I have no idea how God determines the precise amount of punishment called for by a particular amount of guilt. Consequently, the ideas of God's infinite worth and sin's infinite evil have a somewhat abstract feel to me. Nevertheless, I think Edwards's idea makes the best sense of the scriptural facts. Finite sin apparently does indeed deserve endless punishment, and only the death of Jesus brings forgiveness to the guilty.

I know no better explanation of these facts than to say that because God is infinitely worthy, sin is infinitely evil and can be removed only through the punishment of a Being who Himself is of endless worth.

Third, this answer to the question of why punishment must be eternal draws our minds away from the abstract question of justice and punishment and focuses them on what is far more important: the glory and splendor of God. Sin is not simply violation of a law; it is an affront against a God who is infinitely wise, holy, and good. Sin is a hideous and damnable thing because it is rebellion against our Creator and a rejection of His will and His grace.

Even Christians tend to have shamefully small thoughts of the Deity. We fall easily into an attitude of smug familiarity with God, imagining Him to be pretty much as we are—just larger. But the sheer horror of the doctrine of eternal punishment—like the story of the crucifixion of Christ—seems designed to burn the complacency out of our hearts and minds, teaching us a new and proper awe of God. God is not merely holy; He is infinitely holy. He is not merely good; He is so good as to pay an infinite price for our salvation. He does not merely dislike sin; He hates it with a passion that can be fully expressed only on Calvary or in the depths of an everlasting hell. The Bible's doctrine of eternal punishment does not only teach us about punishment; it teaches us about the character of God. As John Piper has written, "The infinite horrors of hell are intended by God to be a vivid demonstration of the infinite value of the glory of God."[14]

IS THE DOCTRINE OF HELL MORALLY INTOLERABLE?

John Stott is one of my favorite Bible expositors, and so it troubles me that he has announced himself a proponent of annihilationism. Stott offers exegetical arguments for his position, but in the end one suspects that his theology may be driven primarily by his visceral revulsion against the idea of everlasting punishment. "Emotionally," he writes, "I find the concept intolerable and do not understand how people can live with it without either cauterizing their emotions or cracking under the strain."[15] This is hardly a biblical or theological argument, but it is one that resonates in the hearts of multitudes of Christians and deserves to be carefully considered.

Even after we have listened patiently to the teaching of the Scriptures on the doctrine of hell, we still shrink from the idea that the fate of a portion of the human race is everlasting, conscious torment. How can we live here and now with such an idea? How can we imagine the redeemed in heaven living with it? Is such a terrible concept really compatible with the goodness of God and with the eternal happiness of God and His elect creatures?

If any aspect of the doctrine of divine justice calls for restraint and humility, it is this one. Or to put it just a little differently, if there is any place in theology where our willingness to submit to the Bible is tested to the utmost, it is surely here. If the Bible did not teach everlasting punishment, then there would be no need for us to tolerate that doctrine. If the Bible does teach it, as I have argued that it does, then we have no right to reject it, no matter how much anguish it may cause us and no matter how great a change it may demand in our living and thinking.

Our sense of its moral intolerability may well move us to look for alternatives to the doctrine of eternal punishment, but if in the end we find that doctrine in the Bible, we have no choice but to learn to tolerate it. A failure to do so might well result in a failure to grow into the people God wants us to be.

Facing Up to the Intolerable

In considering this matter, a good place to start is with the observation that hell is not the only truth that is almost intolerably painful to consider. It is my understanding that at present, about thirty thousand children worldwide die every day of starvation or hunger-related diseases. I have children of my own, and I cannot bear the thought of one of them going without food for even a week; how then can I contemplate the horrendous suffering of the poor children of the world without, to use Stott's phrase, "cauterizing my emotions"? Again, as much as I would like to deny this, it is simple historical fact that during World War II the Nazis brutally murdered some six million Jews. I cannot look at pictures of Auschwitz and Buchenwald without becoming almost physically ill.

I find that my mind won't allow me to dwell for too long on the suffering endured in those camps. In this I am not alone: The world seems eager to forget the Holocaust, as well as other such horrific evils as the massacres of millions under Stalin (in the Soviet Union) and Pol Pot (in Cambodia), and the steady sacrifice of countless millions of unborn children on the altar of "a woman's right to choose."

Yet these evils are real. They are in one sense "intolerable," but in another sense we have no choice but to tolerate them unless we are willing to deny reality. We may well shield the eyes of children from them, but for adults the pathway to moral sanity is not to hide from them but to look at them long and hard, and then to commit ourselves to doing whatever we can either to stop them or to prevent them from recurring.

It would be foolish and irresponsible to suggest that the goodness of God is incompatible with the existence of such horrors; their existence is beyond question. We may and must ask what God demands of us in the light of such evil, but we are not at liberty to use the doctrine of God's goodness to help us pretend that the evil is unreal.

In a similar way, if the doctrine of eternal punishment can be firmly established from Scripture, as virtually all Christians throughout history have argued it can, then we must stop complaining that it is intolerable to us and that it doesn't fit our idea of God, and we must start changing both our lives and our thinking to bring them into line with divinely revealed truth. The question we must ask ourselves is not "Can I tolerate this doctrine?" but "In the light of this doctrine, how ought I to order my life?"

Is it not possible that it is this doctrine alone—the doctrine that human beings must spend eternity in either heaven or hell—that can move us to treat other human beings with the full dignity they deserve? Does not Christian history suggest that it has been those who have been most persuaded of precisely this doctrine who have worked and prayed hardest to bring others to a saving knowledge of Christ? I am far from thinking that the desire to save others from hell is the only or even the most important motive for missions and evangelism. The great focus of the Christian should be on the goal of winning worshipers of Christ from every nation and tribe, not primarily because otherwise they will be lost but because Christ deserves their worship. Nevertheless, compassion for the lost is one proper motive for evangelism, and our experience of this compassion can only be deepened by meditation on the reality of eternal punishment.

Heaven Viewing Hell

But again we must face the question of how the sufferings of hell can be compatible with the joys of heaven. As we saw in the previous chapter, it is an ancient idea—and one well grounded in Scripture —that the redeemed will rejoice over the destruction of the wicked. There is probably no aspect of the doctrine of everlasting punishment that so infuriates its opponents as this. One reads constantly that this idea is "vindictive" and "sadistic." Hans Urs von Balthasar is ashamed and embarrassed that it should ever have entered into the theological tradition.[16] Pinnock says it puts him in mind of a person who would fry a cat in a microwave and laugh at its suffering.[17]

To these criticisms we must raise a couple of objections. First, the simile of the cat in the microwave is very inappropriate. It is impossible to imagine a situation in which it would be just to subject a cat to torture. But if our interpretation of the Bible is correct, the pains suffered by the lost in hell are strictly just. Naturally, it is the justice of hell that theologians like Pinnock wish to dispute, but their case is not made any stronger by the use of highly emotional similes. If it is just for God to inflict everlasting punishment on the wicked, then it is neither vindictive nor sadistic for Him to do so; it is right.

Second, if indeed it is just for God to punish the wicked everlastingly, then it is a certainty that the saints in heaven will perceive that justice and will rejoice in its administration, even as they rejoice in all of God's works and decisions. This does not mean that either they or God will derive glee from watching the torments of the damned. It means that they will agree that God's decision to punish the wicked is right and good, and that the punishment that He allots to each lost person is precisely what that person deserves. They will realize that it is only God's grace that stands between them and a similar fate, and so there will be no element of pride or vindictiveness in their joy.

But the saints will indeed be joyful. A much better picture of this joy than Pinnock's simile of the burned cat is the satisfaction the world felt when the Nazi war criminals received their sentences at Nuremberg. Great crimes had been committed. The laws of both God and man had been flouted. It was necessary and good that the dignity of the law and of the human race be reasserted through the prosecution and punishment of the guilty parties. In the same way, the saints in heaven see the punishment of the damned as the proper reassertion of the dignity of God's law and of God Himself, and they cannot help but rejoice in it.

Preaching the Justice of Eternal Punishment

This is a truth that deserves to be preached, because it has extraordinary power to unmask the conceits of the unconverted heart. Those who scoff at the gospel typically do so from the vantage point of their status as people who are loved and respected by others. They can afford to ignore God's view of them because they already enjoy the good opinion of people. But if they persist in their rebellion against God, one day they will lose the sympathy of the redeemed. They deserve to be told this.

One of Edwards's published sermons, "The End of the Wicked Contemplated by the Righteous," is on precisely this topic. In the course of the sermon Edwards explains clearly that the joy the redeemed in heaven will feel over the punishment of the wicked will in no way derive from sadism or a spirit of revenge, but it will express their gratitude toward God for their own salvation and their clear-eyed understanding of the justice of His judgments. He insists also that in this life we are under obligation to love all people, no matter how evil we may consider them, and to seek their salvation. Nevertheless, Edwards says, a time will indeed come when the redeemed will rejoice in the vindication of God's law through the punishment of the wicked.

Having established these facts, Edwards turns to his unconverted hearers and pleads with them to have mercy on their own souls, insisting that if they continue to spurn the grace of God, in the end they will forfeit not only God's love but also that of even their closest family members and friends:

You that have godly parents, who in this world have tenderly loved you, who were wont to look upon your welfare as their own, and were wont to be grieved for you when any thing calamitous befell you in this world, and especially were greatly concerned for the good of your souls . . . how will you bear to see them in the kingdom of God, crowned with glory? . . . How will you bear to see your parents, who in this life had so dear an affection for you, now without any love to you, approving the sentence of condemnation, when Christ shall with indignation bid you depart, wretched, cursed creatures, into eternal burnings?[18]

Edwards then completes the sermon by reminding his hearers that God Himself invites and implores them to repent and believe, and that if they do so, not only they but also all the inhabitants of heaven will rejoice over their salvation.

Let others complain against Edwards if they wish; to me this is courageous, honest preaching, preaching motivated by sincere love for lost people. Edwards is following here in a long and noble line of Christian preachers who have believed that they had a responsibility to confront people with truth, even if doing so involved a painful work of rooting out the last vestiges of false hope. If it is true that those who reject God subject themselves to everlasting contempt from the entire universe, then people need to hear that truth.

Like Edwards, preachers who speak on this theme must do so with great caution, lest they give the impression that the rejoicing of the redeemed over the punishment of the lost is based on any motive lower than a pure love for God and for truth. Again, like Edwards, they must stress that our responsibility in this life is to love every person and do everything in our power to bring about his or her conversion. But love itself also requires that we tell people as much as we know about the fate that awaits them if they reject God's grace.

THE SPIRITUAL IMPORTANCE OF THE DOCTRINE OF JUDGMENT

A Doctrine That Makes Us Sober and Compassionate

Archibald Alexander once compared our knowledge of biblical truth to the seal on a signet ring and the impression made by that truth on our minds to the impression of the seal in the sealing wax that secures a document. He argued that just as any marring of the seal will be evident in the wax, so any defect in our grasp of biblical doctrine will inevitably reveal itself as a defect in our religious feelings and attitudes.[19]

The analogy is a good one and applies well to the doctrine of eternal punishment. For countless generations, this doctrine has made a deep and discernable impression on the minds and in the lives of Christians. It has helped to make them sober, prayerful, grateful, and compassionate. It has deepened their reverence for God and their love for their fellow human beings. It has contributed gravity to Christian character, a quality not much evident in the contemporary church. Far from shunning this doctrine, I suggest that Christians today need to meditate on it long and hard and allow it to work a transformation in our thinking and living.

Futile Lives

In particular, we need to recognize how profoundly this doctrine establishes the futility of lives continuing without Christ. Here, for example, is a loving couple: They have worked hard to make a good life; they have raised their children to be kind, responsible people; they have gone through the last stages of life hand in hand, enjoying together their retirement. Now they face death with courage and dignity. Yet they do not know God, and if they depart this world without repentance, they will suffer the loss of all those things they have worked to create. Cast into everlasting punishment and deprived of that divine grace which in this life prevented them from becoming worse than they were (and which was the real, though unacknowledged, cause of their happiness), they will come in time to hate and blame one another for their misery. They will also curse God for having ever created them.

Gone will be their happiness, their satisfaction, their love. The ultimate purpose of their existence will turn out not to be any of the good deeds they had done in life but the revelation of the justice of God in punishing their sins.

Or again, here is a man known to all as a philanthropist. He has devoted his life to some great cause; he has labored for world peace or the preservation of the environment. Perhaps he has been an educator or writer or philosopher. Perhaps he has also been a church leader. He leaves this world with the sound of human applause still ringing in his ears, but he enters the next one only to discover that in the sight of God, all of his righteous acts are but filthy rags. Having never entrusted himself to Jesus, having never recognized his need for the forgiveness that only Christ can give, this prince among men cannot stand in the presence of the King and must instead suffer eternal retribution for his rebellion.

A Frightening Specter

Frightening thoughts! Thoughts so far out of line with the self-confident spirit of our age as to be almost incredible. Yet thoughts that become inevitable the moment we begin to take with complete seriousness the teaching of Jesus and His apostles. If Jesus were a fraud, then we might safely banish the frightening specter of eternal retribution. Or again, if the Gospels misrepresent the teaching of Jesus—an utterly unpersuasive claim that will nevertheless always find adherents among those who wish to claim allegiance to Jesus while ignoring His words—then we may put the idea of hell behind us once and for all. But if Jesus was who He claimed to be—the Son of God, the authoritative Teacher of all humankind, and the Savior of the world—then hell is as much a reality as the room in which I am now sitting to write this chapter. And it is, moreover, a reality that awaits a large number of our contemporaries.

Rather than reacting against the doctrine, we should examine our own lives closely to see whether they exhibit the kind of serious attitude toward life in general and toward the salvation of others in particular that the doctrine demands of us. If we find the doctrine intolerable, we must nevertheless tolerate it. If we find it appalling, then we must allow ourselves to be appalled. Indeed, we must meditate, weep, repent, and pray; and then go out in the love and power of the Holy Spirit to invite the lost to come in to the wedding supper of the Lamb.

Patient Father, I am burdened by a sense of my great unfaithfulness as a minister of Jesus Christ. If I have been dull of understanding and slow to believe the teaching of Your Word on the awful reality of judgment, even more have I been culpably reluctant to preach this doctrine with clarity and conviction. In how many sermons, I wonder, have I detracted from the greatness of the gospel by failing to speak frankly of Your wrath? How often have I hindered people from gaining a profound grasp of the wonders of Your grace by my cowardly fear of telling them the terrible and deserved fate from which grace saves us? How often have I presented Christ as a means by which lives already rich and free may become still more satisfying, rather than as the only One who can deliver us from everlasting misery?

Forgive me this dereliction of my duty, Lord. Grant that I and all preachers and teachers of Your Word may become more faithful messengers, determined never to displease or misrepresent You and never fearing to speak Your truth. And grant that Your church, rather than chafing at Your justice, may burn with zeal to present Your offer of salvation to every living human being. In Jesus' name, amen.

NOTES

1. For a sharp indictment of evangelicalism's uncritical use of marketing, see David Wells, *God in the Wasteland* (Grand Rapids: Eerdmans, 1995), 60–87.

2. As Shedd wrote more than a century ago, "The strongest support of the doctrine of Endless Punishment is the teaching of Christ, the Redeemer of man. Though the doctrine is plainly taught in the Pauline Epistles, and other parts of Scripture, yet without the explicit and reiterated statements of God incarnate, it is doubtful whether so awful a truth would have had such a conspicuous place as it always has had in the creed of Christendom. . . . Jesus Christ is the Person who is responsible for the doctrine of Eternal Perdition. He is the Being with whom all opponents of this theological tenet are in conflict. Neither the Christian church, nor the Christian ministry are the authors of it." W. G. T. Shedd, *Dogmatic Theology* (New York: Charles Scribner's Sons, 1888), 675, 680.

3. The comments of Spurgeon are worth meditating on: "We know by observation in our pastoral work that while the mercy of God draws many to him, there are some who are more affected at first by the terrors of the Lord. We have many now, who are members of this Church, walking in holiness and in the fear of God, who listened to sermons upon the softer and more tender topics, and were not affected, but who came under the heavy blows of the hammer of God's law, and their flinty hearts were broken into shivers, and ere long they turned unto the hand which smote them. God has ordained both the terrors of the law and the tenderness of the gospel, that by means of both men may be saved." Charles Spurgeon, sermon no. 682, on Hebrews 10:31, quoted from *The Charles H. Spurgeon Collection,* CD-ROM, vers. 1 (Albany, Ore.: Ages Software, 1998).

4. J. I. Packer, *Knowing God* (Downers Grove, Ill.: InterVarsity, 1973), 138.

5. C. S. Lewis, *The Great Divorce* (New York: Simon & Schuster, 1996), 72.

6. Edwards suggests that just as Lazarus in Jesus' parable was carried by the angels to the bosom of Abraham, it is reasonable to suppose that when a wicked man dies, evil spirits pounce upon his soul and carry it off to hell to torment it. *The Works of Jonathan Edwards,* vol. 2, rev. Edward Hickman (1834; repr., Edinburgh: Banner of Truth, 1986), 881.

7. William Crockett does a very fine job of showing why the New Testament pictures of hell are to be interpreted metaphorically rather than literally, though it seems to me that he abandons too quickly the effort to explain the meaning of the metaphors. See *Four Views On Hell,* ed. William Crockett (Grand Rapids: Zondervan, 1992), 43–81.

8. As quoted in John Gerstner, *Heaven and Hell* (Grand Rapids: Baker, 1980), 61.

9. Shedd's argument is an old one, reaching back at least as far as Thomas Aquinas. See Thomas Aquinas, *Summa Theologica: Complete English Edition in 5 Volumes,* trans. the Fathers of the English Dominican Province (Westminster, Md.: Christian Classics, 1981), part 1, Q. 87, A. 4.

10. W. G. T. Shedd, *The Doctrine of Endless Punishment* (1885; repr., Carlisle, Pa.: Banner of Truth, 1986), 129–30.

11. JEdwards, "The Justice of God in the Damnation of Sinners," *Works,* vol. 1, 669; see also "Justification by Faith Alone," *Works,* vol. 1, 628. Anselm's argument for our infinite obligation to God was slightly different. He reasoned that because God is who He is, disobedience to God could never be right, even if by disobeying God we could save the entire creation. See his *Cur Deus Homo,* chap. 21.

12. Edwards, *Works,* vol. 1, 640.

13. Edward William Fudge and Robert A. Peterson, *Two Views of Hell* (Downers Grove, Ill.: InterVarsity, 2000), 191–92. Pinnock makes a nearly identical argument in Crockett, ed., *Four Views on Hell,* 152–53.

14. John Piper, *Let the Nations Be Glad* (Grand Rapids: Baker, 1993), 22.

15. David L. Edwards and John Stott, *Evangelical Essentials: A Liberal-Evangelical Dialogue* (Downers Grove, Ill.: InterVarsity, 1988), 314.

16. Hans Urs von Balthasar, *Dare We Hope "That All Men Be Saved"?* (San Francisco: Ignatius, 1988), 202.

17. Clark Pinnock, "The Conditional View," Crockett, ed., *Four Views on Hell,* 140.

18. Edwards, *Works,* vol. 2, 211.

19. Archibald Alexander, *Thoughts on Religious Experience* (1844; repr., Edinburgh: Banner of Truth, 1967), xvii.

PART TWO

At His Mercy

If I am ignorant of the nature, extent and limits of what I can and must do with reference to God, I shall be equally ignorant and uncertain of the nature, extent and limits of what God can and will do in me. . . . Now, if I am ignorant of God's works and power, I am ignorant of God Himself; and if I do not know God, I cannot worship, praise, give thanks or serve Him, for I do not know how much I should attribute to myself and how much to Him. We need, therefore, to have in mind a clear-cut distinction between God's power and ours, and God's work and ours, if we would live a godly life.

✝MARTIN LUTHER
The Bondage of the Will

✻

I have my own private opinion that there is no such thing as preaching Christ and Him crucified, unless we preach what is nowadays called Calvinism. It is a nickname to call it Calvinism; Calvinism is the gospel, and nothing else. I do not believe we can preach the gospel . . . unless we preach the sovereignty of God in His dispensation of grace; nor unless we exalt the electing, unchangeable, eternal, immutable, conquering love of Jehovah; nor do I think we can preach the gospel unless we base it upon the special and particular redemption of His elect and chosen people which Christ wrought out upon the Cross; nor can I comprehend a gospel which lets saints fall away after they are called.

✝CHARLES SPURGEON
C. H. Spurgeon: The Early Years

4

HIS CHOICE,
MY CHOICE

*"No one can come to me unless
the Father who sent me draws him.
And I will raise him up at the last day."*

+JOHN 6:44

PREDESTINATION. FOR YEARS the very word made me angry. I didn't just consider the idea wrong; I believed it demonic. It made God into a tyrant and human life into a puppet show.

All human freedom and all pretense of love on God's part were rendered ridiculous by the doctrine of predestination—that God determines who will and who will not be saved. In seminary I debated the point with professors and a pastor, and I thought my arguments to be watertight. A predestining God simply could not be the God of Jesus Christ, who wept over Jerusalem's hardness of heart.

At the same time, however, I had other experiences and thoughts that pointed me in a very different direction. I remember a cold Connecticut night, just a few weeks after my conversion, when a few friends and I were walking back to our dormitory after an evening church service. The conversation turned to predestination, and although each of us found the concept repellent, we also each found that we were not comfortable attributing our conversions to ourselves. It seemed to us that there must be some kind of divine plan behind our choices. Even more, we found that we were intensely uncomfortable with the idea of taking credit for being in Christ, as if we were somehow smarter or more moral than our friends and relatives who were still not believers.

In my case, conversion came about as a result of my reading certain books and following certain trains of thought; once I had become a believer in Christ, I figured those same books and thoughts ought to persuade all who encountered them. I accordingly passed around copies of C. S. Lewis's *Mere Christianity* and various other books to friends and family, and explained the logic of my own belief in letters and long conversations. Yet nobody believed on the basis of those arguments! It was as if a door had opened for me into Lewis's land of Narnia but then closed before anybody else could pass through. It did not seem to me—and still does not—that I was wrong to be persuaded by those arguments. In fact, nobody with whom I discussed them offered any substantial refutation. Yet neither did my friends find the arguments compelling.

The most common response was polite indifference: "We're glad for you, but please don't push your views on us." This was astounding and depressing. It was as if I had discovered an immense treasure and earnestly sought to share it with others, only to find that most acted irritated to be asked even to look at it!

How could I understand this? I knew that the explanation could not lie in any superiority in myself: I was not more moral, honest, or intelligent than those who disagreed with me. My conviction that Christianity is true, my realization that I must put my faith in Jesus, my newfound love for Him and desire to be like Him—all these could not be attributed to any qualities or virtues in me. Where, then, did they come from?

Why Do We Believe?

Confusion and Conflict About God's Role

I mention these personal feelings and experiences because I am convinced that they are representative of the feelings of many, if not most, Christians. The idea of predestination frightens us; it suggests that God is cruel and that human life is meaningless, since God seemingly makes the spiritual choice, not us. Moreover, we know that we have in fact made real and unconstrained choices to believe in Jesus. Nobody forced us; we came to Him because we wanted to. At the same time, we are conflicted. We shrink from ascribing any portion of our salvation to ourselves, and we find it natural to think of our conversions as having been brought about by the power of God and in response to the prayers of others.

The confusion and conflict deepen when we ourselves turn to prayer, because most of us quite readily pray for the conversion of our friends and relatives. We ask that God draw them, convert them, give them new birth, change their hearts—anything to bring them into the kingdom of His Son! We take it for granted that they must come willingly, since to come to Christ unwillingly is not to come at all. Nevertheless, we ask God to *make* them willing to come, and we do not feel that in doing so we are asking Him to violate their freedom. Furthermore, if they do in fact come, we spontaneously and gladly thank God and give Him the credit!

It seems, then, that when we think about predestination in the abstract we find it repugnant, but when we consider the origins of our own faith or pray for others to believe, we almost immediately think and pray like predestinarians.

A Personal Search for Clarity

Eventually I became sufficiently uncomfortable with my confusion over this issue that I decided I must study it more deeply. I was encouraged in this resolution by the discovery that the doctrine of predestination has been held in one form or another by virtually all of the theologians who have been viewed by the church as its greatest thinkers: Augustine, Aquinas, Luther, Calvin, Edwards. We cannot assume that the doctrine is true simply because great leaders have believed it, but the fact that they have believed it should make us hesitant to reject it uncritically, especially since each of them claimed to have found the doctrine in the Bible. That, at least, is how I reasoned.

I began to read the writings of those thinkers on the subject of predestination and free will, and at the same time I began to give serious attention to the passages in the Bible that seemed to point most strongly toward predestinarian conclusions. In time, I came to feel that those conclusions simply cannot be avoided if we are to take the Scriptures with complete seriousness.

This was not a welcome development to me at the time, but over the intervening years I have come to embrace predestination not only as an unavoidable deduction from biblical texts but also as a truth that nourishes and strengthens my soul. I have come slowly to understand why the Reformed tradition of Protestant theology has defended the doctrine with such vehemence. I have moved inch by inch to the point where I can agree with Jonathan Edwards, who said that although he originally hated the idea of divine control over man's salvation, in time he came to a place where absolute sovereignty was what he most loved to ascribe to God.

What follows in this section of the book is, first, an attempt to indicate from Scripture why the doctrine of predestination cannot be avoided, and second, an effort to show how nurturing, encouraging, and strengthening this doctrine really is. In this chapter I will set forth the major competitors to the Reformed or Calvinistic understanding of predestination, explaining briefly in each case why I find them unconvincing. In the next two chapters I will make a biblical case for Calvinism, deal with some moral objections, and also set forth some of the benefits of Calvinistic thinking to the Christian's spiritual health and growth.

TREAD CAREFULLY, THINK PRAYERFULLY!

Before we begin, one word of warning. The doctrine of predestination stirs up powerful emotions in us. Those who love it are at times inclined to speak derogatorily of those who do not, while those who hate the doctrine cannot understand how anybody could be so blind as to fail to see the injury it does to the honor of God and the dignity of human freedom.

Historically, both Calvinists and their adversaries have denounced one another as heretics and have issued dire warnings of the disasters that will befall the church if the opposing views are accepted. Not infrequently, theologians have devoted more energy to depicting one another as either wicked or stupid than to wrestling with the biblical issues. For many people, the very language we use to discuss these issues—"Calvinism," "Reformed theology," "election," "free will"—stimulates tension or anger even before the concepts have been defined. I urge the reader to resist the temptation to allow his or her emotions to become too quickly inflamed over this issue.

No area of theology is more difficult than this one. The doctrine of the Trinity equals predestination in intellectual complexity, but it has far less power to kindle our fears and threaten our pride. It is not at all surprising that there are great differences of opinion in the church about predestination; no doubt there will be so until the Lord returns. We must recognize that there are good and sincere Christians on both (or all) sides of this issue, and then move forward thoughtfully and prayerfully, asking God to enlighten our minds and strengthen our hearts. When we find our studies too taxing or confusing, we should take a break from our efforts to be good theologians and make sure that we are at least good worshipers and good witnesses. And when we find anger and indignation toward our fellow Christians rising in our hearts, we should ask God to make us humble and contrite in spirit.

Our goal is not to win victories over one another. Our goal is to know God rightly and to learn to love both Him and His world.

AN ISSUE OF CHOICE

But how do we approach so large and forbidding a subject as predestination? One relatively simple way is to raise the question of the logical relationship between God's choice of us and our choice of Him. The Bible is quite clear that believers have been chosen by God, as the following texts remind us:

Who shall bring any charge against God's elect? (Romans 8:33)

So too at the present time there is a remnant, chosen by grace. (Romans 11:5)

Blessed be the God and Father of our Lord Jesus Christ, who has blessed us in Christ with every spiritual blessing in the heavenly places, even as he chose us in him before the foundation of the world. (Ephesians 1:3–4)

111

For we know, brothers loved by God, that he has chosen you. (1 Thessalonians 1:4)

But you are a chosen race, a royal priesthood, a holy nation. (1 Peter 2:9)

Those who follow Christ are "God's elect" and part of "a chosen race" (Rom. 8:33; 1 Peter 2:9). Yet both Scripture and practical Christian experience also make it clear that we choose God.

Everywhere in the Bible we are urged to turn to Christ, to believe in Him, to look to Him, and to follow Him; and there is no suggestion anywhere that our decision to accept these invitations is other than free in the sense that it is truly ours. Many Christians know the exact date and even the exact hour when they made their choice to trust in Christ, as well as the train of reasoning that led to that choice.

So there are two choices: God's choice of us, and our choice of Him. But what is the relationship between those choices? Did God choose me because He foresaw that I would choose Him? Or did I choose Him because He previously chose me and then worked in me to cause me to choose Him? Or is it possible that we have to abandon altogether the effort to state the logical connection between these two acts of choice and simply assert both to be true without harmonizing them? Keeping our focus on this issue—the logical relationship between our choice of God and His choice of us—will take us straight to the core of the various competing explanations of predestination.

THE ARMINIAN EXPLANATION: "GOD CHOOSES US BECAUSE HE FORESEES THAT WE WILL CHOOSE HIM."

By far the strongest competitor to the Calvinistic understanding of predestination is Arminianism. Although Arminianism was once a minority position among Protestants, at present the tables have been turned. At least within the United States, a majority of evangelicals hold to an Arminian theology.

Arminianism takes its name from a seventeenth-century Dutch professor, Jacobus Arminius, who took offense at the theology of the Belgic Confession of Faith and the Heidelberg Catechism (and, by extension, the theology of the Protestant Reformers of the sixteenth century).[1] In 1610 some of Arminius's followers, who became known as the "Remonstrants," presented five theses to the state of Holland as a "remonstrance," or protest, against that teaching.

There are variations among Arminian theologians on some of these theses, but they still provide a convenient outline for a presentation of Arminianism. In the numbered headings that follow, I will use Roger Nicole's summary of the Remonstrants' articles.[2]

The Arminian View of Predestination

"I. God elects or reproves on the basis of foreseen faith or unbelief." Here we have the fundamental idea of Arminianism: God's choice of us rests upon His foreknowledge of our choice of Him. God elects those whom He knows will believe in Him and persevere in their faith to the end. From the Arminian point of view, only this understanding of the predestinarian passages of the Bible can save God from the charge of being cruel or arbitrary. Eternal election is a divine reality, but it is, so to speak, an advance confirmation of free human choices. It is the human choice, not the divine one, that is decisive in determining a person's salvation or damnation. Arminians support this idea with the use of such passages as Romans 8:29 ("For those whom he foreknew he also predestined to be conformed to the image of his Son") and 1 Peter 1:1–2 ("To those who are elect exiles . . . according to the foreknowledge of God the Father"), which they interpret to mean that God chooses those whom He, in His perfect knowledge of future events, sees will eventually choose Him.

"II. Christ died for all men and for every man, although only believers are saved." The Remonstrants, like most Arminians since them, rejected universalism as unbiblical. Nevertheless, they were troubled by the Calvinistic idea that Christ died for the elect only, as this seemed to them to place limitations upon God's love. Doesn't the Bible say that God so loved the world that He gave His only Son (John 3:16)? Isn't Jesus Christ described in Scripture as the propitiation "for the sins of the whole world" (1 John 2:2)? And doesn't Scripture make it plain that God is not willing that any should perish but desires that all should come to a knowledge of the truth and be saved (1 Tim. 2:4; 2 Peter 3:9)? The obvious implication, from the Arminian point of view, is that Christ died for each and every human being, but whether any given human being will be saved is determined by the person's own free choice. God has provided salvation for every person; all that remains is for us to receive that salvation through the response of repentance and faith.

"III. Man is so depraved that divine grace is necessary unto faith or any good deed." This article distinguishes the Arminians from Pelagians, who deny that Adam's fall into sin has affected the rest of the human race. To a Pelagian, each of us has the power to believe in Christ and to do other spiritually good deeds without any divine assistance whatsoever. Arminians, on the other hand, insist that Adam's fall has corrupted the entire race, with the result that we can do no spiritual good without God's help. An Arminian would interpret such a passage as John 6:44 ("No one can come to me unless the Father who sent me draws him") to mean that no person will come to faith in Christ unless the Father, acting by the power of the Holy Spirit, woos and persuades that person to exercise his free will and choose to believe.

"IV. This grace may be resisted." On the other hand, Arminians are convinced that the final decision whether to believe or disbelieve lies completely with the human being, and so they insist that the grace by which God calls a person can be resisted. God can invite us into His kingdom, but only we can walk through the door. For God to compel us to believe would be for Him to violate our freedom, and this He will never do. In support of their understanding of this relationship between grace and free will, Arminians point to such texts as Luke 7:30 ("But the Pharisees and the lawyers rejected the purpose of God for themselves") and Acts 7:51 ("You stiff-necked people, uncircumcised in heart and ears, you always resist the Holy Spirit").

"V. Whether all who are truly regenerate will certainly persevere in the faith is a point that needs further investigation." Finally, the Remonstrants found themselves unable to agree on the issue of final perseverance of the saints. Uncertainty on this point has remained among Arminians, with the majority insisting that it is possible for genuine Christians to fall away and be eternally lost and others asserting that the regenerate are eternally secure.

The Attractiveness of Arminianism

Arminianism has a very strong initial attraction. Arminians are able to provide plausible interpretations of many of the biblical passages that concern the relationship between God's will and the human will. Their scheme appeals to our common-sense view of both freedom and justice. Some people choose to believe in Christ, and for that choice they deserve praise. Others choose to reject Him, and their choice merits censure. It is not immediately clear how these facts can be reconciled with a perspective that makes God's choice, rather than the human decision, the determining factor in salvation.

Moreover, Arminianism seems to protect God from even the hint of unfairness or favoritism, since His election means nothing more than His foreknowledge of our self-election. The Calvinist idea of unconditional divine election brings us into immediate and great difficulty over divine fairness; but Arminianism, at least on the surface, frees us from all our fears that God may turn out to be arbitrary or cruel.

TAKING ISSUE WITH THE ARMINIAN VIEW

In spite of this aura of plausibility, I am convinced that the Arminian scheme is quite wrong. I will develop a detailed biblical case against Arminianism and for Calvinism in the next two chapters, but here let me simply raise the issues that most troubled me in my own Arminian days and impelled me to investigate the Calvinist alternative.

Nothing of Which to Boast

First, Arminianism violates the Christian's inner conviction, based both on Scripture and on self-examination, that the ultimate cause of his salvation cannot lie within himself. In 1 Corinthians 4:7 Paul writes, "For who sees anything different in you? What do you have that you did not receive? If then you received it, why do you boast as if you did not receive it?" Paul's point in this passage is to show the Corinthians that they cannot boast, because everything they have, and everything that makes them different from other people, is from God. But the Arminian has to take issue with Paul at this point. The Arminian says, "Well, for the *most part* it is God who makes me different from anyone else, and *most* of what I have I received from Him, and there is really little of which I may properly boast. But as for my decision to trust in Christ, and my faith in Him at this moment, and my confidence that I will continue to believe in Him in the future, these are all from myself, and of them I may boast." I cannot imagine any Christian actually making such a statement, but is that not the conclusion to which Arminianism naturally leads?

The Bible says that "Salvation comes from the LORD" (Jonah 2:9 NIV), but Arminianism, even if unwittingly, says, "Salvation is partly from the Lord and partly from the exercise of human freedom." The Bible says, "For by grace you have been saved through faith. And this is not your own doing; it is the gift of God, not a result of works, so that no one may boast" (Eph. 2:8–9), but Arminianism says, "It is chiefly by grace that we have been saved, but not entirely; and we may very appropriately assume credit for the faith through which we receive salvation since it is an act of our own free will."

Again, I do not claim that Arminians actually make such statements, but neither do I see how they can logically avoid them. If God's choice of me rests ultimately upon His foreknowledge of my choice of Him, then it is just and right for me to take credit for my salvation and to view myself as in some way superior to the person who makes a decision not to believe. Maybe I am smarter than my friends who haven't believed, or maybe I am more virtuous; one way or the other, it is by my own freedom that I differ from those others, and it would be false modesty to refuse to boast. Yet what Christian wants to boast in this way? Arminianism may square with ordinary human notions of justice, but it doesn't square with the Christian understanding of divine grace.

Whatever Happened to God's Initiative in Election?

Second, even in the days when I rejected Calvinism, it seemed to me that Arminianism disposed just a little too easily of the biblical problem of predestination. In the first place, the Arminian view of election seems to create a strange discontinuity between the Old and New Testaments. God's choosing of Israel was clearly a unilateral action on His part and had nothing to do with His foreknowledge that Israel would choose Him. We are given no reason to suppose that God called several other people at the same time He called Abram and that only Abram responded. No, the point of Genesis 12:1 is simply that, out of the mass of humanity, God assumed the initiative to choose this one man. Even more clearly, God's choice of Jacob over Esau was a sovereign decision on God's part; He chose Jacob before the twins were born or had done anything good or bad (Rom. 9:11–13). In Deuteronomy 7:6–8 Moses tells the Israelites that they are God's "treasured possession," chosen out of all the people of the earth. Yet they are not to think that they were chosen because they were numerous; rather, God chose them because He loved them.

Nowhere in Scripture is any higher or prior ground given for their election than this divine love. There is no hint here or anywhere else that they were chosen because of decisions that God foresaw they or their leaders would make.

But if the emphasis in the Old Testament doctrine of election is always on God's initiative, how does it come to mean something so different— a mere aspect of divine foreknowledge—in the New Testament?

The Arminians' Trouble in Interpreting Predestinarian Passages

Furthermore, it is hard to see that divine election really means anything at all on Arminian principles, which makes it difficult to understand why the New Testament devotes so much attention to it. If "God chose us" really just means "God foresaw that we would choose him," then why should the Bible even bother to speak of God's choosing? Let me illustrate the point with two texts of Scripture.

First, look at 1 Corinthians 1:26–31:

> *For consider your calling, brothers: not many of you were wise according to worldly standards, not many were powerful, not many were of noble birth. But God chose what is foolish in the world to shame the wise; God chose what is weak in the world to shame the strong; God chose what is low and despised in the world, even things that are not, to bring to nothing things that are, so that no human being might boast in the presence of God. He is the source of your life in Christ Jesus, whom God made our wisdom and our righteousness and sanctification and redemption. Therefore, as it is written, "Let the one who boasts, boast in the Lord."*

At least on the face of it, this passage is about God's exercise of His prerogative to choose whom He will. He has deliberately chosen people who may be considered weak or foolish in order to shame those who are strong, so that no one may boast before Him. Therefore, the Christians in Corinth should recognize that it is by God's grace that they are in Christ, and they should boast only in Him. On this reading, the passage sets up a relationship of opposition between God's election on the one hand and human boasting on the other. The Corinthians must not boast, not only because the initiative in their election lay with God, but also because their election is, if anything, a sign of their lowliness and weakness.

If Arminianism is correct, however, and God simply chooses those who choose Him, then it seems that we have to radically reinterpret the passage. In this case, what Paul is really saying is that the weak and foolish chose God (as He of course foreknew they would), while the wise and strong did not. Though apparently about God's prerogative to choose whom He will, the passage actually is a discussion of human choices. But if this is so, then what is the point of the discussion? And how does the reference to God's choosing counteract the tendency of the Corinthians to boast?

A Corinthian Christian might, I suppose, say something like this: "Well, perhaps my decision to believe in Christ is in one sense a sign of my 'weakness' or 'foolishness,' but in another and much deeper sense it is evidence of my superiority. The 'wise' ones of the world may look down on me, but I have chosen the better path and have thereby shown that it is they who are the fools." But this leaves the Christian boasting in himself, which is the very thing Paul is trying to avoid! Surely the Calvinist understanding of the passage is the more logical one.

Second, consider Romans 9. In that passage, Paul is anguishing over the unbelief of many of his fellow Jews and trying to explain that unbelief in theological terms.[3] In verses 6–13, Paul seems to deal with the problem by appealing to divine sovereignty: Just as God sovereignly chose Jacob over Esau, so now He is choosing some for faith and leaving others in unbelief. Paul then responds to the objection that rises naturally in every human heart at this point—that God's action is unfair. Let's consider Paul's answer in its entirety:

*What shall we say then? Is there injustice on God's part? By no means!
For he says to Moses, "I will have mercy on whom I have mercy, and I
will have compassion on whom I have compassion." So then it depends
not on human will or exertion, but on God, who has mercy. For the Scripture says to Pharaoh, "For this very purpose I have raised you up, that I
might show my power in you, and that my name might be proclaimed in
all the earth." So then he has mercy on whomever he wills, and he hardens whomever he wills.*

*You will say to me then, "Why does he still find fault? For who can
resist his will?" But who are you, O man, to answer back to God? Will
what is molded say to its molder, "Why have you made me like this?" Has
the potter no right over the clay, to make out of the same lump one vessel
for honored use and another for dishonorable use? What if God, desiring
to show his wrath and to make known his power, has endured with much
patience vessels of wrath prepared for destruction, in order to make
known the riches of his glory for vessels of mercy, which he has prepared
beforehand for glory—even us whom he has called, not from the Jews
only but also from the Gentiles? As indeed he says in Hosea, "Those who
were not my people I will call 'my people,' and her who was not beloved I
will call 'beloved.' And in the very place where it was said to them, 'You
are not my people,' there they will be called 'sons of the living God.'"*
(Romans 9:14–26)

This is a hard passage, and I do not propose to offer a detailed
interpretation. We will take a closer look at it in chapter 9. All I want
to do right now is ask whether Paul's response to his imaginary inter-
rogator makes any sense if Paul's doctrine is Arminian. If all Paul is saying is that God chooses those whom He foresees will believe, then why
is Paul concerned that somebody may accuse God of injustice? If it is
the human decision to believe that is of ultimate significance, why does
Paul feel he needs to insist on God's sovereign rights over His creation?
Why does not Paul simply say something like this, "Oh, you thought
I meant that God sovereignly decides who will and who will not be
saved? Nothing of the sort! God just chooses those who choose Him!"
The fact that Paul does not respond in that way but instead enters
into a defense of God's right to do as He wishes with His creatures is,
I suggest, a powerful indication that the apostle Paul is no Arminian.

I will not belabor the point, but I think the truth is that Arminianism runs into difficulty every time it tries to make sense of biblical passages that refer to election. The reader might wish to take some time to meditate on such passages as Ephesians 1:11, 1 Thessalonians 1:4, and 1 Peter 2:9, asking in each case why the biblical writer has chosen to introduce the idea of election into the discussion. I believe it will be readily seen that in each such passage, election serves either to magnify the sovereign majesty of God and humble the pride of man, or to give believers confidence in God's power to save them fully.

The reader should then ask himself a further question: If Arminianism is true, and election is primarily about our choice for God and only secondarily about His choice for us, how does the Bible's use of this doctrine further the ends of exalting God and humbling and assuring believers? My own conviction is that Arminianism renders the Bible's predestinarian passages meaningless.

So it seems that while Arminianism provides a plausible explanation of *some* biblical passages and *some* portions of Christian experience, it runs into serious difficulty at certain other points. Even if we feel an affinity for Arminianism (as I certainly did at one point and as the reader may now), our desire for a coherent understanding of the Bible should push us to study further.

THE OPEN THEIST EXPLANATION:
"OUR DECISION FOR GOD TAKES HIM BY SURPRISE."

In recent years a new form of Arminianism has appeared, one that is in some ways closer in spirit to process theology than to historic Arminianism.[4] It is characterized by an astonishing willingness to abandon the doctrine of God's omniscience. The argument is very simple: While God certainly knows everything that can be known, the future acts of free creatures are inherently unknowable until they occur. Therefore God cannot know in advance what we will do. And if He cannot know what we will do, He obviously cannot know whether we will decide to believe in Him or whether, having made such a decision, we will persevere in our faith to the end of life. This means that it is necessary for us to completely reinterpret the predestinarian biblical texts in such a way as to avoid the implication that God elects or predestines individuals. Instead, God has elected to have a community of believers, and it is up to us to decide whether to join that community. Advocates of this position include Gregory Boyd, Clark Pinnock, Richard Rice, John Sanders, William Hasker, and David Basinger.[5] They describe their position as "Free-Will Theism" or the "Openness of God" view. I will refer to it as "open theism."

This approach to the problem of the relationship between God's will and ours is so plainly incompatible with both Scripture and the Christian theological tradition that it is hard to believe it will endure for long within the evangelical community. One certainly hopes not. Nevertheless, it is a position that has made considerable headway over the past decade, and so it is wise to touch at least lightly on its most fundamental weakness.

TAKING ISSUE WITH THE OPEN THEIST VIEW

Iron Cages of Metaphysics

As I read the writings of the free-will theists, I am reminded of a passage in George MacDonald's *Creation in Christ* where, after expressing his disgust for the classical understanding of God's justice as demanding punishment for sin, MacDonald cries out, "Away with your doctrines! Away with your salvation from the 'justice' of a God whom it is a horror to imagine! Away with your iron cages of false metaphysics!"[6] The cry of these advocates of open theism is similar: "Away with divine foreknowledge! Away with divine sovereignty! Away with the hard doctrines that come along with the classical doctrine of God!"

The question, however, is whether the open theists themselves have created an iron cage of false metaphysics. They arrive at their position through a syllogism: Human beings are free; the actions of free beings are inherently unknowable until they occur; therefore, God does not know the future. The conclusion seems logical enough, and so on the basis of their logic they go ahead to thoroughly rewrite the Christian faith, thinking that they are thereby liberating Christians from an oppressive theological tradition.

The problem is that their logic, however appealing it may be to them, is simply wrong. The Bible teaches *both* that man has free agency and is responsible for his actions *and* that God foreknows all that comes to pass. These teachers claim that the theological tradition has not allowed the Bible to speak for itself; they point to passages in which God's response to human beings varies as they respond to Him. But these passages can be readily understood within the traditional theological framework, where God perfectly knows the future yet interacts with human beings in time. There is mystery here, but no contradiction. There is, however, a very great contradiction between open theism and the teaching of Scripture, for the Bible is quite plain about God's perfect knowledge of the future.

God's Perfect Foreknowledge

God, according to Scripture, is the One who makes known the end from the beginning (Isa. 46:10), and His knowledge of the future is what distinguishes Him from idols (Isa. 41:21–22; 44:7–8). Throughout the Bible He foretells events centuries before their occurrence—not just natural events, but events that depend largely or entirely upon human decisions. In Isaiah 44:28 He names Cyrus as the ruler who will build up Jerusalem, yet the name of Cyrus and even his existence as a human being depended upon an unimaginably long and complex series of human decisions separating the prophecy from its fulfillment. Similarly, in 1 Kings 13:2 God predicts the birth of Josiah approximately three hundred years before the event. In 2 Kings 19:25 (NIV) He states explicitly that He had "ordained" and "planned" the military victories of the Assyrians long before they occurred.

And so it is throughout the Bible: God foretells the Egyptians' voluntary oppression of Israel (Gen. 15:13), Pharaoh's hardening his heart against Moses (Ex. 3:19), the rejection of Isaiah's message by the Israelites (Isa. 6:9), the rebellion of the Israelites after Moses' death (Deut. 31:16), Judas's voluntary betrayal of Christ (John 6:70–71), and so on. One might possibly respond that in some of these instances God was able to predict with high accuracy what would happen; for example, the prophecy about Pharaoh was based on God's knowledge of the man's stubbornness. But this kind of explanation simply won't work when we are speaking of prophecies of events that lie hundreds of years in the future, at the end of a chain of millions or billions of relevant human choices.

Furthermore, it is very common in Scripture for God to draw special attention to His foreknowledge of human events so as to emphasize His presence and sovereign activity. To take a simple example, in 1 Samuel 9–10 we read of the events surrounding the anointing of Saul as the first king of Israel. After several days of searching for his father's lost donkeys, Saul wanted to return home, but his servant persuaded him to seek direction from a man of God. He found Samuel just as the prophet was about to offer a sacrifice, and Samuel immediately knew who Saul was because of a revelation he had received a day earlier; indeed, Samuel had already told the cook to set aside a choice piece of meat for Saul's consumption. Samuel informed Saul that he was to be the king, anointed him secretly, and then told him precisely what would happen to him when he left Samuel's presence: He would first meet two men near Rachel's tomb who would give him a message, and then he would meet three more men who would offer him gifts.

All the important details of the story—the servant's insistence that they seek guidance from a prophet, their arrival in the town just as Samuel is about to offer his sacrifice, Samuel's preparations for Saul's arrival, and the signs Samuel gave Saul to prove that God had chosen him—depended on human choices. The very fact that God foreknew these choices and worked His will through them proved that Saul was indeed the one He had chosen. God's precise foreknowledge of human choices is not incidental to the story but essential; it is one of its key theological themes.

Divine "Openness" and the Crucifixion

But the utter impossibility of the "openness" position can perhaps be most easily seen if we focus on the central event of the Bible, the crucifixion of Jesus. According to Peter, Jesus was handed over to His enemies "according to the definite plan and foreknowledge of God" (Acts 2:23), and they did to Him what God's "hand and . . . plan had predestined to take place" (Acts 4:28). I doubt whether any reader of the Bible would ever suppose that "predestined" means "decided the day before." Plainly, it means that God made this decision in eternity.

The question we have to ask ourselves is this: If God does not exercise any control over the actions of human beings, and in fact does not even know in advance what we will do, how could He possibly have decided, hundreds of years in advance—let alone in eternity—what should happen to His Son? If God does not know future human acts, then He did not eternally know that there would be such a man as Pilate or even such an empire as Rome, since both human procreation and military conquest depend on human choices. Far less could He have known whether one of Jesus' disciples would decide to betray Jesus, whether the Jewish leaders would receive or reject their Messiah, whether Pilate would protect Jesus or hand Him over for crucifixion, or whether the Roman soldiers would obey the command to nail Him to the cross. To put it bluntly, God did not know that His Son would be crucified for the sins of the world.

Setting aside the problem that God could not even know in advance that human beings would be in need of a savior, the most that could possibly be said of His eternal foreknowledge of that event, on the basis of the doctrine of the openness of God, is that He knew that one day He would send His Son into the world and that, human nature being what it is, it was likely that His Son would be killed by somebody or other, at some time or other, and in some manner or other.

Merely to state the problem in this way is to reveal the hopeless inadequacy of open theism. The advocates of this view presumably do not intend to undermine the Christian faith, but it is difficult to see their proposal as less than catastrophic in its implications.

The crucifixion of Jesus Christ, the hinge pin of history and the indispensable condition of our salvation, was most certainly not left up to the vagaries of human decision! It was ordained from the foundation of the earth, and it is impossible that it might not have occurred. The Bible nowhere suggests or even permits the interpretation that Judas, Caiaphas, Pilate, and the soldiers were unwilling pawns forced by God into the commission of a horrible crime. They acted freely, in accordance with their own motives and purposes. Yet they did what God's hand and plan had predestined should happen.

Open Theism and Human Dignity

The great irony of open theism (as also of its parent, process theology) is that it destroys that which it sets out to protect. The claim is that when we deny divine foreknowledge of human decisions we safeguard the dignity of human freedom. In reality, this denial undermines the kind of dignity the Bible is most eager to grant to us. The Bible consistently portrays God as knowing all things before they happen, and the biblical writers, far from feeling threatened by this truth, take the greatest comfort in it. In Psalm 139 David praises God for His intimate knowledge of him, and the praise reaches its peak in the affirmation that all the days ordained for him were written in God's book before one of them came to be (v. 16). David plainly believes and glories in a God who is in utter control of his life. His comfort and sense of purpose are wrapped up in his faith in a God who has ordained his life and the events of his life. Christian believers have always found encouragement in the realization that nothing can happen to them apart from the plan of God.

Imagine for a moment a young woman who knows that the only reason for her own existence, humanly speaking, is that her mother was violently raped. Imagine further that the mother has never married and is resentful toward her daughter for the disruption she has brought into her own life. What comfort can there be for this young lady? From the standpoint of secular reasoning, she never should have come into the world. She is unwanted by her parents and by the universe itself.

Yet from a biblical point of view, there is much comfort for her. If she comes to faith in Christ, she can know with certainty that she was chosen by God before the very creation of the earth (Eph. 1:4). She can know that God intended her existence and that He loved her even before she existed. She can know that the sordid circumstances surrounding her conception in no way detract from the rightness of her presence in the world or from her dignity as a being planned and created by God. God knows the future and overrules all natural events and human decisions. She is alive because God, from all eternity, decided to create her. Even if her parents do not want her, the God of the universe does and always has (Ps. 27:10). And that means that her life has no less meaning than that of a person born into a happy family.

But what would open theism say to this situation? What comfort could it offer this woman? Only the comfort that God's character is such that He loves all those who, willy-nilly, find their way into existence. The open theist cannot say that God planned her life, that He has loved her with an everlasting love, that He chose her in Christ before the creation of the world, or even that He foresaw that she would be. Open theism steals from her the rich encouragement and high dignity that the Bible would bestow on her and leaves her in a position hardly better than that she would be in if she had no belief in God whatsoever.

Divine Foreknowledge and Human Freedom

So it seems that the advocates of God's "openness" have built themselves a metaphysical iron cage, giving more credence to their own logic than to the text of the Bible. It is simultaneously true that human beings are free agents, fully responsible for their actions and choices, and that God perfectly foreknows those actions and choices. Does this create a philosophical problem? Of course it does. It creates a problem that no theologian has ever been able to solve. If God foreknows our actions, then our actions are predetermined. If predetermined, then it would seem that they are not truly free.

Nonetheless, the Bible teaches both that God foreknows all things and that we are responsible for what we do, and we have no right to deny either of these truths just because we cannot see how they cohere. Although the advocates of open theism claim that it is the Calvinists who have stretched Christian theology on a procrustean bed of deterministic logic, the reality is that it is Calvinism (and on this point traditional Arminianism as well) that humbly accepts the testimony of Scripture.

No, the open theists' "solution" to the problem of predestination comes at far too high a price. We will have to continue our search for an adequate understanding of the Bible's teaching on election.

THE EXPLANATION OF KARL BARTH: "GOD'S DECISION FOR US NEGATES OUR DECISION AGAINST HIM (MAYBE)."

Without question, the most creative and provocative treatment of the doctrine of election of the past century is that of Karl Barth, in his monumental *Church Dogmatics*. Barth unequivocally rejects the Arminian claim that divine election is grounded in foreknowledge of human decision, but he also decisively rejects the Calvinist doctrine of an "absolute decree" by which God eternally and unchangeably determines who will and who will not be saved. Barth proposes that the idea of the absolute decree has obscured the fact that there can be no decision in God prior to His decision to be the God and Father of Jesus Christ. The failure to realize this has led Calvinistic thinkers to an abstract notion of predestination that is more pagan than Christian. For Barth, Jesus Christ is the decree. Furthermore, Christ is the elect man, as well as the electing God; and it is in Christ that all others are elect.

But Christ is not only the elect man; He is also the reprobate man, who has borne in Himself the divine rejection that is the result of sin. In Christ all people are elect, and in Him all are also rejected. And because He has borne our rejection, nothing remains for us but the favor of God. There are those who are "rejected" in the sense that they reject their own election, and these play a constructive temporary role in the world by their unwitting testimony to the rejection borne by Christ. Nevertheless, no one is rejected by God.

In predestination, says Barth, "We shall never find . . . the decreed rejection either of ourselves or of any other men. This is not because we did not deserve rejection, but because God did not will it, because God willed the rejection of His Son in our stead."[7] The rejected man is already forgiven, though he does not realize it, and he cannot be rejected anymore.[8] Barth will not take the step of affirming universal salvation, but neither will he affirm that any will finally be lost. If human beings decide against God, God has nevertheless decided for them in His election of His Son, and His decision for them negates their decision against Him.

The following passage gives a good summary of Barth's thinking:

In Himself, God is free and He remains free. But in His freedom He decides in man's favour for the establishment and preservation of the covenant between Himself and man. He denies and hates the sin of fallen man with whom the covenant is to be made and maintained. But He wills an unequivocal affirmation and love of man himself, and it is in this affirmation and love that the covenant is willed and concluded. He decrees the rejection of the evil-doer, but in predestinating Himself to union with the Son of Man in His Son He decrees that this rejection should be lifted from man and laid upon Himself. In spite of man's unworthiness in himself, He wills and affirms and loves man, yet in so doing He does not will the continuance of man in His unworthiness. . . . It is God who elects man. Man's electing of God can come only second. But man's electing does follow necessarily on the divine electing. In this history, then, there is nothing wholly dark or obscure.[9]

TAKING ISSUE WITH THE BARTHIAN VIEW

Election and Universalism

Barth's treatment of the election has been hailed by some as a major theological breakthrough, a definitive dispelling of the cloud of fear and uncertainty that has hung over the doctrine since the time of Augustine. The New Testament scholar C. E. B. Cranfield, for example, has described it as "magnificent," a proposal "which, once it has been clearly formulated, seems so entirely obvious that it is almost incredible that it had not been proposed and carried through long before."[10]

While acknowledging Barth's brilliance, creativity, and erudition, I believe that we must take issue with this judgment. Barth's proposal is deeply flawed, in at least two ways.

First, as numerous interpreters of Barth have pointed out, the logic of Barth's system seems to lead inexorably to universalism, a theological position which we have already found to be unbiblical. If all are elect in Christ, and if Christ has borne the divine rejection for all, then there remains no rejection—no condemnation—for any person.

At times Barth seems willing to follow this train of reasoning to its obvious conclusion, stating, for example, that in Christ "God's rejection has taken its course and been fulfilled and reached its goal . . . so that it can no longer fall on other men or be their concern." Since Christ has suffered the penalty of the divine rejection, it cannot be the concern of other people to "suffer the execution of this threat, to suffer the eternal damnation which their godlessness deserves. . . . What is laid up for man is eternal life in fellowship with God."[11] Hell, Barth says, triumphed once over Christ, but that was to the end that it might never triumph again over any other person.[12]

In the end, however, Barth draws back from universalism, stating that to insist dogmatically that all will be saved would be to fail to respect "the freedom of divine grace."[13] Barth clearly hopes that all will finally be saved, and in this his position has much in common with and may have inspired von Balthasar's tentative universalism. But unlike von Balthasar, George MacDonald, or the Arminians, Barth has created a system in which it is almost incomprehensible that any person could finally fail to be saved. If God's grace has already embraced all people in Christ, and Christ has already been punished for the sins of the whole world, and if the human electing of God is not something God foresees but rather something that follows necessarily on the divine electing of man, then how can anybody still be lost?

To put it bluntly, Barth makes statements that are difficult, if not impossible, to reconcile with one another. He says that all humanity is elect in Christ. He insists that Christ alone has borne our condemnation, so that no condemnation remains for any person.[14] He further asserts that our response to God's election is guaranteed, so that to be elected in Christ is to be elected to believe in Him.[15] But after all this, he also refuses to affirm universalism! Somehow, in Barth's system, it is possible for elect individuals to refuse to admit their election and to be lost; and somehow this refusal on their part is to be ascribed not to their freedom but to "the freedom of divine grace."

This is not a coherent doctrine, and it is certainly not a solution to the problem of predestination. It leaves us still wondering why it is that some individuals respond to God while others do not. Barth's answer is more Calvinistic than Arminian in that he puts the emphasis on divine grace rather than human freedom. And Barth himself clearly believes his doctrine to be more optimistic than either Calvinism or Arminianism, in that it asserts that every person is already elect. But when Barth leaves us with the bizarre conclusion that it is possible for a person to be elect and yet lost, we realize that he has led us into a maze of confusion from which there is no exit.

The first lesson we should learn from Barth is that if we are not willing to affirm universal salvation, we must not make the mistake of affirming universal election.

The Nature of Divine Love

Underlying this first problem is a deeper one. Barth speaks much of the freedom of God's grace, and in so speaking he sounds very much like a Calvinist. However, the whole point of his rejection of the "absolute decree" is to suggest that God's freedom is so constrained by His love as to render it impossible for God to reject any sinner: "We must resist the temptation to absolutise in some degree the concept [of] choosing or electing. . . . God's freedom is not an abstract freedom, but the freedom of the One who loves in freedom."[16]

What Barth is saying is that we should not suppose that God's freedom is a freedom to make distinctions among His creatures, giving to one what He withholds from another. Instead, divine freedom is the freedom to love, and by implication, that love must extend to each and every one of God's creatures.

Now, no Calvinist could ever be happy with the suggestion that God's decrees are otherwise than expressive of His loving character. But what Calvinism claims and Barth denies is that in view of the fallenness of the human race and our just liability to punishment, God is free to intervene to save some while leaving others to perish. And there is certainly strong scriptural support for such a view, both in Old and New Testament times: "Jacob I loved, but Esau I hated" (Rom. 9:13). "All things have been handed over to me by my Father, and no one knows the Son except the Father, and no one knows the Father except the Son and anyone to whom the Son chooses to reveal him" (Matt. 11:27; see also Rom. 9:22–24; 1 Peter 2:8). Such passages make it clear that God sees no incompatibility between His love for the world and His freedom to make distinctions among His creatures.

Like George MacDonald, Barth is operating with a definition of divine love not derived from the Bible, one that inevitably skews his interpretation of the doctrine of election. Once again, it may not be inappropriate to speak of an "iron cage of false metaphysics." Barth, like MacDonald and like a vast number of modern theologians, starts from an unbiblical and misleading understanding of love, and that is the ultimate reason he finds himself teetering uneasily on the brink of universalism, unable either to clearly affirm or deny that all will finally be saved. Although he is not as blunt about it, Barth, like MacDonald, finds it intolerable that a loving God should allow any to be lost; and this is a very good indication to us that his doctrine does not provide an adequate explanation of the Bible's teaching. I am impressed by Barth's brilliance, but I find it impossible to accept his doctrine.

THE EXPLANATION OF NORMAN GEISLER:
"OUR DECISION AND GOD'S ARE NOT LOGICALLY RELATED."

Yet another attempt to untie the knot of predestination has been offered by the prominent evangelical philosopher and apologist Norman Geisler in his book *Chosen But Free: A Balanced View of Divine Election*. In most respects Dr. Geisler, who calls himself a "moderate Calvinist," actually argues like a classical Arminian, but his book contains one proposal that sets it quite apart from both Arminianism and Calvinism. Geisler claims that it is wrong to make either of the two decisions—God's decision for us or our decision for Him—logically prior to the other. He bases this idea on his interpretation of 1 Peter 1:2 and on the doctrine of "the simplicity of God":

> There is a third alternative [to Calvinism and Arminianism]. It postulates that God's election is neither *based on* His foreknowledge of man's free choices nor exercised *in spite of* it. As the Scriptures declare, we are "elect *according to* the foreknowledge of God" (1 Peter 1:2 NKJV). That is to say, there is no chronological or logical priority of election and foreknowledge. As John Walvoord insightfully commented on 1 Peter 1:2, it "teaches not the logical order of election in relation to foreknowledge but the fact that they are coextensive." In other words, all aspects of the eternal purpose of God are equally timeless.
>
> God is a simple Being, all of whose attributes are one with His invisible essence. Hence, both foreknowledge and predetermination are one in God. Whatever God knows, He determines. And whatever He determines, He knows. . . .
>
> According to the moderate Calvinist's view, whatever God forechooses cannot be based on what He foreknows. Nor can what He foreknows be based on what He *forechose*. Both must be simultaneous, eternal, and coordinate acts of God. Thus, our actions are truly free, and God determined that they would be such. God is totally sovereign

in the sense of actually determining what occurs, and yet man is completely free and responsible for what he chooses.[17]

For Geisler, the controversy between Calvinists and Arminians is based on a misunderstanding of the doctrine of God, and the whole unpleasant matter can be disposed of by recognizing that neither God's foreordination nor His foreknowledge forms the basis for the other.

TAKING ISSUE WITH GEISLER'S EXPLANATION

Chosen But Free is a disappointing book. Geisler's works on philosophy and apologetics have been helpful to countless evangelical Christians, and he has firmly established himself as a careful and thoughtful scholar. I myself have learned much from him. But in this book, Geisler does not attain to his usual standard of scholarship. He misrepresents the nature of the debate over divine sovereignty and human freedom, offers virtually no exegetical support for his own theological beliefs, and sets forth a "solution" to the problem of predestination that is clearly unworkable and unbiblical.[18] Here I will address just two of the problems with Geisler's position.

Misrepresentation of the Debate

First, Geisler misrepresents both Calvinism and the Calvinist/Arminian debate. Although he claims to be charting a course between "extreme Calvinism" and "extreme Arminianism," these terms are highly misleading. What Geisler calls "extreme Calvinism" is really just Calvinism, the assertion that God's choice of the elect is logically prior to their choice for Him. And what Geisler calls "extreme Arminianism" is actually open theism, which classical Arminians would repudiate as vigorously as any Calvinist. This strange redefinition of terms allows Geisler to present himself as a "moderate Calvinist" who is worried about the dire effects of accepting the position at either of the extremes.

In reality, Geisler's position differs from classical Arminianism in only two respects: His confidence in the final perseverance of true believers and his theory that neither the human nor the divine choice can be made the basis of the other. Throughout the book Geisler's primary concern is to warn against the dangers of "extreme Calvinism" (read "Calvinism"), and in most places his arguments are completely indistinguishable from those normally made by Arminians. For Geisler to characterize his position as "moderate Calvinism" seems equivalent to a citizen of Nevada claiming to live in "western New England," or a Londoner describing her city as belonging to "southern Scotland." Geisler is in virtually all respects an Arminian and in virtually no respect a Calvinist. His strange renaming of the historical positions serves only to introduce new confusion into what is already an extremely difficult area of theology.

Divine Simplicity

Second, Geisler's proposal that the divine simplicity prevents us from speaking of a logical relationship between God's foreknowledge and His election is not persuasive. I do not believe that any major theologian has ever suggested such an idea—not even Thomas Aquinas, who is one of Dr. Geisler's favorite thinkers and who made great and effective use of the doctrine of simplicity in other contexts (most notably his doctrine of the Trinity).

It is not hard to see why that is so. If no logical relationship can be stated between God's election of individuals and His knowledge of who will believe, then it must also be true that no logical relationship can be posited between any of God's decrees and His knowledge. On Geisler's theory we would have to say, for example, that God's decision to create the universe is not logically related to His foreknowledge of the universe's existence. God determined to create the universe, and He knew that the universe would indeed exist, but His knowledge in no way depended on His decision. This is absurd. It is certainly true that God knows all things eternally and simultaneously, but it does not follow that there are no logical relationships among the things He knows. With regard to creation, God has known eternally that the universe would exist, and the cause of that knowledge is His knowledge that He would create it. With respect to election, God certainly knows both that He has elected certain people and that they will believe, and His knowledge of these facts is eternal. But that does not mean that it is wrong for us to ask whether His election leads to our faith or our faith leads to His election.

Geisler might respond that the existence of the universe represents a false analogy to the acts of free creatures. The universe cannot exist without direct action on God's part, but an intelligent creature with free will makes decisions independently of God, decisions that God can foreknow without causing. This may be so, but in that case the ground of the argument has shifted, and we are making statements about the nature of human freedom and not about the simplicity of God. If Geisler really wants to safeguard human liberty by reference to the principle of simplicity, he needs to be willing to apply that principle to all of God's decrees and knowledge.

What about the biblical support for Geisler's idea? Geisler mentions only one text, 1 Peter 1:2, and he does not offer any evidence for his contention that it teaches that election is not logically related to foreknowledge. Since he provides no argument, one hardly knows how to refute him. To make his case, Geisler would need to show that (1) the foreknowledge to which Peter is referring is foreknowledge of the individual's decision to believe in Christ, rather than (as frequently in Scripture, e.g., Rom. 11:2) foreknowledge of the person himself; and that (2) the preposition *kata* ("according to"), when it modifies a noun in the accusative case, is incompatible with the presence of a causal relationship between the things it joins, in this case, God's foreknowledge and our election.

Geisler does not even attempt the exegesis that would prove his point. We will consider the nature of God's foreknowledge in this verse in the next chapter. Here let me simply point out that the standard Greek-English lexicon does indeed list as one definition of *kata* "because of, as a result of, on the basis of."[19] This does not prove that the use of *kata* in 1 Peter 1:2 implies a causal relationship between election and foreknowledge, but it does prove that Geisler cannot possibly establish his doctrine on the basis of this preposition alone.[20]

Acceptance of Geisler's principle that decision and foreknowledge are one and the same in God would require us to excise from our Bibles every reference to purposeful action on God's part or, at the very least, to qualify each such reference with the stipulation that there is no logical relationship between God's determination to act and His foreknowledge of His own actions. So "I will harden Pharaoh's heart" (Ex. 7:3) means exactly the same thing as "I know Pharaoh's heart will be hardened." "I will bless you" (Gen. 12:2) tells us nothing more than "I know you will be blessed." "And I will lead the blind in a way that they do not know" (Isa. 42:16) means "I know that the blind will be led." "I am coming soon, bringing my recompense with me, to repay everyone for what he has done" (Rev. 22:12) means "I know that everyone will receive according to what he has done." The position is untenable.

Again, Geisler is a brilliant scholar and a superb guide on apologetics and ethics. Nevertheless, the sooner his "moderate Calvinism" is forgotten, the better.

THE VIEW OF TOZER:
"CALVINISM AND ARMINIANISM ARE NOT INCOMPATIBLE."

Before we move on to explore Calvinism, we should consider one last proposal. In his devotional classic *The Knowledge of the Holy,* A. W. Tozer says that although most Christians have chosen to align themselves with either Calvinism or Arminianism, in reality those two schools of thought are not incompatible with one another:

> Here is my view: God sovereignly decreed that man should be free to exercise moral choice, and man from the beginning has fulfilled that decree by making his choice between good and evil. When he chooses to do evil, he does not thereby countervail the sovereign will of God but fulfills it, inasmuch as the eternal decree decided not which choice the man should make but that he should be free to make it. . . . Certain things have been decreed by the free determination of God, and one of these is the law of choice and consequences. God has decreed that all who willingly commit themselves to His Son Jesus Christ in the obedience of faith shall receive eternal life and become sons of God. He has also decreed that all who love darkness and continue in rebellion against the high authority of heaven shall remain in a state of spiritual alienation and suffer eternal death at last.[21]

There is much here with which we can agree. God has indeed decreed that man should have freedom to exercise moral choice and that our choices should have eternal significance. It is also true that when we exercise our freedom—even in wickedness—we do not countervail but rather fulfill God's sovereign will. And of course it is true that God has decreed that all who believe in Christ shall be saved. All of

135

this is quite right, and by speaking so strongly of God's sovereignty Tozer gives the impression that he is at least half a Calvinist. In the end, though, his position seems indistinguishable from Arminianism.

Although he does not say explicitly that God's election of an individual is based on His foreknowledge of that individual's faith, Tozer implies this by his assertion that God's decree extends only to the person's freedom to choose and not to his or her actual choices. Like the Arminians and like Dr. Geisler, Tozer believes that genuine freedom and responsibility are negated by a doctrine of sovereignty that makes it certain that we will choose in one way or another. He sees God moving sovereignly and inexorably toward the accomplishment of His great aims for the world but doing so without actually determining that any human individual will make any specific choice.

But this creates an obvious problem. Tozer believes strongly in God's omniscience, so the path taken by the open theists is closed to him. Yet he also denies the Calvinist doctrine that our choices are divinely decreed. All that remains to him is to say—precisely as the Arminians have always said—that God foreknows our choices. And if the proper connection between God's will and ours is divine foreknowledge, there is no escaping the Arminian doctrine that God chooses those whom He foresees will choose Him. And so, even though Tozer avoids the language that would immediately identify him as an Arminian, we must conclude that his doctrine does not really represent a compromise or rapprochement between the two major historical approaches to the problem. If Tozer is forced to choose, he will clearly align himself with the Remonstrants.

I have the greatest admiration for A. W. Tozer, but I think that in this matter he has made a fundamental error, and one from which we must learn. It will never do to suggest that Calvinism and Arminianism are compatible with one another, or that they merely represent different theological emphases. The truth is that these are radically different systems of thought, making mutually exclusive claims about the nature of fallen humanity and the relation between God's will and human wills. If Arminianism is right, then Calvinism is wrong; and if Calvinism is right, then Arminianism is wrong. We might possibly decide that both are wrong, but we cannot logically argue that both are right.

THE SEARCH FOR A SATISFYING ANSWER

Here, then, is the point at which we have arrived: We have seen that serious biblical problems exist with the Arminian claim that our decision for God is logically prior to His decision for us. There are even greater problems with the idiosyncratic doctrines of the open theists, of Karl Barth, and of Norman Geisler. Tozer's attempt to reconcile Calvinism and Arminianism is a failure, as will be any similar attempt.

Even if Calvinism strikes us as difficult or forbidding, our search for an intellectually satisfying answer to the puzzle of election has led us to the place where we can no longer hold it at bay. It is time to let the Calvinists speak.

Gentle Father, protect me from the grave sin of distorting the views of thinkers who disagree with me. My analyses of the positions described in this chapter have been brief, but I have sought to be fair. If I have spoken wrongly, make that clear to both my reader and to me. If I have spoken rightly, give us the mental and spiritual tenacity to persevere in our quest to understand Your ways. In Jesus' name, amen.

NOTES

1. It is important to realize that neither the principles of Calvinism nor of Arminianism were originated by the men whose names we now associate with them. All true Calvinists and all true Arminians are persuaded that their own systems of thought are simply the theology of the New Testament, and citations supporting both systems can be found from all periods of church history. Seen in broader historical perspective, Arminianism is a form of semi-Pelagianism, while Calvinism is a refined expression of Augustinianism.

2. Roger Nicole, "Arminianism," *Baker's Dictionary of Theology*, ed. Everett F. Harrison (Grand Rapids: Baker, 1960), 64.

3. It is not credible to suggest, as many do, that Paul's discussion in Romans 9–11 concerns nations only; the sorrow of 9:1–3 makes it clear that it is the salvation of individuals that is on Paul's heart. The reader is encouraged to consult John Piper's defense of the historic understanding of this passage in *The Justification of God: An Exegetical and Theological Study of Romans 9:1–23* (Grand Rapids: Baker, 1993), 56–73. See also Thomas R. Schreiner, "Does Romans 9 Teach Individual Election Unto Salvation?" ed. Thomas R. Schreiner and Bruce A. Ware, *Still Sovereign: Contemporary Perspectives on Election, Foreknowledge, and Grace* (Grand Rapids: Baker, 2000), 89–106.

4. Process theology is a theological movement based on the metaphysics of Alfred North Whitehead. Among its key concepts is the idea that God is growing and changing together with the world. He does not exercise perfect power over the world, nor does He have a precise knowledge of the future. He is, so to speak, just doing the best He can. For a sympathetic introduction to this school of thought, see John B. Cobb Jr. and David Ray Griffin, *Process Theology* (Philadelphia: Westminster, 1976).

5. The literature on open theism is large and growing rapidly. A good place for the reader to start might be the June 2002 edition of the *Journal of the Evangelical Theological Society,* which contains an overview of arguments on both sides.

6. George MacDonald, *Creation in Christ,* ed. Rolland Hein (Wheaton, Ill.: Shaw, 1976), 39.

7. Karl Barth, *Church Dogmatics,* vol. 2, bk. 2, trans., ed. Geoffrey W. Bromiley et al., (Edinburgh: T & T Clark, 1957), 168.

8. Ibid., 450, 453.

9. Ibid., 192.

10. C. E. B. Cranfield, *A Critical and Exegetical Commentary on the Epistle to the Romans,* vol. 2 (Edinburgh: T.&T. Clark, 1979), 448–49.

11. Barth, *Church Dogmatics,* 319.

12. Ibid., 496.

13. Ibid., 417.

14. Ibid., 172.

15. Ibid., 126. See also page 178: "The purpose and meaning of the divine election of grace consists in the fact that the one who is elected from all eternity can and does elect God in return."

16. Ibid., 25.

17. Norman Geisler, *Chosen But Free: A Balanced View of Divine Election* (Minneapolis: Bethany, 1999), 52–53.

18. James R. White has written a comprehensive critique of Geisler's book, and I encourage the interested reader to obtain it. James R. White, *The Potter's Freedom: A Defense of the Reformation and a Rebuttal of Norman Geisler's* Chosen But Free (Amityville, N.Y.: Calvary, 2000).

19. Walter Bauer, *A Greek-English Lexicon of the New Testament and Other Early Christian Literature,* 2nd ed., ed. William F. Arndt, F. Wilbur Gingrich, and Frederick W. Dankerj (Chicago: Univ. of Chicago, 1979), 407.

20. The passage Geisler alludes to in the work of John Walvoord also provides absolutely no exegetical support for the contention that there exists no logical relationship between God's foreknowledge and His election. See Lewis Sperry Chafer and John F. Walvoord, *Major Bible Themes* (Grand Rapids: Zondervan, 1974), 233.

21. A. W. Tozer, *The Knowledge of the Holy* (San Francisco: Harper & Row, 1961), 118–19.

5

NOT OF
HUMAN WILL
OR EXERTION

For he says to Moses, "I will have mercy on whom I have mercy,
and I will have compassion on whom I have compassion."
So then it depends not on human will or exertion,
but on God, who has mercy.

✝ROMANS 9:15–16

WE HAVE SAID THAT A GOOD WAY to approach the issue of predestination is to seek the logical relationship between God's choice
of us and our choice of Him. We have found reason to be suspicious
of both the Arminian claim that God chooses those whom He foresees
will choose Him and Norman Geisler's idea that no logical relationship between the choices may be posited. Calvinism states bluntly that
it is God's choice that is primary and fundamental. We choose to believe in Him because He has already chosen us and acted to produce
faith in us. God is in every sense the initiator of our salvation: He elects
us in eternity, sends His Son to die for us, leads us to repentance and
faith by the regeneration of the Holy Spirit, and ensures our continuation in belief to the end of life. Salvation is of the Lord. We are saved
entirely by grace.

It will be remembered from the last chapter that the Arminians, in their rejection of the Belgic Confession, set forth their views in the form of five propositions. In response to the Arminians, the Calvinistic theologians at the Synod of Dort put forward five propositions of their own. It has become customary to refer to these propositions with the use of the acrostic "TULIP": Total Depravity, Unconditional Election, Limited Atonement, Irresistible Grace, and Perseverance of the Saints. Calvinists tend to agree that these phrases are misleading and do not really comprise a good statement of their position, but because the acrostic has the virtue of being memorable, few are willing to completely abandon it.

In what follows I will follow this conventional arrangement of ideas, but I will supplement the acrostic with terms that seem to express more accurately the convictions of the Reformed theological tradition. I implore the reader not to react blindly to the terms themselves. Do not become infuriated with the words "total depravity" or "limited atonement" until you are quite sure you know what they mean and why multitudes of Christians have believed them to be expressive of important biblical truths.

TOTAL DEPRAVITY/SPIRITUAL INABILITY

The Remonstrants asserted that the fall of man rendered human beings unable to think, will, or do anything truly good without divine assistance, and they affirmed that "all good deeds or movements, that can be conceived, must be ascribed to the grace of God in Christ."[1] They went on, however, to insist that this grace of God can be resisted, which necessarily implies that it is left to man to either resist or cooperate with divine grace.

Arminian Versus Reformed Thinking

Later Arminians have tended to stress this point more strongly than the Remonstrants, arguing that while the Fall badly damaged human nature, so that no person will find his or her way to God without divine assistance, nevertheless we remain capable of deciding freely for or against faith in Christ. To Arminians, this degree of spiritual ability is implied both by the Bible's repeated calls to sinners to repent—admonitions that seem to them pointless if in fact we *cannot* repent—and by the fact that we are held responsible for our choices. From the Arminian point of view, it would be unjust of God to condemn a person who was literally incapable of repenting and believing on his own.

The Reformed understanding of human nature is much more pessimistic. All sons and daughters of Adam, according to the canons of the Synod of Dort, "are conceived in sin, and are by nature children of wrath, incapable of any saving good, prone to evil, dead in sin, and in bondage thereto; and, without the regenerating grace of the Holy Spirit, they are neither able nor willing to return to God, to reform the depravity of their nature, nor to dispose themselves to reformation"[2] Or, in the words of the Westminster Confession of Faith, "Man, by his fall into a state of sin, hath wholly lost all ability of will to any spiritual good accompanying salvation: so as, a natural man, being altogether averse from that good, and dead in sin, is not able, by his own strength, to convert himself, or to prepare himself thereunto."[3]

The core idea of these statements is that until God regenerates us (gives us spiritual rebirth), we have neither the ability nor the inclination to cooperate with His grace. Regeneration must be a "monergistic" work of God (meaning that in regeneration we are passive and God alone is working), because the Fall has rendered us totally unable to do anything of spiritual or saving value. In regeneration we neither cooperate nor resist; we are acted upon and changed by the Holy Spirit. He raises us from the dead and gives us new life and new hearts, and it is *then* that we begin to cooperate with Him by repenting, believing the gospel, and seeking God.

Thus, apart from the Spirit's prior, unilateral work in us, we would never of ourselves turn to Christ. Without this special work of the Spirit we are capable of deeds that, seen in themselves and without reference to the attitudes toward God that lie behind them, can be considered good. The non-Christian mother loves and cares for her child. The non-Christian soldier willingly lays down his life for his country and his companions. These acts, however, are not saving. What the unconverted person will never do is turn to Christ in repentance and faith.

Such doctrine as this may strike us as extreme. I believe, though, that it is fully warranted from the Scriptures.

Neither Able nor Willing . . .

Calvinism does not teach that fallen human beings are incapable of making intellectual sense of the Christian faith. What it asserts is that in our fallen state we are incapable of desiring God. We run from God, not to Him, and we suppress and reject our knowledge of Him (Rom. 1:18). We may well seek the gifts of God, but God Himself we hate; that is why Paul insists that "no one understands; no one seeks for God. All have turned aside; together they have become worthless; no one does good, not even one" (Rom. 3:11–12).

Lest we think that Paul is speaking in hyperbole in Romans 3, we need to see that he gives a very specific and unambiguous statement of his doctrine elsewhere. Consider two texts:

> For those who live according to the flesh set their minds on the things of the flesh, but those who live according to the Spirit set their minds on the things of the Spirit. To set the mind on the flesh is death, but to set the mind on the Spirit is life and peace. For the mind that is set on the flesh is hostile to God, for it does not submit to God's law; indeed, it cannot. Those who are in the flesh cannot please God. (Romans 8:5–8)

> The natural person does not accept the things of the Spirit of God, for they are folly to him, and he is not able to understand them because they are spiritually discerned. (1 Corinthians 2:14)

Look carefully at the statements Paul makes about "those who live according to the flesh," or "the natural person." He says that such a person's mind is set on what his nature desires, but the desires of that nature are contrary to those of the Spirit. The person's mind is hostile to God, neither willing nor able to submit to God's Law, and so it is incapable of pleasing God. Moreover, it does not accept the things that come from God; in at least one sense, it doesn't even understand them. We cannot suppose that Paul means that unregenerate people are incapable of understanding the gospel intellectually; rather, he is saying that they cannot see its truth and beauty.[4] They find the gospel foolish and unattractive, and all their desires are set against it.

If this is so, then how will such a person ever cooperate with divine grace and receive Christ? He does not want Christ. He does not see any beauty in Christ. He does not want to be subject to Christ, nor does he want to believe that his sins needed to be atoned for by Christ. He desires Christ neither as Savior nor as Lord; in fact, all he really wants to do with Christ is forget Him, or else reinterpret Him so as to fit Him into some man-made religious system. He hears the outward call of the gospel, but his desires are set against those of the Spirit, and so he rejects that call. He is hostile to God and does not want to be reconciled to Him.

And what distinguishes the Christian from this "natural person"? The Holy Spirit. The Christian has the Holy Spirit; the natural man does not. The difference between the two is not chalked up to the different uses the two make of their freedom to choose; it is ascribed to God. Before we have the Holy Spirit, our minds are fixed on the desires of the sinful nature. After we receive the Spirit, our minds are controlled by the Spirit. It is not that we first change our minds about God and are then given the Holy Spirit, but rather that it is the presence of the Spirit in us that enables us to understand the things of God and receive them. We do not change ourselves—how could we, when in our inmost being we are hostile to God? Rather, He changes us.

. . . Unless the Father Enables Us

Paul's teaching is in complete accord with that of Jesus. No one, says Jesus, "knows the Father except the Son and anyone to whom the Son chooses to reveal him" (Matt. 11:27). Indeed, unless God enables us, we will never believe. Consider Jesus' teaching in John 6:35–40:

> Jesus said to them, "I am the bread of life; whoever comes to me shall not hunger, and whoever believes in me shall never thirst. But I said to you that you have seen me and yet do not believe. All that the Father gives me will come to me, and whoever comes to me I will never cast out. For I have come down from heaven, not to do my own will but the will of him who sent me. And this is the will of him who sent me, that I should lose nothing of all that he has given me, but raise it up on the last day. For this is the will of my Father, that everyone who looks on the Son and believes in him should have eternal life, and I will raise him up on the last day."

Jesus affirms that all who believe in Him will be saved. But many do not believe. Why not? Because they have not chosen to cooperate with God's grace? That is not Jesus' line of explanation. Instead, He says that no one can come to Him unless drawn by the Father. Jesus, in other words, refers salvation not to the exercise of human free will but to the power of God. He expresses the same point even more strongly in verse 65 of the same chapter, where He says, "This is why I told you that no one can come to me unless it is granted him by the Father." No one can come—no one is *capable* of coming (that is the force of the Greek)—unless the power to do so has been given to him by God.

God gives this power to some but not to all. Those to whom He gives it will certainly believe: "All that the Father gives me will come to me." Those to whom He does not give the power will not believe. Jesus' words do not leave room for the possibility that some may come to Him without power being given to them by God, nor do they allow that some to whom that power has been given will nevertheless refuse to come.

In this statement, Jesus shows no interest at all in defending the autonomy of the human will. His focus is entirely on the sovereignty of God. Human beings are oriented away from God, so much so that they are incapable of believing rightly in Christ. For all that, some will most certainly believe, and the reason why they will believe is that God will give them power to do so.

Fallen man's inability to repent and believe is implied throughout the Scriptures. More extensive treatments of the doctrine generally discuss such passages as Genesis 6:5; Jeremiah 17:9; John 3:3, 19; 8:43–47; Ephesians 2:1; and Colossians 2:13. For my part, I believe the doctrine is firmly established by the texts we have looked at already. The mind of sinful man is death; it is incapable of submitting to or pleasing God. Those controlled by such a mind—and all who are unregenerate fall into this category—do not seek God. Because they do not seek or desire God, it is impossible for them to come to Christ unless God empowers them to do so. All who are so empowered will come; those who are not, will not.

Is This Fair?

The Pelagian and Arminian response to this doctrine is to insist that it is simply unfair and therefore wrong. A just God would never command us to repent and believe if repentance and belief were beyond our ability. The presence of the command necessarily proves our ability to obey; otherwise, God would be engaging in cruel mockery to impose it. If we cannot believe that God is unjust, then we must reject the idea of the complete spiritual inability of fallen human beings, no matter how clearly the Bible may seem to teach it.

The difficulty in this line of reasoning lies in the fact that this is not the only place where God commands the impossible. The most dramatic example comes in the story of the raising of Lazarus (John 11:40–44). Jesus stands before the open tomb and commands Lazarus to get up and come out, something a dead man is obviously unable to do unless the command is accompanied by divine power. Lazarus does indeed rise and come out—and in doing so he exercises his will in obeying the command—yet the glory belongs entirely to God, because without God's power Lazarus would be helpless.

This is a good picture of what Calvinists believe happens in conversion: God commands people who are dead in sins and transgressions to repent and believe the gospel, and with the command comes, if God wills it, the power to obey.

But Jesus' word to Lazarus is not the only case in which a human being is commanded to do something that is impossible for him without divine power. Jesus tells us that we must be perfect, even as God is perfect (Matt. 5:48), yet none of us can be perfect. Worse, He tells us that the greatest commandments, the commandments in which all the other commandments are summarized, are these: "You shall love the Lord your God with all your heart and with all your soul and with all your mind and with all your strength. . . [and] you shall love your neighbor as yourself" (Mark 12:30–31). We are no more capable of obeying these commands than Lazarus was of raising himself from the dead! Our hope and prayer is that God will work in us to make us increasingly capable of fulfilling the commands, but we are aware of our complete inability to do so without His power.

In fact, the imposition of commands that are beyond our ability seems to be God's way of bringing us to recognize our need for Him. Jesus' dealings with the rich young ruler (Luke 18:18–25) are understood by most interpreters as intended to destroy the man's self-confidence and show him his spiritual poverty. He claimed to have kept all the commands from his youth, but Jesus' challenge to him to sell his possessions revealed that he was in fact an idolater who had not succeeded in obeying even the first of them. Jesus no doubt wanted him to see that he needed forgiveness for his failure to keep the commandments, but He also wanted him to see that without divine power he would never succeed in keeping them.

We can only hope that the young man went away from Jesus thinking to himself, *But if I have not in fact kept the commandments, in spite of all my efforts, then where will I ever find the power to do so?* And we hope further that the more he meditated on that question, the more he realized that he would never succeed in keeping the commandments unless God gave him the power he lacked, and that this realization drove him back again to Christ.

Here is how Martin Luther put it: "Reason thinks that a man is mocked by an impossible commandment, whereas I maintain that by this means man is admonished and awakened to see his own impotence."[5]

UNCONDITIONAL ELECTION

If human beings are in voluntary rebellion against God, such that they are not capable even of desiring to submit to Him, then it follows necessarily that God's choosing of those who will believe cannot be based on His foreknowledge of their choices. If God does not first act in us, we will not believe. And if we will not believe, then it is obvious that our belief cannot form the foundation of God's decision to choose us. There is, in fact, nothing good in us for God to foreknow, apart from that which He graciously decides to do in us. Our election is unconditional, rooted not in any acts or decisions that might commend us to God but solely in His own good pleasure. The ultimate reason that one person believes and another does not is to be found in the will of God; no higher explanation may be given.

The unconditional nature of election is implied in the passage we just looked at in John 6: Those who come to Jesus do so not because of any goodness in themselves but because the Father has given them to the Son. The same doctrine, though viewed this time from the perspective of the action of the Son in the calling of the elect, is taught in Jesus' statement in Matthew 11:27 that no one knows the Father except the Son "and anyone to whom the Son chooses to reveal him."

If there seems to be a contradiction between the characterization of the elect as, on the one hand, those whom the Father has given to the Son, and, on the other hand, those to whom the Son chooses to reveal the Father, it is resolved in Jesus' prayer in John 17:2: "You have given him [the Son] authority over all flesh, to give eternal life to all whom you have given him." The Father has given the elect to the Son, and the Son, in concurrence with the Father's power and in obedience to His will, reveals the Father to them and gives them eternal life. The Father and the Son are both involved in the work of choosing and calling.

In none of these passages, however, is it suggested or even allowed that the cause of election is to be located in the ones who are chosen. The emphasis is clearly on the divine initiative in salvation, and as with other passages we have looked at already, the imposition of Arminian assumptions on these verses renders them almost incomprehensible. John 17:2 emphatically does *not* mean "For You granted Him authority over all people to be able to observe the self-election of those You foreknew would believe."

Paul's doctrine is the same:

> *Blessed be the God and Father of our Lord Jesus Christ, who has blessed us in Christ with every spiritual blessing in the heavenly places, even as he chose us in him before the foundation of the world, that we should be holy and blameless before him. In love he predestined us for adoption through Jesus Christ, according to the purpose of his will, to the praise of his glorious grace, with which he has blessed us in the Beloved. . . . In him we have obtained an inheritance, having been predestined according to the purpose of him who works all things according to the counsel of his will, so that we who were the first to hope in Christ might be to the praise of his glory.* (Ephesians 1:3–6, 11–12)

The predestinarian nature of this passage is obvious: "He chose us. . . . In love he predestined us . . . having been predestined." And when Paul reaches for the ground of God's gracious choice of His people, the apostle locates it in the "purpose" or "counsel" of God's will.

There is not a whisper here of an election based on divine foreknowledge of human choices. God chooses His people for His own pleasure and will, to the end that His grace may be praised. If God chose those whom He foresaw would choose Him or would in some other way distinguish themselves from their fellow human beings, then their election would redound to their praise. As it is, election is designed to bring praise to God, as the One who freely gives grace to the undeserving and the One whose sovereign power enables Him to work out all things in conformity with the counsel of His will.

Paul's understanding of the relationship between divine election and human faith is expressed in 2 Thessalonians 2:13: "But we ought always to give thanks to God for you, brothers beloved by the Lord, because God chose you as the firstfruits to be saved, through sanctification by the Spirit and belief in the truth." Paul does not say that he ought to thank the Thessalonians for believing, but that he ought to thank God for choosing them; and he sees their belief in divine truth as one of the means by which their election by God is expressed and fulfilled in their salvation. The logical order is that God first chose them and then, because He had chosen them, they believed. Their salvation comes by the sanctifying work of the Spirit and by their own belief in the truth, both of which are results of their having been chosen by God from the beginning.

The same doctrine is also proclaimed, as we saw in the last chapter, in Romans 9:1–33. Contrary to the thinking of many commentators, Paul is speaking not solely or even primarily of the election of the nation of Israel over the nation that sprang from Jacob's brother Esau. Instead, he uses the choosing of Jacob as an illustration of the principle of unconditional election—a principle that alone explains why so many of Paul's Jewish contemporaries, for whom Paul felt "sorrow and unceasing anguish" (v. 2), had failed to believe in their Messiah. The fundamental assertion of the passage is to be found in verse 18: "So then he has mercy on whomever he wills, and he hardens whomever he wills." From one lump of clay—fallen, sinful humanity—God fashions vessels for noble purposes and vessels for common use. It is God who makes the one group of people to differ from the other, and whether we fall into the first group or the second is determined not by human desire or effort but by divine mercy.

If Paul's readers wish to dispute this doctrine, then they need to understand that they are talking back to God Himself. As we saw earlier, if Paul had viewed salvation as the Arminians do, this would have been the perfect place for him to say so. Instead, he takes the opportunity to express in the strongest possible terms the unconditional nature of election.

Election is not by human desire or effort but by grace. It is an expression of God's freedom to show mercy where He will. It has nothing whatever to do with foreseen faith; it has everything to do with God's plan and sovereign power.

Divine Choice According to Foreknowledge: Romans 8:28–30

But what of the texts that speak specifically of a divine choice that is according to foreknowledge? I do not believe that either of them actually gives support to the Arminian interpretation of election. Let's look first at Romans 8:28–30:

> And we know that for those who love God all things work together for good, for those who are called according to his purpose. For those whom he foreknew he also predestined to be conformed to the image of his Son, in order that he might be the firstborn among many brothers. And those whom he predestined he also called, and those whom he called he also justified, and those whom he justified he also glorified.

Verses 29–30 establish a "chain of salvation." Those who are foreknown are predestined; those who are predestined are called; those who are called are justified; those who are justified are glorified. Because the chain begins with foreknowledge, it has often been used by Arminians to defend the idea that God predestines those whom He knows will choose Him. There are, however, large problems with this interpretation.

The first problem is that Paul puts Arminians in the position of making two statements they really don't want to make: that all who are called are justified, and all who are justified are finally saved. The Arminian idea, let us remember, is that the call of the gospel goes out to all people, but it is received by some and rejected by others as a result of the use of their free will. Moreover, the majority of Arminians hold that it is possible for a person to be a true Christian, justified and forgiven, and yet fall away and be finally lost. But how do these ideas comport with this passage? When Paul describes a group of people as being, for example, "those whom [God] predestined," he can only logically be understood as meaning "*all* whom God predestined." It would wreak havoc with the passage if we supposed that Paul meant that *some* whom God foreknew were predestined, *some* whom He predestined were called, and so forth. Plainly Paul is saying that *all* whom God called He justified, and *all* whom He justified He glorified. But how can Paul make such statements if the calling in question is one that human beings are capable of resisting and if justification can be lost?

It seems very clear that this is yet another of those passages in Paul's writings in which he is intensely interested in exalting the sovereign power of God and not at all concerned to defend human "free will." Paul is saying that when God sets out to save a person, He does not stop halfway. Those whom He wants to save, He saves. He predestines them, calls them, justifies them, and glorifies them. Their complete salvation is assured by God Himself. The point is much the same as that made by Jesus when He promised that He would lose none whom the Father had given Him but would raise them up at the Last Day (John 6:39). The passage is not, in my view, compatible with a consistent Arminianism.

But what of that word *foreknew*? Doesn't it establish the Arminian position beyond doubt? Not at all. If Arminians cannot explain the rest of the passage, we should not be too quick to assume that they are correct in their interpretation of this one word. They tell us that it means that God predestines those whom He knows will choose to believe in Him. But what Paul actually says is that God predestines those whom He *knows*. The object of the verb "to know" is "whom." Whom He foreknew, He predestined. The emphasis is not on God's foreknowledge of human decisions or actions, but on His foreknowledge of *persons*.

And what does it mean for God to foreknow a person? Our best guidance is found in the fact that in the Bible, to "know" a person is often the same thing as to love or choose him. As Vos notes in *Biblical Theology*, "The Shemitic and Biblical idea [of love] is to have the reality of something practically interwoven with the inner experience of life. Hence 'to know' can stand in the Biblical idiom for 'to love,' 'to single out in love.'"[6] Some English translations of Amos 3:2 have God saying to Israel: "You only have I chosen of all the families of the earth," but the word translated "chosen" is literally "known." It is possible to translate the Hebrew with the word "chosen" because when God says that He has known Israel alone of all the families of the earth, He means that with them alone has He entered into a loving, covenantal relationship. His knowing, loving, and choosing are the same thing.

In Genesis 4:1 the same Hebrew word for knowing is used to express the idea of sexual intercourse between Adam and Eve. And in numerous other locations, in both Testaments, the Bible uses the verb "to know" in a manner that is almost synonymous with "love." Concerning the relationship between God's knowledge and love, the reader may wish to meditate on such verses as Exodus 2:25; Psalms 1:6; 144:3; Jeremiah 1:5; Hosea 13:5; Matthew 7:23; Romans 11:2; 1 Corinthians 8:3; Galatians 4:9; 2 Timothy 2:19; and 1 John 3:1.

If we interpret Paul's use of "foreknow" along these lines, the passage makes perfect sense. Those whom God has eternally loved He has predestined to be conformed to the image of His Son. That they may attain that end, He first calls them (and His calling is effectual, in that it results in their coming to faith), then justifies them (based on their faith), and finally glorifies them in His presence. The passage is not about God's response to foreseen human actions. It is about God's sovereign power to save those He has chosen.

Divine Choice According to Foreknowledge: 1 Peter 1:2

What about 1 Peter 1:2, which states that believers are elect "according to the foreknowledge of God the Father"? Again we should notice that there is nothing in the text to suggest that what is foreknown is the actions or choices of those chosen. The Arminian has to first insert this idea into the verse before it can be found there. Without this insertion, Peter can be most readily understood as making the same affirmation as Paul: that God predestines those whom He has eternally loved and chosen.

It is significant that in 1 Peter 1:20, the apostle refers to Jesus as having been "foreknown" before the foundation of the world. In this verse Peter uses *proginosko*, the same verb translated "foreknew" in Romans 8:29 and the verbal form of the noun "foreknowledge" in 1 Peter 1:2. God's foreknowledge of Jesus is surely not a mere prescience of Jesus' actions. It has to do with God's eternal love toward Him and choice of Him.

As one who has wrestled long and hard with the doctrine of unconditional election, to the point of feeling at times that I could not see how I could love a God who acts in such a manner, I fully appreciate the attractiveness of the idea that God elects those whom He foresees will elect Him. But I do not believe that the idea is biblical. It is not taught in Romans 8:29 or 1 Peter 1:2; and if not there, then where? It is, in fact, a mere human invention that has grown out of our discomfort with the doctrine of the Bible.

What the Bible says about divine election is that it is just that: *divine election*. From before the creation of the world, God has determined whom He will call to faith and whom He will leave in unbelief. This decision is not based on anything we have done or will do; it is based solely in God's good pleasure and is intended to bring Him glory.

Concerning God's Will and Our Will

Even if the Bible does not directly teach that election is a matter of God's foreseeing the use we will make of our free will, are there not other texts that undermine the Calvinist understanding of predestination? Two passages often cited by Arminians are the following:

> *First of all, then, I urge that supplications, prayers, intercessions, and thanksgivings be made for all people, for kings and all who are in high positions, that we may lead a peaceful and quiet life, godly and dignified in every way. This is good, and it is pleasing in the sight of God our Savior, who desires all people to be saved and to come to the knowledge of the truth.* (1 Timothy 2:1–4)

> *The Lord is not slow to fulfill his promise as some count slowness, but is patient toward you, not wishing that any should perish, but that all should reach repentance.* (2 Peter 3:9)

It is argued that since these passages teach that God desires the salvation of all people, we must assume that what distinguishes the saved from the lost is not the decree of God but the different uses made by the two groups of their freedom to choose.

Much ink has been spilled over these passages, and I do not suppose that I am able to offer an interpretation of either of them that will be satisfying to all. I would, however, make a few observations. First, we need to note that neither of these texts says anything about human free will. In fact, neither text tells us anything at all about what causes one group of people to receive Christ and another group to reject Him. In view of the fact that such passages as John 6, Ephesians 1, and Romans 9 speak so explicitly of the unconditional nature of election, we should be very slow to read a different doctrine into these two texts.

Second, there seem to me to be only two reasonable interpretations of these passages, each of which fits well with Calvinism. Suppose first that when Paul and Peter speak of God as desiring the salvation of all, they are speaking of what would be pleasing to Him. This interpretation seems the correct one, and it is perfectly compatible with Calvinism, which states that God frequently ordains that which, considered in itself, does not please Him. God was not happy to see His Son unjustly condemned and killed, and yet He certainly ordained the Crucifixion for the sake of the greater good that would come from it. It did not gladden His heart to watch Jesus suffer and die, yet the Scripture says flatly that it was His will to "crush him" and "put him to grief," that He might be a guilt offering for the sins of the world (Isa. 53:10).

In the same way, it makes perfect sense to believe that God genuinely hates for any person to be lost, and genuinely desires that all should be saved, and yet, for the greater good of the universe, does not ordain the salvation of each and every person.[7]

But if, on the other hand, we understand God's will in these passages to be His "will of decree," His sovereign will that ordains what must certainly come to pass, then Paul and Peter are saying that God is not willing for any of His elect to be lost. In this case, "all people" in 1 Timothy 2:4 and "any" in 2 Peter 3:9 do not refer to each and every human being who has ever lived, or even every human being alive at the time the Epistles were written, but rather all the elect from all nations and all times. God wants prayer to be made for all people (and especially political leaders, whose decisions can influence the spread of the gospel), in order that the elect may be brought to faith, and He is delaying the return of Christ until that goal is reached.[8]

In the first of these interpretations, we take God's will to be His good pleasure, and we take "all people" to refer literally to each and every human being. In the second, we take God's will to be His sovereign decree, and we take "all people" to refer to the elect. Either way, the text fits well with Calvinist doctrine. But what other interpretation is available to us? If we suppose God's will to be His sovereign decree and take "all people" to refer to each and every human being, then the inevitable conclusion will be universalism, which we have already seen to be unbiblical. These texts do nothing to undermine the doctrine of unconditional election, and they do nothing to establish Arminianism.

"But What About My Child?"

One further observation may be in order. What often impels us toward Arminianism and causes us to oppose election is our desire to believe that God is doing all He can to save as many as possible. Yet both Calvinism and Arminianism teach that God has imposed limitations on the use of His power to save; where they differ is in what they believe to be the basis of those limitations. The Calvinist believes that God could save all but does not, and that His decision not to save all grows from His gracious desire to make a full revelation of His character. (I will have more to say about this in chapter 9.) The Arminian also believes that God could save all but does not, but insists that the basis of God's self-limitation is His desire to give us the dignity of autonomous free choice.

Notice that whether we are Calvinists or Arminians, all of us must face the truth that God *could* save all but doesn't.

I think this is an important point, as it seems that anger against the doctrine of election often grows out of anxiety over the lost condition of our own loved ones. In my pastoral counseling I have witnessed this anger, a noisy insistence that God "desires all to be saved." The counselee usually feels anxious about a spiritually lost family member. Perhaps it is a child who has left the church, or a parent who is indifferent to Christ, or a sibling or spouse who views the believer's faith with contempt; in any case, the Christian wants to feel that God is just as anxious for that person's salvation as he or she is. Calvinism seems to us to imply that God is indifferent to our prayers, while

Arminianism appears to teach that God stands wholeheartedly on our side.

But matters are more complicated than this. The Calvinist God does indeed have power to save your and my loved ones, and He encourages us to come to Him in prayer on their behalf. Yet He does not give us certainty that they will finally believe. Ultimately, He tells you and me to entrust them to Him. And what of the Arminian God? He also has power to save our loved ones, but He has decided that He cannot do so without violating the human will. So He stands back and watches to see which way our loved ones will choose.

Both of these theologies allow me to believe that God would be pleased with my loved one's salvation, but both also insist that I live without certainty that he or she will in fact be saved. Arminianism does not free me from the knowledge that God *could* save my loved one but will not necessarily do so. For myself, I find the Calvinist position more comforting than the Arminian, because I would rather put my hope in a sovereign God than in the fallen will of the person whose salvation I desire.[9]

Is God Arbitrary?

Unconditional election inevitably raises two questions in our minds. First, if election depends solely on God and not at all on us, then why doesn't God elect everybody? I will consider this question in chapter 9 of the book. Second, doesn't this doctrine make God arbitrary? If His decision to choose one person over another is completely unrelated to the character or decisions of those two people, then isn't God behaving like a tyrant? How can we respect and revere a God who acts in this manner?

Opponents of Calvinism have tended to wax hot and eloquent on this theme. Charles Wesley spoke for many when he accused Calvinists of believing that:

> The God of Love pass'd by
> The most of those that fell,
> Ordained poor Reprobates to die,
> And forc'd them into Hell.[10]

This objection is identical to that of Paul's imaginary dialogue partner in Romans 9:19: "You will say to me then, 'Why does he still find fault? For who can resist his will?'" Wesley expressed the complaint more poetically and irascibly, but it is precisely the same complaint: It is unfair for God to exercise sovereignty in man's salvation. If God chooses some and passes over others, He is behaving unjustly, and so the damnation of the lost, who do not "resist his will," is to be laid at His feet; in Wesley's phrase, God forces them into hell. Now I am not interested in mocking Wesley or anyone else who feels as he did. I have had those feelings myself and have expressed them vigorously. I wish only to point out that this objection to unconditional election was fully anticipated by Paul in his clearest exposition of that doctrine.

No doubt Paul had heard it hundreds of times in the course of his ministry, and he knew that it would continue to be heard until the return of Christ. It represents a reflexive reaction of the human soul against the doctrine of election. But the very fact that Paul responds to this objection, and does so in very stern terms—"But who are you, O man, to answer back to God?" (v. 20)— should make us cautious about giving free rein to our anger.

As I see it, we have an important choice here, one very similar to the choice we have to make with respect to the doctrine of eternal punishment. We can become indignant, reject the doctrine, castigate those who hold it, and loudly insist that whatever the Bible may teach, it doesn't teach *that!* Or we can humble and quiet ourselves before God and ask Him to give us power to understand what we are capable of understanding and to continue trusting when understanding fails us. There is more at stake here than mere doctrine. Our response to God's assertion of His own sovereignty will affect our spiritual growth and development, our attitude toward Scripture, and our approach to preaching the gospel. Let us take care that we not be found "answering back to God."

The second thing to notice about this objection that God is arbitrary is the adjective itself: The term "arbitrary" is emotionally laden. It suggests to us a person who is out of control or one whose actions conform to no moral principles. A drunken father behaves arbitrarily when he takes out his frustrations on his wife and his baby daughter. A dictator acts arbitrarily when he murders an entire echelon of leaders to root out the one or two who may be plotting against him. Now obviously the Bible never posits such behavior of God, and no well-instructed Calvinist has ever believed such blasphemy. God's character is infinitely holy; He is righteous in all His deeds. Though His judgments are unsearchable and His ways inscrutable (Rom. 11:33), it is a fundamental premise of Christian faith that God is wholly and unalterably good. Again and again Scripture declares that truth, and Jesus exemplified it. God may never properly be described as arbitrary.

Why Election Seems Arbitrary

And yet, from our perspective, election does seem arbitrary. Why? First, because we suppose that if the reason for our election does not lie in us, then there must not be any reason at all.

However, that does not follow. We may be confident that God has reasons for His choices, but we must recognize that He is not obligated to reveal them to us. All we need to know is that we are not chosen because of any goodness in ourselves; our salvation is entirely of grace.

Second, we view election as arbitrary because we swiftly forget our guilt and liability to punishment, or shift ultimate responsibility for our guilt to God. God, we say, ordained us to fall. He created some of us for the express purpose of damning us. He forces us into hell against our will. We are innocent victims of God's cruel design.

Of course, this is nonsense. It is true, as we saw in the first chapter, that accepting the justice of God's decision to let Adam represent us requires an act of faith. And very often, objections to election actually turn out to be objections to this doctrine: "I never chose to be born a sinner; how can God hold me accountable for my actions?" But there is no evading the fact that we are indeed sinners, who sin deliberately and gladly. We have no basis for saying that God should view us as innocent of our sins simply because we have been sinners from birth. Nor is there any evading the Bible's insistence on our guilt and our liability to punishment. All have sinned; the wages of sin is death; we all deserve hell.

What the doctrine of election says is that although all deserve hell, God has graciously chosen to give heaven to some. He didn't need to do that. He could justly have allowed us to go our way and then brought on us the wrath our sins deserve. But instead He has chosen a great multitude to be saved and given His Son to die in their place. He now calls them out of their spiritual death and rebellion and gives them eternal life. They do not deserve this grace, and they can take no credit for their having received it. It is a gift, pure and simple. As for those who have not been chosen, they will have nothing of which to complain, for they will be treated with strict justice.

Understanding this is hard. The mind keeps seeking a way to shift blame for sin onto God's shoulders. The heart keeps whining that it is not just for God not to save all. But the truth of the situation is that we are all, justly, on death row: We are guilty as charged. If all are executed, that is simple justice. If some are executed and others have their sentences commuted, then the first group receives justice and the second receives mercy. No one is treated unjustly.

How does God determine who will fall into the first category and who into the second? Again, He determines this according to His own wisdom, telling us only that our election gives us absolutely no grounds for boasting. To impugn His exercise of His sovereign right as arbitrary is to fall into blasphemy. Our job is to diligently make our own calling and election sure (2 Peter 1:10), to rejoice in God's goodness toward us, and to participate in His work of calling the lost to faith.

Ah, Sovereign Lord! The doctrine of eternal punishment terrifies, but the doctrine of unconditional election shatters. We thought we were the masters of our own fate; we supposed that we could be saved whenever we pleased. But now we find—and our hearts confirm the Bible's teaching in this—that unless You act to save us, we will be lost. We are trapped in ourselves until You set us free. We are the willing victims of our own insane animosity to You. We claim to seek You even when we are hiding from You, and we pretend to desire Your truth even when we are devising ways of suppressing it. If You change us, we will live. If You abandon us to our free will, we will perish.

Father, grant that those of us who are Christians may never detract from Your glory by supposing that our faith is anything other than Your free gift. And grant that those who do not yet know You may recognize their true position—under Your judgment and at Your mercy—and may realize the urgency of seeking Your grace. To the glory of Jesus, amen.

NOTES

1. "The Five Arminian Articles," article IV, in Philip Schaff, *The Creeds of Christendom,* vol. 3, *The Evangelical Protestant Creeds* (Grand Rapids: Baker, 1985), 547.

2. Ibid., 588.

3. *Westminster Confession of Faith* (Glasgow: Free Presbyterian, 1973), chap. 9, art. 3.

4. Commentator Charles Hodge says of 1 Corinthians 2:14: "To know is to discern the nature of any thing, whether as true, or good, or beautiful. This is in accordance with the constant usage of scripture. . . . What, therefore, the apostle here affirms of the natural or unrenewed man is, that he cannot discern the truth, excellence, or beauty of divine things. He cannot do it. It is not simply that he does not do it; or that he will not do it, but he cannot. . . . The difficulty in his case is not in the will alone, but in his whole inward state." Charles Hodge, *Commentary on 1 Corinthians,* Master Christian Library, version 8, Ages Digital Library, 2000 (Rio, Wisconsin).

5. Martin Luther, *Bondage of the Will,* 158. Samuel Davies commented on this truth in a sermon on Jeremiah 5:3: "Oh! when shall we see the vanity and self-confidence of sinners mortified? When shall we see them deeply sensible of their weakness and helplessness? It may seem strange, but it is undoubtedly true, that they will never strive in earnest till they are sensible that all their strivings are not sufficient, but that God must perform the work in them. When they see that it is God alone who must work in them both to will and to do, then, and not till then, they will earnestly cry to him for his assistance, and use all means to obtain it." Samuel Davies, "A Time of Unusual Sickness and Mortality Improved," *Sermons by the Rev. Samuel Davies,* vol. 3 (Morgan, Pa.: Soli Deo Gloria, 1995), 251.

6. Geerhardus Vos, *Biblical Theology* (Edinburgh: Banner of Truth, 1996), 8.

7. John Piper advances this understanding of these passages in "Divine Election and God's Desire for All to Be Saved," ed. Thomas R. Schreiner and Bruce A. Ware, *The Grace of God, the Bondage of the Will,* vol. 1 (Grand Rapids: Baker, 1995), 107–32. See also John Murray's pamphlet, *The Free Offer of the Gospel* (Edinburgh: Banner of Truth, 2001), 23–29.

8. A classic statement of this approach to these passages may be found in John Owen, *The Death of Death in the Death of Christ* (Edinburgh: The Banner of Truth Trust, 1959), 231–37.

9. My advice to Christians who are praying for their loved ones to come to Christ is that they must never give up. Do not entertain the thought that the one you love is not elect. Instead, come to Christ repeatedly and urgently, laying before Him in all humility your love for this person and your earnest desire that he or she be saved. God is not lacking in love; make sure that you are not either.

10. Charles Wesley, "The Horrible Decree," in *The New Oxford Book of Christian Verse,* Donald Davie, ed. (Oxford, England: Oxford Univ. Press, 1981), 161.

6

HE WHO
BEGAN A
GOOD WORK

*And I am sure of this, that he who began a good work in you
will bring it to completion at the day of Jesus Christ,*

+PHILIPPIANS 1:6

OF ALL THE "FIVE POINTS" of Calvinism, the one that has aroused the greatest animosity is the doctrine that Christ died for the elect rather than for all persons in the world. The doctrine is called *limited atonement* in the TULIP acrostic, though many Calvinist theologians prefer the term a *definite* (or circumscribed) *atonement*.

Calvinists affirm that the death of Christ was for all people in the sense that it was intended for the salvation of a vast multitude from every nation, tribe, language, and people. It was for all in the further sense that it is for every person who desires salvation on God's terms. There is no possibility that a person might repent of his sins and trust in Christ, only to discover that Christ did not in fact die for him. Again, the death of Jesus has universal importance in the still further sense that from it there have flowed temporal benefits that are gradually reaching into every society on earth; the whole world is a better place for what happened on Calvary. And certainly no Calvinist has ever denied that the death of Christ was of sufficient value to provide for the salvation of all human beings.

Yet Calvinists have argued from Scripture, from the logic of election, and from the nature of the Atonement itself that it devalues the death of Jesus to suppose that He died for those who will not be saved. And this denial—or more accurately, the assertion that the Atonement was designed by God to save His elect rather than the entire human race—tends to infuriate the opponents of Calvinism. One occasionally meets a person who refers to himself as a "four-point Calvinist" because of his inability to believe the doctrine of definite atonement.

LIMITED ATONEMENT/DEFINITE ATONEMENT

A Troubling Doctrine

Why does this doctrine trouble us so deeply? One reason lies in the unfortunate terminology that has traditionally been used to describe it: *limited atonement.* To many people the adjective "limited" suggests either that Calvinists are small-hearted people who want to keep Jesus to themselves, or else that the God of the Calvinists is a small-hearted God. But Calvinists have rightly pointed out that Calvinism and Arminianism both "limit" the Atonement, though in different ways. Calvinism says that Christ died for the elect, and His death guarantees their salvation. The limitation in this case is in the number of persons for whom the Atonement was designed and executed. Arminians, on the other hand, say that Christ died for everybody who has ever lived, but His death guarantees the salvation of none. Here, too, there is limitation, namely on the power of the Atonement to save. If Jesus died for all human beings indiscriminately, including millions who will never be saved, then His atonement is clearly of very limited efficacy. In fact, in the Arminian understanding, the death of Christ does not *save* anyone; it simply makes it possible for God to forgive those who use their free will to repent and believe. God does not ensure the salvation of any person in particular, and in principle it is quite possible that in spite of Jesus' having died for all, none will finally be saved.

One theologian has written that for the Calvinist, the Atonement "is like a narrow bridge which goes all the way across the stream," while for the Arminian it is "like a great wide bridge that goes only half-way across."[1] Unless we are willing to affirm universal salvation, we cannot have a doctrine of the Atonement that does not involve some type of limitation.

But a second great reason for our discomfort with "particular" atonement is that it appears to be contradicted by the Bible, which teaches that Jesus died for "the world" (John 1:29; 3:16; 6:33, 51; Rom. 11:12, 15; 2 Cor. 5:19), for all people (Rom. 5:18; 1 Cor. 15:22; 2 Cor. 5:14; 1 Tim. 2:4, 6; Heb. 2:9), for "us all" (Rom. 8:32), and for the sins of "the whole world" (1 John 2:2). Such texts leave us with the impression that Christ died for every person, and so opponents of the doctrine of definite atonement portray it as an example of Calvinistic logic run amok. Surely, they say, nobody would dare to place a limitation on the love of God for all people unless he had already made himself a prisoner in an "iron cage" of false Calvinistic metaphysics.

And perhaps there is a third explanation for our distaste for this doctrine. Many of us first heard the gospel presented in terms such as these: "Christ showed His love by dying for you; therefore, you should reciprocate and believe in Him"—and when we learned to share our faith with others, that was the message we committed to memory. For many Christians today, the idea that Jesus paid for the sins of each and every human being lies so close to the heart of the Christian message that they can't imagine what it would be to preach the gospel without it. If we could not know whether Jesus had died for a particular person, how could we persuade him of God's love for him? How could we invite him to faith in Christ? And how could we even know that God was acting sincerely in authorizing us to offer such an invitation? To Christians reared on Arminian preaching and Arminian courses in evangelism, the doctrine of definite atonement sounds both heretical and unpreachable.

A brief consideration of this topic will never suffice. The reader who wants to really understand the nature and extent of the Atonement will have to go far beyond my discussion here. He or she will have to delve into many disputed texts and the arguments on both sides of the controversy, and will have to determine which perspective finally makes the most sense. My own conviction, however, is that

Calvinism does the better job of interpreting the teaching of Scripture on this topic. In what follows I will attempt to provide a simple outline of the Calvinist argument, as well as some thoughts on the implications of this doctrine for preaching.

The Logic of the Atonement

Let's begin by considering the logic of the doctrine. Some claim that definite atonement is a monstrosity of Calvinistic logic. In reality, both Arminianism and Calvinism are self-consistent logical systems.

If human beings are capable of responding to God's grace on their own, and if election means only God's acceptance of those He foresees will turn to Him, then the only atonement that is necessary is one that permits God to forgive those who so respond (Arminianism). But if, on the other hand, fallen human beings are in bondage to their sinful nature, incapable of understanding spiritual things, submitting to God's Law, or doing anything pleasing to Him; and if election is truly a matter of God's unconditional choice—if, in short, God has given a people to His Son—then we would expect an atonement that actually saves the lost (Calvinism). From the point of view of a Calvinistic understanding of the Scriptures, it is the Arminian atonement that seems a monstrosity, because it promises fallen men and women no power to raise them from their spiritual death. If a woman were lying at the bottom of a deep well, with no strength to climb out, it would not comfort her much to hear somebody at the top shouting, "Good news! There is nothing to prevent me giving you a hand once you get to the top!" From the Calvinist perspective, the help offered by an Arminian atonement is worthless.

The Calvinist atonement, in contrast, is one that actually saves the lost. Jesus' death satisfied the claims of divine justice against the sins of the elect and purchased for them all that is required for their salvation: effectual calling, faith, justification, sanctification, and eventual glorification with Christ in heaven. All these blessings of salvation flow to them from the Cross. Christ has paid for their sins. He has descended to the very bottom of the well on their behalf, and He will by no means fail to rescue them. "And this is the will of him who sent me, that I should lose nothing of all that he has given me, but raise it up on the last day" (John 6:39).

From the Calvinist point of view, it is Arminianism that presents logical impossibilities. Arminianism tells us that Jesus died for multitudes that will never be saved, including millions who never so much as heard of Him. It tells us that in the case of those who are lost, the death of Jesus, represented in Scripture as an act whereby He took upon Himself the punishment that should have been ours (Isa. 53:5), was ineffective. Christ has suffered once for their sins, but they will now have to suffer for those same sins in hell.

The Arminian atonement has the initial appearance of being very generous, but the more closely we look at it, the less we are impressed. Does it guarantee the salvation of any person? No. Does it guarantee that those for whom Christ died will have the opportunity to hear of Him and respond to Him? No. Does it in any way remove or even lessen the sufferings of the lost? No. In reality, the Arminian atonement does not *atone*. It merely clears the way for God to accept those who are able to lift themselves by their own bootstraps. The Calvinist does not believe that any fallen person has such power, and so he views the Arminian atonement as unsuited to the salvation of sinners and insulting to Christ.

The Atonement in the Scriptures

What do the Scriptures say? Is the Atonement presented in the Bible as a divine act that saves sinners or as the removal of an obstacle that prevents sinners from saving themselves? I do not think there can be any serious question that the former view is correct.

We are easily confused on this point. God has ordained that we may not be saved apart from faith in Christ, and so we are quick to suppose that faith is our independent contribution to our salvation rather than, as is the case, one of the blessings Christ purchased for us. But when the Scriptures speak of the Atonement, they emphasize the efficacy of Christ's death to produce salvation. Jesus "gave himself for our sins to deliver us from the present evil age" (Gal. 1:4); He "redeemed us from the curse of the law by becoming a curse for us" (Gal. 3:13); He reconciled us to God when we were still God's enemies (Rom. 5:10).

If we say that Christ did these things for all people, we find ourselves in impossible difficulties, because not everybody has been rescued from this present evil age or has been redeemed from the curse of the Law or has been reconciled to God. These are the blessings purchased by the death of Christ, yet they are blessings enjoyed only by the elect. The Bible nowhere suggests that the death of Christ was intended to produce certain blessings in those who believe and other blessings in those who do not. Those for whom Christ died are forgiven, reconciled, freed, and redeemed. With His blood Christ has purchased people for God from every tribe and language and people and nation, and those whom He purchased are made a kingdom and priests (Rev. 5:9–10). He gave Himself up for His church (Eph. 5:25).

We cannot universalize these statements to include all human beings without rendering them nonsensical, since not everyone is saved and not everyone is included in Christ's kingdom or in His church. Nor can we argue that the blessings of Jesus' death are held hostage by our human decision whether or not to believe. Doing so adds a thought that is as alien to the Bible as the notion that election is based on foreknowledge of human choices. The Bible teaches that if Christ died for a person, that person will be saved.

Perhaps the matter will be clearer if we look closely at Romans 8:28–39:

> And we know that for those who love God all things work together for good, for those who are called according to his purpose. For those whom he foreknew he also predestined to be conformed to the image of his Son, in order that he might be the firstborn among many brothers. And those whom he predestined he also called, and those whom he called he also justified, and those whom he justified he also glorified.
>
> What then shall we say to these things? If God is for us, who can be against us? He who did not spare his own Son but gave him up for us all, how will he not also with him graciously give us all things? Who shall bring any charge against God's elect? It is God who justifies. Who is to condemn? Christ Jesus is the one who died—more than that, who was raised—who is at the right hand of God, who indeed is interceding for us. Who shall separate us from the love of Christ? Shall tribulation, or distress, or persecution, or famine, or nakedness, or danger, or sword? . . .
>
> No, in all these things we are more than conquerors through him who loved us. For I am sure that neither death nor life, nor angels nor rulers, nor things present nor things to come, nor powers, nor height nor depth,

nor anything else in all creation, will be able to separate us from the love
of God in Christ Jesus our Lord.

What is Paul's main point in this passage? It is that believers are
secure in Jesus Christ. Nothing in all creation can separate them from
God's love for them. What is the foundation of this love? God's foreknowledge and predestination of them from all eternity. They will
always be loved because they have always been loved. And what is the
guarantee and proof of this love? The death of Christ. If God gave
His Son for them, then they may be fully assured that He will graciously give them all else they may need to bring them safely to heaven.
Because of the death of Christ, their sins are forgiven, and no one may
bring accusation against them. Because of the death of Christ, they
may count on God's presence and protecting power in all of the struggles of life and also in the pains of death. Because Christ died for them,
they have nothing whatsoever to fear; they may know that they were
chosen in eternity and that they will be eternally loved.

Can these things be said of those who never come to Christ? Does
it make any sense at all to say of a person who is in hell that nothing
can separate him from the love of God that is in Christ Jesus? Obviously not. But if we cannot make such a statement about the person
who is lost, neither can we say that Christ died for him, for the death
of Christ on a person's behalf is the guarantee that these blessings
are his. If God gave His Son for us, then He will most assuredly give
us all things. But if we do not have those things—things belonging
to salvation—then what evidence do we have that Christ died on our
behalf? I do not think there is any evading the conclusion that Christ
died for the elect.

"But," says the Arminian, "you are overlooking one thing: The
blessings God gives are blessings that come through faith." True
enough, but where does faith come from? Faith is our human act; God
does not exercise faith on our behalf. But the implication of the passage is that faith is one of the things guaranteed to those whom God
has chosen. If all whom God predestines He calls and all whom He
calls He justifies, and if justification comes through faith, then it follows that God will ensure that those whom He has predestined will
indeed come to faith; otherwise, they could not be justified. It is certainly true that we will not be saved unless we believe in Jesus Christ,

but it is also true that if God has chosen us and Christ has died for us, we will believe.[2]

What then of the passages that say that Christ died for "all" or for "the world"? Here we must be cautious. It is a simple thing for opponents of definite atonement to quote these passages and announce that they have overthrown Calvinist doctrine. But words must be interpreted in context, and we have abundant evidence that "all" and "world" do not in every case in Scripture refer to each and every human being who has ever lived.

In Romans 8:32 Paul says that God has given up His Son "for us all." What does this mean? In context, it is clear that Paul is referring to believers, those people who actually receive the benefits of the death of Christ. He is not speaking of all human beings. Similarly, when Jesus says in John 12:32 that when He is lifted up He will draw "all people" to Himself, He cannot be understood to mean that all human beings will come to him in faith. Or again, as we saw in chapter 2, it is a misreading of Romans 5:18—"Therefore, as one trespass led to condemnation for all men, so one act of righteousness leads to justification and life for all men"—to understand Paul to say that all will be saved. Paul's point, rather, is that people are saved through Christ in a manner analogous to the way they are lost through Adam. All who are Adam's children stand under condemnation; all who are Christ's spiritual children will be justified.

In other passages in Scripture, terms like "all" and "world" are used to refer to all types or races of people, or to Gentiles as well as Jews, or to people in all parts of the world—not to each and every individual human being. It is not possible to look here at every passage that could be construed as teaching universal atonement; there are too many of them. But I encourage the reader who wants to pursue the issue further not to jump to Arminian conclusions without careful study of those passages in their context. My own judgment is that some of them can be reconciled to an Arminian interpretation, but none compels us to adopt that interpretation.

Is Definite Atonement Preachable?

Finally, we must consider the objection that belief in definite atonement makes it impossible to preach the gospel. We have become so accustomed to telling unbelievers that Christ died for them that most of us are unaware that the gospel has not always been presented in this way. We search in vain for such statements in the sermons of George Whitefield, Jonathan Edwards, Samuel Davies, Charles Spurgeon, or other great Calvinistic evangelists of the past. We learn that many of our greatest missionaries—William Carey, Adoniram Judson, Hudson Taylor—were staunch defenders of Calvinistic orthodoxy. And yet it seems to us that they were preaching a defective gospel! How is it possible for us to move the hearts of the unbelieving unless we first tell them that Christ so loved them that He died for them?

First, let's recognize that if the Bible does not say that Christ made atonement for each and every person, then we are not authorized to tell the unbeliever that Christ died for him. We are authorized to tell him that he is a sinner. We are authorized to tell him that Christ died for sinners and now invites all to come to Him for salvation. We are authorized to promise that if he will repent and believe, he can know that Christ died for him—that, as the older theologians would have put it, he has an "interest" in Christ.

Finally, we are authorized and commanded to express these truths with all the passion and love of which we are capable. When Christ told us to "compel" them to come in (Luke 14:23), He meant that we are to urge and warn and persuade with all vehemence and sincerity. But we ought not to think that the Holy Spirit needs us to doctor His truth in order to move the hearts of the ungodly. Our commission is to offer Christ, not to make statements the truth of which we cannot verify.

Trying to Preach the Arminian Gospel

Second, any good effect that might be accomplished by telling the unbeliever that Christ died for him is quickly lost when he learns that Christ has, on this understanding, done nothing more for him than He has done for millions who are even now in hell. The Calvinist can preach a Christ who saves, a Christ who, if He is for us, will ensure that we can by no means be lost; and the Calvinist preacher can passionately invite the unbeliever to turn to this Christ for the salvation He alone can give. But the Arminian first tries to win the heart of the unbeliever by telling him that Christ loved him enough to die for him, and then quickly undermines the force of that statement by admitting that what Christ did for him, Christ did for everyone, which means that He cannot be counted on to exercise any more saving grace in the life of the potential convert than He did in Judas's life. This type of presentation is hardly suited to raising the unbeliever's confidence in or respect for Jesus Christ.

In fact, the Arminian gospel presentation immediately throws the unbeliever back on his own spiritual resources, rather than telling him to look to an all-powerful Christ. If Christ died for all, yet not all are saved, then clearly it is up to us to save ourselves by deciding to believe in Him. We can't expect Christ to help us with this; He has already done His part by dying for all people, including many who are now lost. Plainly, the initiative is now with us. If we will not save ourselves, no one can.

Thus the Arminian preacher sets off to exalt the love of Christ by declaring His universal atonement, but he ends by pushing Christ to the background and exalting the independent will of man.

And there is one more difficulty with the Arminian approach. The older, Calvinistic evangelism tended to be very wary of false professions of faith. Believing that the only real conversion is the one that is the result of a monergistic, divine work in the soul, and believing that there are all manner of false conversions corresponding to the poor soils in Jesus' parable of the sower, this evangelism excelled in teaching people how to "test" themselves and "make [their] calling and election sure" (2 Cor. 13:5; 2 Peter 1:10).[3] It was not quick to count converts, and it was careful to avoid giving the impression that a person could be saved by raising his hand, going to the altar in a public meeting, or even praying a certain type of prayer. Pastors in this tradition examined candidates carefully before admitting them to church membership, often waiting months or even years to allow the fruits of faith to be revealed.

At its worst, this type of evangelism probably produced unnecessary anxiety in the hearts of timid Christians who never felt satisfied with the evidence of their own conversion or whose pastors were unskilled at helping with the work of discernment. But at its best, Calvinistic preaching undoubtedly helped countless people persevere in the quest for salvation until they had truly substantial evidence that they were reconciled to God.

In Arminian evangelism, by contrast, hardly any effort is made to discern the wheat from the chaff. If Christ died for all, and it is left to us to decide whether we are elect, then any "decision for Christ" is to be taken at face value, and any method that can bring a person to make such a decision is valid. I once heard the pastor of a large, influential church boast that he could lead anyone to Christ, provided only that he could find the key to that person's heart. What he apparently meant was that he could make anyone "decide" for Christ if only he could find the most pressing "felt need" in that person's life. Some people are lonely; Christ can fill their loneliness. Others are fearful; Christ can take away their fear. Still others have low self-esteem; Christ can make them feel good about themselves. Find the individual's need, show her how Christ can meet that need, and you can get her to say yes to Jesus.

For many Arminian evangelicals, that is sufficient. A person who says yes to Jesus is by definition a Christian. She may need some more "follow-up" and discipling, but the validity of her conversion is not to be questioned. The probable result is that multitudes who call themselves Christians are deceived about their standing with God.

Preaching the Definite Atonement

Can the Calvinistic gospel be preached? Emphatically yes. We do not need to know who is elect and who is not, nor do we need to tell the unbeliever that Christ died for her. All we need to know is that Christ has purchased for Himself a multitude of people too great to be counted, and He has commanded us to seek them out. We offer salvation to all. We proclaim to all that "God so loved the world that he [sent] his one and only Son, that whoever believes in him shall not perish but have eternal life" (John 3:16 NIV), and we invite all who hear to believe. When they ask how they may be saved, we tell them to look away from themselves to an all-powerful Christ who is able to give them new life and save them to the uttermost.

We pray, preach, teach, admonish, urge, and warn; and we continue doing these things until they know themselves to be new creatures in Christ, not simply because of a decision they have made but because of the testimony of the Holy Spirit and the evidence of a transformed life.[4]

IRRESISTIBLE GRACE/EFFECTUAL CALLING

Because of what has already been said, it will be possible for us to cover the last two "points of Calvinism" more swiftly. The fourth point is that when God determines to give a soul new life, the grace by which He does so cannot be resisted. Calvinists know well that the Bible teaches that it is possible for both believers and unbelievers to resist the Spirit in a variety of ways. We can "grieve" and "quench" Him (Eph. 4:30; 1 Thess. 5:19), and we can oppose His purposes in the world (Acts 7:51). Nevertheless, if fallen human beings are incapable of understanding or loving the things of God, it follows necessarily that they will never turn to Him unless He works unilaterally in their hearts to overcome their enmity.

Unless a person is born again, he cannot see the kingdom of heaven; and this birth, like our first birth, is an activity in which we are passive. We are born, not of our own will but of the Spirit, who blows where He will (John 3:1–8); and once we are born, we naturally develop the characteristics of the new life we have been given, beginning with repentance and faith in Jesus Christ.

Does God "Violate" the Human Will?

This doctrine is constantly denounced by Arminians as teaching that God "violates" the will of the human being. We saw in chapter 2 that C. S. Lewis based his rejection of universalism on the belief that God cannot ensure the salvation of any individual without violating his or her freedom. Another writer, John White, has told us that in praying for our loved ones who are not Christians we may ask God to open their eyes, burn away their self-deceptions, and rend asunder the dark caverns of their minds, but

> we may not ask him to force a man, woman, or child to love and trust him. To deliver them from overwhelming temptation: yes. To give them every opportunity: yes. To reveal His beauty, His tenderness, His forgiveness: yes. But to force a man against his will to bow the knee: not in this life. And to force a man to trust him: never.[5]

In his book *Chosen but Free,* Geisler never tires of accusing Calvinists of believing in a divine tyrant who crushes our humanity by dragging us kicking and screaming into the kingdom of God.

What should we say to this? Certainly it is true that God changes the will; if He did not, then nobody would ever believe. The leopard doesn't change his spots. People who hate God do not make an independent choice to stop hating Him. Those who are dead in sins and transgressions do not suddenly decide to make themselves alive. If the Bible's teaching about the extent of human depravity is to be taken seriously, then we have to believe that God's work in His elect children is a work that cannot be resisted.

But does this mean that it should be described as a violation of their will? This is a strange way to characterize a work of pure, unsolicited compassion! Sin is a moral disease, a sickness unto death. We cannot cure ourselves of it any more than we can prevent ourselves from succumbing to physical death. If God chooses to cure us, shall we complain that in doing so He has diminished us? Should we not rather thank Him for His mercy?

Cilantro and Grace

Perhaps a homey example will help. I love Mexican, Chinese, and southeast Asian food. However, I detest one ingredient frequently used in all those cuisines: cilantro. Even a small sprig of cilantro on top of a steamed fish or in a bowl of salsa or soup is sufficient to make me lose my appetite for the dish.

I am not proud of my inability to like cilantro. In fact, I consider it a grave defect. Cilantro is one of God's good gifts to humanity, and most people are able to enjoy it. The fact that I cannot suggests that there is something wrong with me.

I would be happy to be able to change. But I can't. Give me two bowls of soup, one with cilantro and the other without, and I will never choose the one with the green leaves floating in it! I would like to be able to like cilantro, but I cannot.

Now suppose that God, in His mercy, should decide to change me. Suppose I wake up tomorrow *craving* cilantro, wanting it in my soup, on my fish, even in my cereal! Will I complain that God has violated me by bringing about this change in my tastes? No, I will thank Him;

and I will thank Him again every time I am served a dish with cilantro in it. In fact, I intend to thank God for everything He does in me to allow me greater freedom to enjoy Him or His creation.

Of course, it is one thing to hate cilantro and another thing to hate God. My dislike of cilantro may have some chemical cause, while my enmity to God is located solely in my will. Perhaps it seems less objectionable for God to "violate" my taste buds than to have Him make a great change in my heart. But in both cases we are speaking of defects over which we ourselves have no control. And while defective taste buds will at most cause me some embarrassment or discomfort in dining situations, a defective will, one hostile to both God's authority and His grace, will damn me forever. Looking back on my own life, I have no doubt whatsoever that had God not worked irresistibly in me, I would not be a Christian today. And I do not feel violated. I feel grateful.

Indeed, I hope God will continue to "violate" my will! I do not yet love God—nor other people—as I ought to. My will is permeated with selfishness and pride. I am capable of desiring to love God perfectly, but I am not capable of doing so, nor do I have power to change myself. If I am ever to be suited for the life of heaven, I need God to work still more changes in my soul. "Give me an undivided heart, that I may fear your name!" (Ps. 86:11).

I realize, of course, that the will is active in sanctification in ways that it is not in regeneration. In regeneration the will is wholly passive, whereas in sanctification we actively cooperate with the Spirit and exert our will to put our sins to death. But the contrast should not be overemphasized. The unconverted person is not capable of desiring God, but he is capable of realizing that unless God causes him to desire Him, he will be lost. He can't convert himself, but he can ask God to convert him. And similarly, in sanctification we are capable of desiring far more than we can accomplish. In both cases, we are in some degree the passive objects of the work of the Holy Spirit. It makes little sense for us to accept our need for divine transformation in sanctification while rejecting it in the more basic sphere of regeneration.

I urge the reader not to take offense at the doctrine of irresistible grace. If you are not yet a Christian, ask God to make you one. If you are, thank Him that He has graciously liberated you from your congenital and suicidal hatred of Him and granted you repentance leading to the knowledge of the truth (2 Tim. 2:25).

PRESERVATION/PERSEVERANCE OF THE SAINTS

The last of the points on our TULIP concerns our continuation in the life of faith. Arminians generally believe that it is possible for a person to be genuinely regenerated and converted and yet to fall away and be finally lost. Calvinists consider such a notion a grave insult to Christ.

Calvinists understand that perseverance requires the full engagement of the human will. Scripture repeatedly urges us to persevere and warns us of the dangers of apostasy. Still, the Calvinist places his ultimate hope for salvation in the power of God, not in his own frail will.

Biblical Evidence

For biblical proof of the doctrine that God will preserve His saints to the end, we may look first to Romans 8, the passage we have considered twice before. If God glorifies all whom He justifies, and if He graciously gives "all things" to them to whom He has given Christ and promises that nothing can separate them from His love, then it follows necessarily that He is assuming responsibility for protecting them from apostasy. To deny that conclusion, we would need to thoroughly rewrite the passage to say that He glorifies *some* of those He justifies, gives *some* things to those for whom Christ died, and will not permit *some* things to separate them from His love.

Instead, the apostle Paul writes to the Philippian believers that the God who begins a good work in a person's life can be trusted to carry it on to completion (Phil. 1:6). Those who are justified by Christ's blood will be infallibly protected from divine wrath (Rom. 5:9).

This is also the only possible conclusion to be drawn from Jesus' promise that He will lose none of those whom the Father has given Him but will raise them up at the Last Day (John 6:39). All whom the Father gives will come to Him (v. 37), and none will be lost. Again, Jesus speaks of those the Father has given Him as His sheep, and He promises that they "will never perish" (John 10:28). Those who argue against the preservation of the saints suggest that Jesus means that they shall never perish unless they choose to; no one else can snatch them from Christ's hand, but they can snatch themselves. But Jesus' statements are categorical and do not allow for this unspoken exception. He will lose *none*. They will *never* perish. Jesus, the Good Shepherd, assumes full responsibility for His flock, protecting them not only from wolves but also from their own waywardness.

Consider one more passage. In Ephesians 1, Paul tells us that Christians have been chosen by God from before the creation of the world to be holy and blameless in His sight (v. 4). He has predestined them to be adopted as His sons (v. 5). He has given them His Holy Spirit as a guarantee of their eternal inheritance (v. 14), and He has set to work in them the same mighty power by which He raised Christ from the dead (vv. 19–20).

Is it conceivable that in spite of all this, they may still fall away and be lost? Is it possible for God to predestine us to holiness, and yet we do not become holy? Can He adopt us as children and then disown us? Can He give us a guarantee of salvation and then renege on His promise? Is the human will so strong as to overcome divine power? Surely not! What more does God need to say to assure us that He will uphold us to the end?

Our Responsibility to Persevere

Why do we stumble over this doctrine? Two reasons: God's warning and those who seem to fall away from faith. First, it seems to us that if our preservation in faith is guaranteed by God, then there should be no need for Him to warn us against falling away. The presence of texts exhorting us to persevere seems an argument against the doctrine. But this is not a weighty objection. When God ordains an end, He also ordains the means by which that end is to be attained. For each of us He has ordained a certain span of days, but that does not mean that we do not need to eat to stay alive. Similarly, if He has ordained that we shall be saved, He has also ordained that we shall work out our salvation by stirring ourselves up to trust and obey.

No doubt God could preserve us without our expending any effort, but He does not choose to act in that way. He prefers to grant us the dignity of cooperation with His purposes, thereby teaching us to care for the things he cares for.

When my daughter, Sarah, was little and we were crossing a street together, I commanded her to hold tightly to my hand and warned her of the consequences should she let go. I spoke to her in this way so that she might grow and mature. But I loved Sarah too much to permit her to turn loose of my hand and run into oncoming traffic, and she knew that. I demanded Sarah's cooperation, but I assumed the ultimate responsibility for her safety. So it is with the God who promises to lead us safely to heaven.

Or consider a biblical example. David was promised the kingship, which meant that Saul would surely not be allowed to kill him; yet David had to dodge Saul's spear and flee from his bedroom in order to stay alive. His ultimate confidence that he would survive and become king was in God, but that did not exempt him from the responsibility of exerting his every effort to fulfill God's plan. In the same way, God wants us to be fully engaged in working out our salvation, but He also wants us to put our confidence in Him and not in ourselves.

The Problem of Backsliding

Second, we are troubled by the fact that people who at least appear to be Christians do at times fall away. Some eventually return to the faith; others never do. How, we wonder, can this be squared with the doctrine of preservation?

From an experiential point of view, this is one of the toughest issues in the Christian life. There are few things more painful than watching someone we love fall away from a close walk with Christ. When, as often happens, the period of backsliding lasts for years or even decades, the suffering of Christian family members and friends can be as intense as if their loved one had become fatally ill or permanently impaired. I do not want to appear to deal with this issue in an offhand way, as if it were all a simple matter of theology. The person who inquires into the meaning of the doctrine of perseverance is often really asking the anguished question, "Will my son come back to Christ?"

Unfortunately, that is a question that is normally impossible for us to answer. There are two possible explanations of any given case of backsliding, and we cannot usually know which applies. The one possibility is that the person was never a Christian to start with. It is clear from the parable of the soils (Matt. 13:1–23) that some apparent believers are not believers at all; they may receive the Word with joy and appear to want to walk with Christ, only at some later time to fall completely away. John refers to this same phenomenon when he speaks of those who "went out from us, but they were not of us; for if they had been of us, they would have continued with us. But they went out, that it might become plain that they all are not of us" (1 John 2:19). The implication is that before they left, they gave every appearance of being believers. This is a good reason for parents and pastors to do all they can to help those in their care to be sure of their calling and election.

The other possibility is that the person is indeed a Christian, but God is allowing him to fall away for a time in order that he may learn the bitterness of sin and the sweetness of forgiveness. There can be no question that genuine believers can, for a time, fall into very serious sin. David committed both adultery and murder. Peter denied all acquaintance with Jesus at the very moment when the Lord most desired his companionship. Although we may never use this as an excuse for sin, it seems that God often allows His children to wander for the sake of teaching them to value their salvation. While they are wandering, though, neither they nor anyone else has sufficient evidence to be confident of their salvation. Assurance of salvation is available only to those who are bearing the fruit of repentance.

However a particular case of backsliding is to be explained, the phenomenon itself should not shake our confidence in the promise and ability of God to preserve His own. Christ has died for us and is even now interceding for us, and there is no possibility of our being finally lost.

DIVINE PREDESTINATION AND HUMAN ACTIVITY

Fatalism: Twisting a Doctrine

One more objection to predestination needs to be stated and answered. It is often argued that Calvinism is fatalistic, that it produces passivity and lethargy in those who accept its premises. If God has determined who will and who will not believe, then what is the point of prayer and evangelism? If God has ordained that His people will never fall away, where is the need for watchfulness and effort in the Christian life?

The best way to answer these questions is to point out that every biblical doctrine can be exaggerated and twisted. Jews and Muslims are convinced that Christians are polytheists, yet Christians know that the doctrine of the Trinity does not lead to polytheism, since the same Scriptures that teach us that there are three who are God also teach us that God is one. We cheerfully admit our inability to fully understand the eternal relationships among the Father, Son, and Holy Spirit, but we nevertheless know that we are in no danger of believing in multiple deities.

Or again, it was the complaint of Roman Catholics at the time of the Reformation that the doctrine of justification by faith alone would lead inevitably to indifference to God's Law. A person who thought that he had only to believe to be saved would never make any serious effort toward a holy life. Yet well-instructed Protestants know that the charge misses the mark. While it may indeed be the case that some people deceive themselves with the idea that their faith relieves them of the responsibility to seek God, those who have genuinely entered into relationship with God through faith will find the biblical call to holiness to be natural, welcome, and compelling. They will *want* to be holy and will be satisfied with nothing less than holiness.

Similarly, while outsiders to the Calvinistic system may be utterly confident that Calvinism leads inevitably toward fatalism, those who embrace the system know that the accusation is false. And why is it false? Because the same Bible that declares that God is the ultimate source of our salvation also insists on the necessity of human effort toward salvation. We are commanded to pray, to preach, to bear witness; we are also enjoined to believe, to hold fast to our faith, and to persevere to the end of life. Having come to recognize that Arminians are wrong to emphasize human responsibility while denying divine sovereignty, the Calvinist is not greatly inclined to commit the opposite error of denying the texts that urge him to work.

God Uses Means

At a practical level, the bridge between the doctrines of divine sovereignty and human responsibility is the recognition that God uses means to accomplish His purposes. God ordained that I should become a Christian in September of 1979, but He also ordained the means by which this would be accomplished. Among other things, He used the decision of C. S. Lewis in the 1940s to deliver the series of radio messages that later became *Mere Christianity,* John Stott's later decision to write a fine book called *Basic Christianity,* the courage of several Christian friends in witnessing to me, and the prayers of many people, including some whom I did not know and do not know even today. Those people did not bring me to Christ; God did that. But He used their efforts. He made them the means of my salvation.

Now, if God brought me to Christ in that manner, why should I doubt that He wishes to use me in similar ways in the lives of other people? If I needed the intellectual arguments of C. S. Lewis and John Stott, the personal encouragement of my friends, and the mysterious power of prayer to bring me to faith, then should I not bend every effort to be a good apologist and evangelist myself, in order that God may use me to accomplish His purposes in the lives of others? Should I not in fact be encouraged to do so by the knowledge that God has willed to make such means effective in the salvation of souls?

Or again, if the Bible informs me that it is God who is working in me to will and to act according to His good purpose, how does this truth absolve me of the responsibility to "work out [my] own salvation with fear and trembling" (Phil. 2:12)? Why should Christ's promise that He will not lose any of those the Father has given Him cause me to ignore Paul's warning to me to watch my life and doctrine closely, that I may save myself and my hearers (1 Tim. 4:16)?

Avoiding Fatalism

Can the doctrine of predestination be perverted into fatalism? Of course it can, just as trinitarianism can be perverted into tritheism, justification by faith alone can be perverted into antinomianism, and the doctrine that God sometimes heals bodies in response to faith can be perverted into the idea that all who are not healed are guilty of faithlessness. Every doctrine can be perverted. And it is probably true that the most natural direction for the perversion of predestination is toward fatalism.

However, the biblical doctrine of predestination is not fatalistic, nor does it lead inevitably toward fatalism. Placed in proper, biblical balance with the doctrine of human responsibility, predestination produces the kind of bold confidence in God that enables us to persevere in the disciplines of the Christian life.

CONCLUSION: THE GOODNESS OF GOD

One day some years ago, I was browsing in the bookstore at Fuller Theological Seminary. A young woman burst through the door and, in obvious distress, asked the clerk for help in finding books to refute Calvinism. I well understood her anguish. It is bad enough to believe that the lost will suffer everlasting, conscious torment in hell. Believing that God could save them—yet doesn't—makes matters a good deal worse. And although this is an implication of both Arminianism (where God voluntarily ties His own hands for the sake of our freedom) and Calvinism (where God elects unconditionally), it is certainly in the encounter with Calvinism that we become most aware of the dilemma.

As I remarked at the beginning of chapter 4, my initial impression of Calvinism was that it makes God into an ogre and reduces human freedom and dignity to a sham. The first time I opened a copy of the Westminster Confession of Faith and read its statements on the divine decree, I felt as though I could not breathe. I did not come fully to terms with the doctrine of predestination until I learned to see it in the perspective of God's great purpose for creating the universe, a topic we will deal with in chapter 9. But even now, before we have considered that topic, it is possible to dispel some of the gloom that seems to surround the doctrine.

Accepting Blame for Our Sins

A first observation is that the Calvinist God, contrary to the accusation of Charles Wesley, does not force anyone into hell. God did not force Adam and Eve to sin (though He certainly did ordain that this should happen), nor does He force you or me to sin. We sin because we want to, and if we go to hell, it will be because of our own free choices. As wrong as it is to say that Calvinists believe that God "violates" the human will of the elect in order to save them, it would be far more wrong to suggest that He violates the will of the reprobate in order to damn them. He simply leaves them alone. He lets them do as they please. To borrow from C. S. Lewis, He says to them, "Thy will be done."

No damned person will ever be able to blame God for his damnation; he will be forced to confess that hell is what he has chosen, and his punishment is what he deserves.

A Reason for Praise

Second, the doctrine of predestination is always presented in the Bible not as a topic for abstract speculation but as a matter for praise and adoration. Read through the first chapter of Ephesians. The passage is thoroughly predestinarian, yet it is also one of the greatest expressions of praise found anywhere in the Bible. In fact, the doctrine of election lies at the heart of the praise: God is praised precisely because He has chosen us, predestined us, redeemed us, lavished grace upon us, and given us a promise that can never be broken. Strip the passage of its "Calvinism," and Paul would no longer have anything for which to give thanks! The apostle teaches believers to rejoice in the knowledge that their salvation is a completely free gift given at God's own discretion and for His own glory.

Far from gnashing our teeth at God's sovereignty, we ought to adore Him for the love that moved Him to send His Son to redeem us. We should confess that we were previously "dead in . . . trespasses and sins," by nature "children of wrath," and that now we are alive in Christ purely by virtue of the richness of God's mercy (Eph. 2:1–5). We are brands plucked from the burning. The doctrine of predestination is intended to humble and gladden us, and to lead us to worship.

Learning to Love a Sovereign God

To the person still struggling with predestination, the suggestion that it could be a source of rejoicing seems incredible. "How can I love a God who has power to save all yet does not do so?" But the doctrine is clearly and unambiguously taught in the Bible, and a decision to reject it will, ultimately, lead you away from God rather than toward Him.

If you want to rail against predestination and against those who believe the doctrine, you will certainly have plenty of company—yet not, if I may dare to say so, the very best company. The most careful students of the Bible have believed in divine election because it is, beyond all doubt, a biblical doctrine. It is taught explicitly, plainly, emphatically, and repeatedly. The Bible doesn't say that God chooses us because He foresees that we will be holy or do good works, but that He chooses us that we may *become* holy and do good works (Eph. 1:1–4; John 15:16). It doesn't say that He chooses us because he foresees that we will have faith; it says that He ordains us to eternal life, and because of this, we believe (Acts 13:48). The Bible says that God saves us "not because of our works but because of His own purpose and grace," a grace given us in Christ Jesus "before the ages began" (2 Tim. 1:9). And it teaches that God acts in this way for His own good pleasure (Matt. 11:26). He has mercy on whom He will have mercy.

God is not ashamed of the doctrine of predestination; He is glorified by it. We must be careful not to stumble over it.

Fitting predestination together with all else we know of the goodness of God and the responsibility of man may be difficult work. It may be work that we will not complete in this life. But it is work that must be done. We cannot reject any part of God's truth without impoverishing ourselves, and we may be very certain that when all aspects of truth are finally seen in their proper relationships, the vision will be blindingly beautiful. So we must persevere.

One practical suggestion in seeking the biblical truth: Make sure your intellectual efforts are at least matched by your efforts in prayer. Open your Bible to Ephesians 1–2, or Romans 9–11, or John 6 and begin to give God glory for your salvation. Confess that you were once dead in sins and transgressions, the natural object of God's anger. Confess that your mind was hostile to God, and that the things of the Spirit made no sense to you. Confess that God could have justly left you in your darkness and condemned you for your sins.

Then thank God for what He has done for you by His grace. Praise Him for choosing you before the foundation of the world and sending His Son to die for you. Thank Him for foreknowing you, predestining you, calling you, and justifying you; and thank Him that you have been given His Spirit as a guarantee that He will bring His work in you to completion and glorify you with the saints in heaven. Rejoice in these great truths and in the sheer pleasure of knowing that your salvation is entirely from God. He alone has made you to differ from those who do not believe.

The opponents of election would like to deny you the joy of thus reveling in God's grace, on the grounds that you are indulging in selfish fantasies of God's special favor. "At first blush," writes Norman Geisler, "one is impressed by a God that supposedly loves him more than others and has elected him to eternal salvation. But upon further reflection, he cannot help but wonder why, if this God is so loving, He does not so love the world."[6] Geisler's solution, of course, is that God has done absolutely nothing more for His elect than for those who are eternally lost, which means that you must not thank God for your being a Christian. You may thank God for "providing" salvation, but you must thank yourself for being wise or good enough to receive it. I urge you to not listen to such doctrine. Sooner or later we must learn to let God be God. If we can grant Him that right in our prayers, as we give thanks for all He has done for us, then it will not be long before our theology will fall into line with our hearts.

Gracious Father, let others boast of their free will and their decisions; as for me, I will boast in the Lord. I know that I am responsible for believing in Christ, but I would never have believed had You not first enabled me. I know that I am responsible for persevering in faith, but my hope that I will succeed is based entirely on Your promise to complete what You have begun in me. I know that I am responsible to pray for the lost and invite them to Christ, but I also know that unless You empower them, they will not come. I do not understand all of these things. I see, but only as through a glass, darkly. Yet I understand enough to believe, and I see enough to adore. And in the end, that is all I need.

Give me sufficient light to walk a straight path, and I will be satisfied. Let me not dishonor You, whether by assuming credit for that which only You can do or by falling into listless fatalism. Let me pray as if all depended on You, and work as if all depended on me. Let me love You with all my heart and my neighbor as myself. To the glory of Your Son, amen.

NOTES

1. Lorraine Boettner, *The Reformed Doctrine of Predestination* (Philipsburg, N.J.: P & R Publishing, 1932), 153.

2. Although many modern scholars disagree, I think the most natural reading of Ephesians 2:8 is that faith is the gift of God. This appears to have been the dominant interpretation among the ancient Greek Fathers, and it alone prevents the clause "And this is not your own doing; it is the gift of God" from being a mere repetition of the statement that it is by grace we have been saved. Regardless of which interpretation of Ephesians 2:8 is taken, the gratuitous nature of faith is implied in Philippians 1:29; Acts 5:31; 11:18; and 2 Timothy 2:25. See the discussion in Sinclair B. Ferguson, *The Holy Spirit* (Downers Grove, Ill.: Inter-Varsity, 1996), 126–29.

3. Although contemporary evangelicals are largely unaware of it, we are the heirs to a rich literature aimed at helping people in this work of self-examination. The literature reaches its high point, in my opinion, in Jonathan Edwards's book *The Religious Affections* (repr., Edinburgh: Banner of Truth, 2001).

4. The best way to learn how to preach evangelistically is to study the sermons of great preachers. I have benefited most from reading the sermons of Charles Spurgeon, Asahel Nettleton, and Samuel Davies. I have also learned a great deal from J. I. Packer's "Introductory Essay" to John Owen's *The Death of Death in the Death of Christ,* and from two books by Iain Murray: *The Forgotten Spurgeon* (1966; repr., Edinburgh: Banner of Truth, 1986) and *Spurgeon Versus Hyper-Calvinism: The Battle for Gospel Preaching* (Edinburgh: Banner of Truth, 1995).

5. John White, *Parents in Pain* (Downers Grove, Ill.: InterVarsity, 1979), 47–48.

6. Norman Geisler, *Chosen But Free: A Balanced View of Divine Election* (Minneapolis: Bethany, 1999), 135.

PART THREE

Within His Embrace

We strongly reject, therefore, every explanation of the death of
Christ which does not have at its center the principle of
"satisfaction through substitution," indeed divine self-satisfac-
tion through divine self-substitution. . . . The theological words
"satisfaction" and "substitution" need to be carefully defined and
safeguarded, but they cannot in any circumstances be given up.
The biblical gospel of atonement is of God satisfying
himself by substituting himself for us.

✝JOHN STOTT
The Cross of Christ

⸙

It is a thing infinitely good in itself that God's glory should
be *known* by a glorious society of created beings.

✝JONATHAN EDWARDS
"The End for Which God Created the World"

7

THE CHASTISEMENT THAT BROUGHT US PEACE

But he was wounded for our transgressions; he was crushed for our iniquities; upon him was the chastisement that brought us peace, and with his stripes we are healed.

+ISAIAH 53:5

THEOLOGY IS THE MOST personally demanding of sciences. To grow in knowledge of God we must also grow in knowledge of ourselves, and the knowledge we must acquire is largely painful and unwelcome.

For instance, we must learn that we are sinners in the hands of a justly angry God—and that our sins are an evil of infinite proportions. Further, we must learn that apart from His grace we are hopelessly locked in antagonism toward Him and will remain in that state to all eternity. And we must discover that even when we have come to faith in Christ, our hearts remain deceitful.

All these truths, strange and difficult as they may be, must be integrated into mind and heart and daily living in order for us to see God as He truly is.

If we rebel against this knowledge at any point, our minds may well continue spinning out theology, but the theology will be distorted. If we stumble over our guilt and ill-desert, we will manufacture a god who doesn't take sin seriously. If we reject the Bible's teaching on the bondage of the will, we will create a god who does not so much save us as give us the opportunity to save ourselves. Our unwillingness to face the hard words of the Bible about sin, judgment, punishment, and human depravity will inevitably lead us to develop a view of God that conforms to our self-righteousness and leaves our pride intact. We will make God in our own image.

THE PERVASIVE DOCTRINE OF THE ATONEMENT

Nowhere is this more evident or tragic than in the efforts of theologians to make sense of the work of Jesus for our salvation. The Bible consistently portrays Christ's life as the basis for our imputed righteousness and His death as a substitutionary sacrifice offered to free us from guilt and wrath. Jesus paid the price we should have paid; He died the death we should have died; He suffered the punishment we deserved. He stood in our place and satisfied the demands of God's justice on our behalf, so that we may be free of the condemnation our sins have merited.

This is the pervasive doctrine of Scripture, and it is taught so clearly and in such a profusion of ways that it is difficult to see how anyone can read the Bible and miss it. In the Old Testament there are types and promises: the Levitical sacrifices, the Passover, the Day of Atonement, the redemption of God's people from slavery, the prophecy of a Suffering Servant who would suffer and die in the place of His people. In the New Testament, Jesus is presented as the fulfillment of all these types and promises. He is the true sacrificial Lamb; His death is the purchase price of our redemption; He is the Suffering Servant.

Throughout the biblical teaching there is great stress on certain key concepts: that Jesus is our substitute, that His death was a punishment for sins, that the Cross expiates our guilt and propitiates God's wrath against us.

These truths lie at the heart of the gospel, for they reveal the height and depth of God's love for us. Meditation on them should fill our hearts with gratitude and joy.

THE THEOLOGIANS AND THE ATONEMENT

Despite the clarity, pervasiveness, and beauty of these concepts, many theologians refuse to accept them; and their theology suffers terribly as a result. We have already seen that the denial of the biblical truth that human beings are unable to turn to Christ without God's first regenerating them leads directly to a universalistic doctrine of the Atonement, in which Jesus is seen as having done nothing more for those who actually believe and are saved than for those who are finally lost. The Arminian atonement is really not atonement at all, but merely an invitation to us to exercise our own free will to save ourselves.

A "Subjective" Atonement?

But it is also the case that the inability to see that it is right for God to punish sinners—regardless of whether that punishment is intended for their reform—will introduce equally serious distortions into our understanding of Christ's death. George MacDonald was apparently charged with rejecting the doctrine of the Atonement. He responded with characteristic eloquence and indignation but in terms that could not possibly have satisfied his accusers:

> I believe that Jesus Christ *is* our atonement; that through Him we are reconciled to, made one with God. There is not one word in the New Testament about reconciling God to us; it is we that have to be reconciled to God. . . .
>
> Did not the Lord cast Himself into the eternal gulf of evil yawning between the children and the Father? Did He not bring the Father to us, let us look on our eternal Sire in the face of His true Son, that we might have that in our hearts which alone could make us love Him—a true sight of Him? Did He not insist on the one truth of the universe, the one saving truth, that God was just what He was? Did He not hold to that assertion to the last, in the face of contradiction and death? Did He not thus lay down His life persuading us to lay down ours at the feet of the Father? Has not His very life by which He died passed into those who have received Him, and re-created theirs, so that now they live with the life which alone is life? Did He not foil and slay evil by letting all the waves and billows of its horrid sea break upon Him,

go over Him, and die without rebound—spend their rage, fall defeated, and cease? Verily, He made atonement.[1]

What is MacDonald saying? He is saying that Jesus made atonement in the sense of showing us the love of God and therefore persuading us to repent. When we see the death of Jesus on the cross, we suddenly realize just how good God is, and we are brought to a desire to repent of our sins and lay down our lives at the feet of this Father who loves us so greatly. The death of Jesus has a "subjective" impact, in that it moves our hearts. It exerts a moral influence over us.[2] But it does not create any objective change in our standing with God. God stood ready to forgive us even without the death of Christ. The Cross changes our hearts, but it in no way alters God's fundamental relationship to us. It does not turn aside His wrath or remove our guilt. From the tenor of MacDonald's writings it is clear that he viewed the "objective" understanding of the Atonement—that it truly effects a change in God's relation to sinners—as a primitive, ignoble, insulting idea not worthy of the God and Father of Jesus Christ.

MacDonald is not alone. The core idea of modern liberal theology is that the Bible may no longer serve as an authoritative source of knowledge about God; instead, the theologian must work "creatively" with the biblical materials and with his or her own experience of life to develop a portrait of God and of the world. When this procedure is followed, the Bible's teaching on divine judgment against human sin is always the very first part of the biblical revelation to be jettisoned. It is the most offensive part of the Bible, and so it is the first to go, even though this concept provides the key dynamic of the Bible's story. The Bible is a book about God's creation of human beings, our fall into sin, God's hatred of our sin and determination to punish it, and His own action on our behalf to redeem us from our plight. Theologians who will not accept this story line have to invent a new one of their own, which means, among other things, that they must reinterpret the life and death of Jesus in nonbiblical terms.

Jürgen Moltmann may serve as a good example of this tendency. His book *The Crucified God* is a three-hundred-page examination of the Cross. Moltmann argues that meditation on God's love as displayed on the Cross can free us from certain psychological compulsions. Further, because the Cross reveals God as loving and as willing to identify with the oppressed, it may also help us to overcome political injustice and the wanton destruction of the physical environment. All this is good and well. But Moltmann rejects the idea that Christ died as a substitutionary sacrifice for our sins, and he utterly refuses to deal with the Bible's teaching about divine wrath. Jesus, he says, died as an example of "representative suffering"; that is, He showed us that God suffers whenever people suffer. He did not die to pay our debt but to provide us a model of self-sacrifice.

Moltmann's only justification for this twisting of biblical doctrine is the unsupported assertion that the earliest Christian confession was simply that Jesus died "for us," not "for our sins," and, consequently, that the idea of a substitutionary, penal atonement was not part of the earliest Christian preaching.[3] Moltmann is willing to write an entire theology of the Cross without ever facing up to the Bible's own explicit explanation of the Atonement.

A Fuzzy Focus: The Moral Influence of the Cross

Now, MacDonald was not wrong in saying that the Cross exercises a moral influence over those who believe in it. The New Testament frequently urges Christians to live in a manner worthy of Jesus' death on our behalf: We are to live for Him who died for us (2 Cor. 5:15); we are also to adopt His same spirit of humility in our dealings with others (Phil. 2:5–8). And Moltmann is certainly not mistaken in thinking that the cross of Christ has unparalleled power to bring both psychological wholeness and political peace. The problem is that these theologians want to seize the secondary benefits of the Cross without dealing with its primary significance. Their focus is fuzzy. They want to focus on the Cross's influence on our psyches and our politics before they have properly explored its impact on our relationship with God.

Such theologians are like the person who, mired in a painful quarrel with a friend, impatiently wants to quickly "move on" and "let bygones be bygones," without ever facing up to his or her own guilt in the affair. They want to skirt the real issues, and they are annoyed with people who are unwilling to follow them.

We need to do better than this. We need to let God teach us the meaning of Jesus' work on our behalf. In doing so, we will enter deeply into the sheer wonder and joy of the glorious gospel of Christ. Thus, let's clearly focus on the essential nature of the Atonement in biblical categories.

THE ATONEMENT:
A NEW, OBJECTIVE RELATIONSHIP WITH GOD

We must begin with the objectivity of the Atonement. It is quite true that receiving Christ brings about enormous changes in the hearts of those who believe. But the reason it does so is that Christ, by His death, has changed our relationship with God. We cannot say that the Atonement converts God from a God of wrath to a God of love, since it is God's love that moved Him to make atonement for us. But we can and must say that the Atonement removes real barriers to our being accepted by Him and experiencing peace with Him.

The Expiation of our Guilt

One of these barriers is our guilt. All human beings are guilty of sin; sin cries out for punishment, and God has stated unequivocally that He will not clear the guilty (Nah. 1:3). Unless our guilt is dealt with, we must suffer eternally.

Jesus, however, is "the Lamb of God, who takes away the sin of the world" (John 1:29). In His death, we are told, He "bore the sin of many" (Isa. 53:12). He came to "save his people from their sins" (Matt. 1:21). For our sake God "made him to be sin who knew no sin, so that in him we might become the righteousness of God" (2 Cor. 5:21). Jesus has given Himself for our sins (Gal. 1:4); He has made purification for sins (Heb. 1:3); He has taken away sins by His self-sacrifice (Heb. 9:26); He "has freed us from our sins by His blood" (Rev. 1:5).

What is the meaning of these expressions—taking away sin, bearing sin, saving us from sin, being made sin, giving Himself for sin, freeing us from sin?

They certainly do not mean that Jesus became a sinner. They mean that He has expiated our guilt. Those who trust in Him are treated as if they had not sinned. They are declared righteous. Their guilt, as a hindrance to their enjoying fellowship with a holy God, has been removed. The legal problem caused by their sin has been solved through the death of Jesus on the Cross.

The Propitiation of God's Wrath

Another barrier to our acceptance with God is His holy revulsion against our sins. Because God's Law is an expression of His own character and Being, our transgressions arouse in Him an intense anger. This anger is variously described in Scripture as indignation, wrath, and fury: "God is a righteous judge, and a God who feels indignation every day" (Ps. 7:11); "Whoever believes in the Son has eternal life; whoever does not obey the Son shall not see life, but the wrath of God remains on him" (John 3:36); "But for those who are self-seeking and do not obey the truth, but obey unrighteousness, there will be wrath and fury" (Rom. 2:8). Because it is our sins that evoke God's wrath, there is nothing we can do to appease or propitiate God. As long as we remain in our sins, we are very properly "children of wrath" (Eph. 2:3).

But Jesus is our *propitiation*. By His death he propitiated, or satisfied, the wrath of God. Although many modern English translations obscure this truth, it is presented in the New Testament with great urgency. In Romans 3:25–26, Paul tells us that God put Jesus forward as "a propitiation by his blood," in order that God might maintain His justice while simultaneously justifying those with faith in Christ. The author to the Hebrews writes that Jesus "had to be made like his brothers in every respect, so that he might become a merciful and faithful high priest in the service of God, to make propitiation for the sins of the people" (Heb. 2:17). The same word is used twice in 1 John: Jesus "is the propitiation for our sins" (1 John 2:2); and again, "In this is love, not that we have loved God but that he loved us and sent his Son to be the propitiation for our sins" (1 John 4:10). What these texts say is that the death of Jesus is the means by which God's wrath is averted from us.

Many scholars have rejected the idea of propitiation on the grounds that it seems to attribute to God an anger that is irrational and sub-Christian. Others have complained that to speak of the Son as propitiating God by His death is to introduce an unacceptable division into the divine Trinity. These are the principal reasons why so many

English Bibles have replaced "propitiation" with such terms as "expiation" or "atoning sacrifice."

In fact, these objections have little force. There can be no doubt that the proper translation of the Greek *hilasmos* is indeed "propitiation," and careful observation of the passages in which it is used should remove all basis for complaint that the concept is unworthy of God.[4] God's wrath is not the least irrational; it is, very simply, His settled, holy, implacable opposition to evil. And while the propitiation of that wrath does indeed require the shedding of Jesus' blood, the Bible everywhere makes clear that it was by agreement of the Father and the Son that the Son laid down His life. It is God the Father who set Jesus forth as a propitiation; it was Jesus who, as our merciful and faithful High Priest, voluntarily made propitiation for us. In essence, the meaning of propitiation is that the triune God has turned His wrath upon Himself in order that it might not be poured out on us.

Reconciliation

If expiation is the removal of our guilt, and propitiation the removal of God's wrath, reconciliation is the consequent renewal of relationship between God and us. Because we are no longer regarded as guilty and are no longer objects of wrath, there is now no barrier to hinder us from coming to God and experiencing peace with Him. Reconciliation is the restoration of right relations between God and His creatures.

But is reconciliation an objective matter or a subjective one? The answer is that it is both. When we come to faith in Christ, our enmity toward God is ended; and we find that we are, in our own hearts and minds, at peace with God. This is subjective reconciliation. But the emphasis in the New Testament is not on the reconciliation toward God that occurs subjectively in us. Rather, the Bible places stress on the truth that God is now reconciled *toward* us. The death of Jesus has opened the way for God to embrace those from whom He was previously estranged by their sin.

This is seen most readily in 2 Corinthians 5:18–21, where we learn that "in Christ God was reconciling the world to himself, not counting their trespasses against them" (v. 19). It is true, of course, that the knowledge that God no longer counts our trespasses against us leads us to abandon our enmity toward Him. But that is not Paul's point. Rather, he is saying that when God acted in Christ to remove the guilt of our transgressions, that in itself was His act of reconciliation. God made Christ, who knew no sin, to be sin for us, "so that in him we might become the righteousness of God" (v. 21); it is this transfer of our legal liability to Christ that takes away the basis for God's estrangement from us. When Paul urges his readers to be reconciled to God (v. 20), he is urging them to believe the gospel message of forgiveness through Christ and to enter into the experience of reconciliation with God that Christ's death has made possible.[5]

MacDonald was right to say that the Bible does not speak of us acting to reconcile God to ourselves; that would be impossible. But the essence of the doctrine of reconciliation is that God has taken the initiative to reconcile *Himself* to us. As Millard Erickson expresses it, "The process of reconciliation is primarily God's turning in favor toward man."[6]

The Necessity of the Atonement

One more indication that we must view the Atonement primarily as effecting an objective change in our relationship to God is the fact that Scripture appears to view the Atonement as necessary to our salvation. We must speak carefully here. It would never be appropriate to say that it was necessary for God to save us, as if there were some moral principle or law that constrained Him to undertake our redemption. We need to remember that we are guilty before God, which means that He may justly punish us forever for our sins. He is not required to provide a solution to our guilt.

But the fact is that God loves us and desires our salvation. And numerous passages of Scripture strongly imply that to forgive us on any lower grounds than the death of His Son would be a contradiction of God's own nature and character.

Jesus describes it as "necessary" that He should suffer the things foretold by the prophets and then enter into His glory (Luke 24:26). He says also that just "as Moses lifted up the serpent in the wilderness, so *must* the Son of Man be lifted up, that whoever believes in him . . . should not perish but have eternal life" (John 3:14–16; emphasis added). In the Garden of Gethsemane, He asks that, "if it be possible," the cup may pass from Him, yet He resigns Himself to the will of the Father, in which such is apparently not possible (Matt. 26:39–42).

The Epistles also seem to teach that it is only on the basis of Jesus' death that God can forgive sinners. Only the offering of Christ as a propitiation permits God simultaneously to affirm His justice and justify the one who has faith in Jesus (Rom. 3:26). According to the author to the Hebrews, it is impossible for the blood of bulls and goats to take away sins (Heb. 10:4). Yet without the shedding of blood there is no forgiveness of sins, and so it was "necessary" for better sacrifices —all the aspects of sacrifice involved in the death of Jesus—to be offered (Heb. 9:22–23).

It seems, in other words, that the problem created by our sin is one that can be solved in no other way than through the obedience and sacrificial death of the perfect Son of God. Although God is both all-powerful and unconstrained by any law or necessity outside of Himself, it would be a betrayal of His own holy nature to forgive us on any lower grounds than these. He cannot do it. And if that is so, then the primary meaning of the Atonement is that in Christ, God has acted to satisfy the requirements of His own nature, that He may justly give to us the salvation He desires for us to enjoy.

THE ATONEMENT: CHRIST AS OUR SUBSTITUTE

We have said that the Atonement is objective. It does not merely affect our feelings toward God; it provides the basis for the renewal of our relationship with Him. In addition, we must state plainly that the Atonement is substitutionary. That is to say, Jesus died as our substitute. He put Himself in our place. He not only died *for* us; He also died *instead of* us.

The Meaning of the Old Testament Sacrifices

We see the substitutionary nature of Jesus' death as soon as we begin meditating on the Old Testament sacrificial system and its relationship to the death of Christ. In the New Testament we are told repeatedly that we are to interpret Jesus' death in terms of sacrifice. Ephesians 5:2 reports that Jesus offered Himself as a "fragrant sacrifice and offering" to God. Hebrews 9:26 tells us that Jesus "appeared once for all at the end of the ages to put away sin by the sacrifice of himself." Indeed, the major part of the book of Hebrews is concerned to demonstrate that Jesus fulfills the Old Testament types of both priest and sacrifice. And most allusions in the New Testament to the "blood" of Jesus are reminders that He died as a sacrifice. Plainly, we are being instructed to study the sacrifices in order to understand what Jesus has done for us.

When we look at the manner in which animal sacrifices were offered under the old covenant, we notice two elements that indicate that the animal being sacrificed was a substitute for the one making the sacrifice. First, the worshiper was to lay his hand on the head of the animal before slaughtering it (Lev. 1:4; 3:2, 8; 4:24; etc.). Although Scripture does not make the meaning of this action explicit, it appears to imply the symbolic transfer of the worshiper's sins to the animal that was being sacrificed.[7] Next, the worshiper killed the animal as a way of expressing his recognition that his sins were deserving of death (Lev. 1:5). Taken together, these rituals signaled that the worshiper's sins had been laid upon the animal, which must now die to make atonement for them.

The idea of substitution is seen even more clearly in the rituals of the Day of Atonement. On this day the high priest was to offer a bull as a sacrifice for himself, then kill a goat to make atonement for the Holy Place, which had been desecrated by the sins of the people. He was then to take a second goat, lay both his hands on its head, "and confess over it all the iniquities of the people of Israel, and all their transgressions, all their sins" (Lev. 16:21). By so doing, he was symbolically putting those sins and transgressions on the head of the goat, which was then sent into the wilderness to bear the people's iniquities away (Lev. 16:20–22). When the New Testament picks up the story, it insists that the blood of bulls and goats cannot actually take away sins (Heb. 10:4), and therefore Jesus had to make a better sacrifice than these. Christ fulfills the role of the scapegoat by bearing the sins of many (Heb. 9:28). The sin-bearing of the scapegoat was provisional and symbolic; the sin-bearing of Jesus is permanent and real.

The Passover, too, teaches the idea of substitution. The Lord "pass[ed] through" Egypt and took the lives of the firstborn of all Egyptian families, but He "pass[ed] over" each Israelite family that had sacrificed a lamb and placed its blood on its doorposts (Ex. 12:21–23). In their case, the lamb had been substituted for their firstborn children; it died in their place. This is the likely background for John the Baptist's designation of Jesus as "the Lamb of God, who takes away the sin of the world" (John 1:29). And Paul associates Christ directly with the Passover lamb when he declares to the Corinthians that "Christ, our Passover lamb, has been sacrificed" (1 Cor. 5:7). We have been "passed over" by God's wrath because Jesus has died instead of us.

The sacrificial system also provides the background for the teaching of Isaiah 53, which Jesus explicitly applied to Himself (Luke 22:37; see Isa. 53:12). The passage speaks of God's Servant, whose sufferings were misinterpreted by those around Him as punishment for His own sins but were actually the result of His identification with his people. Verse 6 tells us that God has laid on His Servant "the iniquity of us all." Verse 10 describes the Servant's death as an offering for sin, and in verses 11 and 12 it is repeated that He has borne the sin of many.

Verse 5 presents the idea of substitution most clearly: "But he was wounded for our transgressions; he was crushed for our iniquities; upon him was the chastisement that brought us peace, and with his stripes we are healed." This is as much as to say that our guilt was transferred to Jesus, and He took upon Himself the punishment that should have been ours. He died instead of us.

Redemption and Ransom

The principle of substitution can also be seen in the Bible's use of the concepts of redemption and ransom to describe Christ's work on our behalf. The fundamental idea behind these concepts is of the payment of a price to obtain the release of property or of a person. In the case of property, the release was from its being lost to its original owner or its family (Lev. 25:29–33; Ruth 4:4). In the case of persons, the release might be from slavery (Ex. 6:6; Lev. 25:48; Deut. 7:8), the death penalty (Ex. 21:29–30), or death itself (Ps. 49:15). In each case, release was obtained only through the payment of a price, either a monetary sum or the sacrifice of an animal.

This provides the background for Jesus' saying that He came to give His life as a "ransom" for many (Matt. 20:28; Mark 10:45), and the similar statement in 1 Timothy 2:6 that He gave Himself "as a ransom for all." There is no need to ask to whom the ransom was paid; the point being made is simply that Jesus paid a price—a terrible price—to obtain our release from the consequences of our sins. The substitutionary nature of this price becomes especially clear in Galatians 3:13, where we read that "Christ redeemed us from the curse of the law by becoming a curse for us." The curse should have fallen on us, but Jesus redeemed us by taking it upon Himself.

From what, exactly, has Christ redeemed us? From both the penalty of sin (the "curse"), and its power. In Ephesians 1:7 and Colossians 1:14, redemption is defined as the forgiveness of sins, but in Titus 2:14 we read that Jesus "gave himself for us to redeem us from all lawlessness and to purify for himself a people for his own possession who are zealous for good works." We were previously under sentence of death for our sins; now we have been forgiven. And we were previously slaves to sin; now we have been set free (Rom. 6:20–22; Gal. 5:1). This was accomplished by Christ's self-substitution on our behalf.

Jesus' Righteousness

Finally, we see the principle of substitution in the transfer of Jesus' perfect righteousness to those who believe in Him. Although many theological treatments of the Atonement focus solely on the meaning of Jesus' death, it is more true to the New Testament to view His entire life, from Incarnation to ascension, as directed toward the reconciling of men and women to God. In particular, Jesus' perfect righteousness, obtained through a life of absolute obedience to God and imputed to those who trust in Him, is viewed in the Bible as the basis on which God views us as deserving eternal life. In Philippians 3:9–11, Paul states that he wants to be found in Christ, not having a righteousness of his own that comes from the Law, "but that which comes through faith in Christ, the righteousness from God that depends on faith," to the end that he may attain the resurrection from the dead. As theologian Wayne Grudem comments, "It is not just moral neutrality that Paul knows he needs from Christ (that is, a clean slate with sins forgiven), but a positive moral righteousness. And he knows that that cannot come from himself but must come through faith in Christ."[8]

Again, the substitutionary nature of Jesus' action on our behalf is very clear. We are capable neither of rendering God the perfect obedience that is due to him nor of paying the penalty for our transgressions. Jesus has stepped in to take our place, dying the death we should have died and also living the life we should have lived.

THE ATONEMENT:
CHRIST RECEIVING OUR PUNISHMENT

By this time it may seem redundant to insist that Jesus was punished for us; yet that point is crucial, and objections to it must be answered. In theological terms the Atonement is objective, substitutionary, and *penal*— Jesus took on Himself the punishment that should have been ours.[9] The wages of sin is death (Rom. 6:23), and death is what Jesus was given.

But isn't this unjust? If we have sinned, how can it be right for God to treat us as if we had not? And if Jesus is sinless, how can He justly be treated as guilty? Doesn't the doctrine of substitutionary atonement portray God as resorting to a legal fiction?

In answer, it is important first to ensure that we do not understand the doctrine wrongly. The idea is not that Jesus literally became guilty of our sins but rather that He voluntarily accepted legal liability for them. And when we trust in Christ and are declared righteous, that does not mean that our character has already been made holy (although that will necessarily follow as we live out our faith through obedience to Jesus), but that we have been granted a righteous standing before God. God is not pretending that Jesus is guilty and we are righteous; He is freeing us from the legal consequences of our sin by allowing those consequences to fall on His Son, and simultaneously granting us the status the Son has earned for us. We will look at this matter more carefully in chapter 8, when we consider the doctrine of imputed righteousness.

In addition, this is yet another place where we do well to humble ourselves to learn from the Word of God, rather than presuming to instruct the Lord in the doctrine of justice. God has told us plainly that He made Him who knew no sin to be sin, "so that in him we might become the righteousness of God" (2 Cor. 5:21). If God has said it, it is so, regardless of whether we are capable of fully grasping the nature of the transaction. Our proper response is gratitude, praise, and humble faith—not complaints against God's justice.

Another argument against the understanding of the Atonement as penal and substitutionary is that it portrays the Father as treating His Son cruelly. In one recent version of this complaint, some feminist theologians have accused traditional Christianity of promoting child abuse. Only an abusive, tyrannical father, they say, would ever subject his son to undeserved suffering. By writing such a relationship into the very structure of our faith, we Christians have laid the groundwork for fathers everywhere to imagine that they have the right to similarly misuse their children.

Once again, though, we need to remind ourselves that the Atonement is the work of the entire triune God. The Father did not seize a reluctant or terrified Son and force Him to become our substitute; no, the Son voluntarily offered Himself as a sacrifice in anticipation of the joy set before Him, the joy of an eternity spent with His Father and with the great multitude He would redeem. No one took Jesus' life from Him; He laid it down of His own accord (John 10:18). All three persons of the Holy Trinity acted in concert and full agreement with one another to redeem us and reconcile us to God.

We could be redeemed in no other way than through the perfect life and sacrificial death of God's own Son; and so the Father, the Son, and the Spirit together planned and carried out this salvation. To call the Cross an instance of child abuse is to fail to appreciate both the necessity of Christ's death and His full willingness to die on our behalf.

THE ATONEMENT SUMMARIZED: DIVINE JUSTICE SATISFIED

Historically, theologians have summarized the meaning of the Atonement by saying that Christ has fully satisfied divine justice on behalf of those who believe in Him. God's justice—His very nature and character—calls for sinners to be punished with a punishment commensurate with the heinousness of their sin.

Since sin against an infinitely glorious God is an infinite evil, satisfaction can be obtained only through eternal punishment or through the punishment of a Being who is Himself of infinite worth. Those who die in their sins will spend eternity satisfying divine justice for their sins. Those who trust in Christ will find that in their case the justice of God has already been satisfied in full.

The Glory of the Cross

When we have stated that the Atonement is objective, substitutionary, and penal, we have come to the very heart of the Christian gospel. We now find ourselves gazing directly into the unfathomable love of God. "In this is love, not that we have loved God but that he loved us and sent his Son to be the propitiation for our sins" (1 John 4:10). Nothing but the astounding perversity of the fallen human mind can account for the readiness of so many people to part with this doctrine. We should instead cling to it with all our hearts and proclaim it with all our strength. To attempt to define the love of God without the Cross is foolishness, and to build a theology on any other foundation than Christ and Him crucified is idolatry.

There is nothing like this in any other religion or philosophy under heaven. There are religions that know something of the strictness of God's law but nothing of His grace, and others that so emphasize love as altogether to eliminate holiness. Only the Christian faith, through its doctrine of the propitiatory death of Christ, shows us God as He truly is: perfectly holy and utterly uncompromising in His aversion to evil, yet simultaneously loving and gracious beyond our wildest dreams.

It is a ravishing vision. To live in the light of this truth, vitally related to this holy, loving God, is the beginning of everlasting felicity. "But the path of the righteous is like the light of dawn, which shines brighter and brighter until full day" (Prov. 4:18).

O my God, my holy, loving, gracious triune God! The doctrine of the Cross makes my heart sing for joy; would that I had a poet's skill to put that joy into words suited to the grandeur of Your grace! Thank You for the Atonement!

I thank You, loving Father, for sending the Son as a propitiation for my sins. I thank You, Lord Jesus, for freely shedding Your blood for my redemption. I thank You, eternal Spirit, for opening my heart to grasp and receive this inexpressible gift.

Above all, I thank You, dear God, for the sheer, startling beauty of Your moral nature: Your blinding holiness, Your unfathomable compassion, and their astonishing resolution in the agony of Golgotha. Let me live ever close to the Cross, not that I may wallow in my guilt, but that I may exult in Your holy love. And let me radiate that love to all around me, that they, too, may see Your light and enter into Your grace. Amen.

NOTES

1. George MacDonald, *Creation in Christ,* ed. Rolland Hein (Wheaton, Ill.: Shaw, 1976), 78–79.

2. The "moral influence" theory of the Atonement can be traced back to the medieval theologian Peter Abelard.

3. Jürgen Moltmann, *The Crucified God,* trans. R. A. Wilson and John Bowden (Minneapolis: Fortress, 1993), 181–85.

4. For a detailed discussion of the biblical concept of propitiation, see Leon Morris, *The Apostolic Preaching of the Cross* (Grand Rapids: Eerdmans, 1965), chapters 5 and 6, or Leon Morris, *The Atonement* (Downers Grove, Ill: InterVarsity, 1983), chapter 7.

5. John Murray, *Redemption Accomplished and Applied* (Grand Rapids: Eerdmans, 1955), 33–42.

6. Millard Erickson, *Christian Theology* (Grand Rapids: Baker, 1985), 815.

7. Morris, *The Atonement,* 45–47.

8. Wayne Grudem, *Systematic Theology: An Introduction to Biblical Doctrine* (Grand Rapids: Zondervan, 1994), 571.

9. "It is clear from Old Testament usage that to 'bear sin' means neither to sympathize with sinners, nor to identify with their pain, nor to express their penitence, nor to be persecuted on account of human sinfulness (as others have argued), nor even to suffer the consequences of sin in personal or social terms, but specifically to endure its penal consequences, to undergo its penalty." John Stott, *The Cross of Christ* (Downers Grove, Ill: InterVarsity, 1986), 143.

8

REDEMPTION
THROUGH
HIS BLOOD

❧

In him we have redemption through his blood, the forgiveness
of our trespasses, according to the riches of his grace.

✝EPHESIANS 1:7

IN OUR JOURNEY TO DISCOVER God's good plans for our welfare, we have turned a corner. We began our journey (chapter 1) with the observation that fallen human beings are not naturally children of God. God, we learned, justly regards us as sinners who have violated His Law and now deserve punishment for our deeds. We then proceeded to examine the nature of the punishment the Bible says we deserve—the agonizingly difficult topic of hell. In truth, chapters 2 and 3 were as hard for me to write as they probably were for you to read.

But in chapter 7 we reached an important turning point. We discovered that the same God whose holy character calls for sin to be punished has now taken our deserved punishment on Himself. He has expiated our guilt and propitiated His wrath. He has satisfied His justice. In Christ, says Paul, "God was reconciling the world to himself" (2 Cor. 5:19). The more we meditate on this truth, the greater should be our reverence for this holy, compassionate God and the greater our desire to know Him. If He truly loves us enough to make propitiation for us, then we would be fools to let anything hinder us from growing in understanding of His grace to us in Christ.

Having turned the corner, let's consider where divine justice leads us. We need to grasp not only the greatness of His wrath against sin but also the abundance of His love toward those who are in Christ. We have seen something of God's severity; now let us look deeper into the depths of His kindness.

Paul insists that the God "who did not spare his own Son, but gave him up for us all" will now surely, along "with him, graciously give us all things" (Rom. 8:32). And what are those "all things"? It might seem that an examination of that question should lie outside the bounds of an inquiry into divine justice, but I do not think that is so. Our goal is to know God.

How does Jesus' death two thousand years ago become a source of new life for us today? How do the effects of the Atonement become ours?

GOD DRAWS US TO CHRIST

The gospel of Jesus Christ is freely offered by God to all people everywhere. God wishes that every person should come to repentance (2 Peter 3:9). The tears Jesus wept over Jerusalem were by no means insincere or hypocritical; they represented both His and His Father's grief over the people's perverse unwillingness to come to Jesus and be saved (Matt. 23:37). Again and again in the Bible, we learn that God takes no pleasure in the death of the wicked; He prefers that they turn from their ways and live (Ezek. 33:11). He desires that all be saved and "come to the knowledge of the truth" (1 Tim. 2:4)[1]

To that end, God wants churches planted, missionaries sent out, the Scriptures translated, and disciples made of every nation. God's people are to go out into the highways and hedges to *compel* people to come in, that the wedding banquet of the Lamb may be packed (Luke 14:23). The invitation is to be taken to *all* people. Indeed, people everywhere are not merely invited but *commanded* to repent and believe (Acts 17:30).

Yet the painful, stubborn fact is that people reject the gospel.

Why? Is the message defective? Not at all! Surely nothing could be more wonderful than the invitation to experience intimate friendship with the Creator of the universe. No more thrilling prospect can be imagined than that God Himself should set aside the barriers that stand between us and Him and call us into a fellowship of everlasting joy. Where in all of the religions and philosophies of the world can one find a story so moving and heartening as that of Jesus' voluntary death for sinners? How could any message be more perfectly calculated to meet our deepest needs—for truth, forgiveness, knowledge of our Maker, hope for the future, liberation from sin's power, freedom from the fear of death—than the message of the Cross?

If there is any defect in the gospel, I have never found it. The more I understand the gospel, and the more I see how firmly grounded it is in history and how perfectly suited to the human condition, the more I love this message. At times I feel utterly baffled that there should be any who reject Christ.

A Defect in the Human Heart

But reject Him they do, and if it is not because of a defect in the truth, it has to be because of a defect in the heart. The fallen human heart, as we have seen already, is hostile to God. It hears of His holy law and its fear is kindled; and so it runs from Him in terror. It learns of His grace in Jesus and its pride is stung; and so it flees from Calvary as well as Sinai.

Whether God threatens or entreats us, we back away from Him as wounded animals shrink from the veterinarian. We "suppress the truth" by our unrighteousness (Rom. 1:18). Jesus was hated when He was on earth because He declared that the world's deeds are evil, and He is still hated today for the very same reason. The mechanisms of denial and disbelief that led to His crucifixion and to the persecution of His first followers are as operative and powerful in the twenty-first century as they were in the first.

And because this is so, the message of the gospel, for all of its inherent glory and beauty, does not draw people to Christ unless it is accompanied by the secret working of the Holy Spirit in their hearts. God "desires all people to be saved and to come to the knowledge of the truth" (1 Tim. 2:4), but that simply will not happen unless He "grant[s] them repentance leading to a knowledge of the truth" (2 Tim. 2:25). Only the work of God can overcome our resistance to God. No one can come to Jesus unless it is granted him by the Father (John 6:65). God must call us with a calling that is effectual, a calling that carries with it the power to raise us from the dead.

Conviction of Sin

The process normally begins with the Holy Spirit's work of conviction (John 16:8). We are exposed to the gospel message, and as its truth penetrates our hearts, the Spirit makes us aware of our sin, Christ's righteousness, and our liability to judgment. We begin to see ourselves in God's perspective, and the sight frightens us. This is what John Newton was speaking of in his famous line, "'Twas grace that taught my heart to fear." At the same time, the Holy Spirit makes us aware of who Christ is and what He has done and leads us to the realization that His death so long ago is of the utmost relevance to us today.

There is no single pattern for the conviction of sin. We should not expect God to work the same way in different hearts. Some people agonize for long periods under a crushing sense of divine displeasure, while others are given only the lightest touch of pain. In my own case, I first became convinced through rational arguments that God does exist and then immediately began to worry about how I could be confident that God would accept me beyond death.

I took it for granted that God will ban from His kingdom the great tyrants of history—Nero, Hitler, and so forth—but I was not quite sure just how evil one must be to merit that fate. Was it possible that He would reject me? I was not terrified, nor did I have what I would now consider a very deep view of either my own sinful character or God's holiness. But I was certainly troubled, and that trouble was sufficient to shake my self-righteousness.

Although I still viewed the word *sin* as hopelessly quaint, I was beginning to see myself as a person who was both guilty before God and incapable of self-reformation. And when I started to look closely at the life and words of Jesus, that sense of my unworthiness and helplessness just grew. By the time I heard the message of the Cross, I was ready for it. I knew I needed forgiveness and the power to change my life.

While acknowledging the Holy Spirit's freedom to work in each person according to His own perfect wisdom, I believe that some such awareness is indispensable if a person is to properly understand the gospel and sincerely receive Jesus. The prodigal son has to come to his senses before it occurs to him to turn home.

Regeneration

But conviction is not the same as faith. It is one thing to become aware of our plight as sinners before a holy God; it is something else altogether to willingly and gladly entrust ourselves to Jesus for salvation. A person may experience conviction of sin and yet never come to faith in Christ. We may see the truth in an intellectual way and yet hate it. Without a fundamental change in our nature, we will still reject God's grace, and our conviction of sin will simply become the basis for our greater condemnation. We don't just need knowledge; we need a new principle of life. And new life is what God has provided for us.

Theologians generally refer to the impartation of this new life as *regeneration*. Although the word primarily suggests to us the idea of being "born again," the Bible actually unfolds its meaning under three images. First, the Scriptures present the image of *birth:* "But to all who did receive him, who believed in his name, he gave the right to become children of God" (John 1:12); "You have been born again, not of perishable seed but of imperishable, through the living and abiding word of God" (1 Peter 1:23). Second, the Scriptures present the image of *creation:* "For neither circumcision counts for anything, nor uncircumcision, but a new creation" (Gal. 6:15); "Therefore, if anyone is in Christ, he is a new creation. The old has passed away; behold, the new has come" (2 Cor. 5:17). Finally we encounter the image of *resurrection:* "But God, being rich in mercy . . . even when we were dead in our trespasses, made us alive together with Christ" (Eph. 2:4–5). "We know that we have passed out of death into life" (1 John 3:14).

These three images have two important features in common. First, they all indicate that in regeneration we are passive. Whether in the natural realm or the spiritual, we cannot give birth to, create, or resurrect ourselves. Regeneration is God's work. It is not something we do but something that is done in us. Although we usually translate Jesus' words in John 3:3 as saying that no one can see the kingdom of God unless he is born "again," the Greek word *anothen* may also legitimately be rendered "from above." It is likely that John intends us to understand *both* meanings of the word. Regeneration is a second birth, and it is a birth "from above," brought about by the utterly mysterious working of the Holy Spirit, who, like the wind, blows wherever He pleases (John 3:8).

It would make no more sense to say that our faith caused us to be born again than to say that a baby's cry caused it to be delivered from the womb. In regeneration God is active, and we are wholly passive. As Archibald Alexander wrote,

> Among all the preposterous notions which a new and crude theology has poured forth so profusely in our day, there is none more absurd than that a dead sinner can beget new life in himself. The very idea of a man's becoming his own father in the spiritual regeneration is as unreasonable as such a supposition in relation to our first birth. Away with all such soul-destroying, God-dishonouring sentiments![2]

In addition, the three images emphasize the greatness of the transformation God produces in us. He gives us new life; He creates us afresh; He raises us from death. We are still the people we were before our regeneration; our personalities are not fundamentally altered. But we are changed. We now love what we used to hate (God's holy character and His gracious provision for our salvation), and we hate what we used to love (rebellion in every form and variety). Our hearts of stone have been taken away, and we have been given hearts of flesh (Ezek. 19:11; 36:26).

Unless our regeneration took place when we were too young to be conscious of it, we will be aware of a significant change in our whole approach to life. Previously we could not "see" the kingdom of God (John 3:3), but now we are aware of God's work in the world and are eager to participate in it. Previously we were hostile to God and could not submit to His Law (Rom. 8:5–8); now we desire the pure spiritual milk of His Word, that we may grow up in our salvation (1 Peter 2:2).

Previously we were comfortable with sin; now we yearn to be holy (1 John 3:9). We are new creatures, and with John Newton we gladly sing, "I once was lost but now am found; was blind but now I see."

Some people experience this change abruptly, while for others it seems to occur over a period of time. No doubt regeneration itself is an instantaneous act on God's part, but our consciousness that we have been regenerated may develop at different paces in different people. Sooner or later, though, we realize that something has happened in us that has changed us forever.

GOD GIVES US POWER TO RESPOND

Faith

Regeneration is God's work, but faith and repentance are ours. *We* believe in Christ, and *we* turn from sin. Yet faith and repentance follow inevitably upon regeneration and are the manner in which our rebirth registers upon our consciousness. All those whom the Father has given to the Son *will* come to Him (John 6:37), which means that they will exercise faith in Him and humble themselves before Him. As John Murray has written, regeneration "is the renewing of the heart and mind, and the renewed heart and mind must act according to their nature."[3] Whereas previously it was natural to us to hide from Christ and make excuses for not believing in Him, now the natural thing is to throw ourselves on Him. Both faith and repentance are described in Scripture as "granted" to us (Phil. 1:29; 2 Tim. 2:25), not because God believes or repents for us, but because the change He effects in us causes us to *want* to give ourselves to Christ and become like Him.

Faith is often analyzed as consisting of knowledge, assent, and trust. We must know something of the gospel; we must believe it to be true; and we must entrust ourselves to Christ on the basis of that truth. All three of these elements are important, but today there is a special need to emphasize the indispensability of knowledge. In popular culture, "faith" is often stripped of its biblical meaning and treated as something virtuous in and of itself, regardless of its content or object. We are encouraged to maintain faith in ourselves, or even simply to "have faith" (which seems to mean that we are to have faith in faith!).

Meanwhile, at an academic level many so-called "inclusivist" theologians argue that people who have never heard of Christ may nevertheless be saved by Him, provided only that they have "faith" in *something*. What that something is seems unimportant. It may be the god of some other religious tradition, or perhaps even just some vague idea of a reality that transcends human knowledge. What is important is that people *have faith*—that their spirits reach out to something above them. When God sees such faith, He regards those people as if their faith already reposed in Christ.[4]

Both popular culture and the inclusivist theologians are plainly wrong. In the New Testament, "faith" always means faith *in Christ*. As Paul says in Romans 10:17, "Faith comes from hearing, and hearing through the word of Christ." This means that before we can exercise biblical, saving faith, we must have some knowledge of who Christ is and what He has done. At a minimum, it would seem necessary to know that He is the eternal Son of God, that He gave His life as a sacrifice for the sins of the world, and that He rose from the dead. We learn of Christ from a preacher, a book, or a friend, and then we place our trust in that same Christ of whom we have learned.

Christian faith is faith in the trūe Christ, faith that results in our consciously seeking to follow Christ and remain in Him. We have no basis for believing that any other kind of faith can ever connect a person savingly with Christ. There are no "anonymous Christians," just millions of people who, until they are given the opportunity to hear and respond to the gospel, will remain "without hope and without God" in this world (Eph. 2:12 NIV).

All who call on the name of the Lord will be saved, but "how are they to call on him in whom they have not believed? And how are they to believe in him of whom they have never heard? And how are they to hear without someone preaching? And how are they to preach unless they are sent? As it is written, 'How beautiful are the feet of those who preach the good news!'" (Rom. 10:13–15). Saving faith requires knowledge of the good news.

Repentance

Faith and repentance are closely intertwined. The two can be distinguished but never separated from one another. Faith is resting in

Christ, looking to Him alone for a right standing before God. We trust that His death can cover our sins and His righteousness can gain us a title to eternal life. We look nowhere else than to Him for peace with God and all the benefits that flow from that peace. We depend on Him to help us through the "dangers, toils, and snares" of this life, and to lead us at last to the Father's house, where He has gone to prepare a place for us (John 14:2).

Repentance, on the other hand, is turning from sin. Turning *to* Jesus means turning *away* from a life in which Jesus is in any way unwelcome or irrelevant. It means rejecting any thought, word, or deed of which we know He would disapprove, as well as every rebellious effort to make sense of life without Him. Repentance involves hating and grieving over our sins and striving to be free of them. It may well involve tears; it certainly involves effort. Like faith, it is not the work of a moment but of a lifetime. One might say that faith is the regenerate soul's steady, constantly renewed embrace of Christ, while repentance is its constant, hard-fought rejection of sin.

In the contemporary church scene, the whole idea of repentance seems somewhat outmoded. Services of worship have become "celebration services," in which little room can be found for prayers of confession, for music in a minor key, or even for silent reflection. We have become more concerned about acting cheerful than about coming honestly into the presence of God. In many circles, even baptismal testimonies often seem devoid of the note of true contrition. From kindergarten our culture has taught us solemnly that we must hold ourselves in the highest esteem and deny ourselves no pleasure; how then can we be so harsh with ourselves as to grieve over past sins or set our faces against future transgression? Surely God is not such a killjoy as that! Surely His chief interest in our lives is in bolstering our self-esteem.

I am not arguing that public worship ought to be morbidly focused upon sin and judgment. I believe that the dominant activity of our worship should not be "celebration," which has no clear object, but *praise*—conscious, focused adoration of our holy, omnipotent, gracious, triune God. The tone of worship should be joyful. But repentance ought to be the steady undercurrent of our worship and of our lives, in a way that it generally does not now seem to be.

One of my prayers for myself, my family, and my church is that we will become more and more like Job, who saw the greatness of God and then despised himself and repented in dust and ashes (Job 42:6), or like Isaiah, who beheld the holiness of the Lord and cried out, "Woe is me! For I am lost; for I am a man of unclean lips, and I dwell in the midst of a people of unclean lips; for my eyes have seen the King, the Lord of hosts!" (Isa. 6:5). I yearn for experiences of worship in which the presence of the Lord is so powerfully manifest that we will be unable to "celebrate" but will simply bow before Him in tearful humility and gratitude, conscious of our shameful guilt and corruption, even as His grace overwhelms us.

Too often we celebrate life in a dream world—where we are already good people and Christ exists to help us become a little better and a little happier. May God shatter that illusion and grant us true repentance!

He Declares Us Righteous

Very well. God has awakened us to our need for salvation, and He has placed within us the kernel of a new life that has begun to germinate in faith and repentance. But when we turn to God, what welcome will we find? God rightly demands of us that we perfectly obey His holy Law, but we have not done so! We have sinned against Him every day we have lived, and even now, when we find that we wish to be free of sin, we remain entangled in its power. We may find it encouraging to learn that Jesus led a perfect life and then died for the ungodly. But how can sinners like ourselves be made right with God?

The historic Protestant answer to this question is that as soon as we begin to exercise faith in Christ, God justifies us on the basis of that faith. *Justification* is a legal declaration, a statement on God's part that He not only forgives us but also views us as possessing all of the righteousness of Christ. In itself, justification does not make us inherently righteous or holy. God does intend to remake our character after the image of Christ; that is the act of His grace that we call sanctification. Justification has to do with our status before the Law. It is a declaration that God regards us as no longer standing under the condemnation we have earned by our disobedience.

How can this be? If we are guilty, how can we be declared not guilty? If we are unrighteous, how can we be treated as righteous? The answer is that God views believers as united with Christ, standing in such a relationship to Him that He becomes their representative before God.

Adam once stood as our representative, and by his disobedience all of us became sinners, not only in the sense that we are prone to sin but also in the sense that the guilt of Adam's sin has been imputed to us (Rom. 5:19). Now, however, we have a new representative, Jesus Christ. Unlike Adam, Jesus lived a perfectly holy life before God, keeping God's Law in every detail. Further, in spite of His own moral perfection, Jesus died a sacrificial death for the expiation of sin and the propitiation of divine wrath. This was God's plan and purpose, His way of satisfying His justice (Rom. 3:25–26). Christ's death allows God simultaneously to demonstrate His righteousness and justify those who are united to Christ by faith. God accepts Jesus' death as full payment for our sins and His righteousness as a substitute for our unrighteousness. God not only forgives us; He regards us as if we had perfectly fulfilled the requirements of His Law!

Like the Prodigal Son, we come to God sheepishly and fearfully, hoping that He may possibly cancel our debt and accept us as servants. Instead, He receives us with joy, puts new robes on our backs and sandals on our feet, and treats us as if we had never strayed.

Is Imputation a "Contemptible Legalism"?

Many people have stumbled over the truth that Christ's righteousness is credited, or imputed, to the unrighteous. Roman Catholic theology has insisted that justification is not a legal declaration at all but the infusion of Christ's righteousness into our lives. George MacDonald, in somewhat similar fashion, views the classic Protestant doctrine as a miserable fiction by which Christians defend themselves from God's demand that they actually *become* righteous:

> They say first, God must punish the sinner, for justice requires it; then they say He does not punish the sinner, but punishes a perfectly righteous man instead, attributes His righteousness to the sinner, and so continues just. Was there ever such a confusion, such an inversion of right and wrong! Justice *could not* treat a righteous man as an

unrighteous; neither, if justice required the punishment of sin, *could* justice let the sinner go unpunished. To lay the pain upon the righteous in the name of justice is simply monstrous. No wonder unbelief is rampant. Believe in Moloch if you will, but call him Moloch, not justice.

Be sure that the thing God gives, the righteousness that is of God, is a real thing and not a contemptible legalism. Pray God I have no righteousness imputed to me. Let me be regarded as the sinner I am; for nothing will serve my need but to be made a righteous man, one that will no more sin.[5]

MacDonald insists that when Paul says that Abraham's faith was credited to him for righteousness (Rom. 4:3), he simply means that faith *is* righteousness. And since faith brings a person into contact with God, who is able to help him in all his efforts to be righteous, it is appropriate to call a person who has faith a righteous person, even if he is still incomplete in righteousness

As always, MacDonald's rhetoric is powerful. But there are enormous problems in his analysis. To begin with, we have already seen (in chapter 1) that God's justice does indeed require the punishment of sin. It is just not true to say, as MacDonald does, that God is concerned only to destroy sin within us. We have sinned against God and deserve to be punished eternally. If God will *not* impute Christ's righteousness to us but instead treats us as our sins deserve, then we are lost. MacDonald's doctrine appears noble, but in reality it cuts away the very basis of Christian hope. I sincerely hope (and believe) that God did not listen to MacDonald's foolish prayer that Christ's righteousness not be imputed to him.

Second, in insisting that God cannot justly punish Christ in our place, MacDonald is ignoring Paul's argument in Romans 5:12–21, which develops the parallel between Christ and Adam. You and I did not take the forbidden fruit in Eden, but we are treated as if we did. Death—the punishment threatened to Adam—has come upon all of his descendants. Plainly, in some very real way God viewed Adam as representing all of us. And this, Paul says, is the key to understanding the manner in which Christ's righteousness becomes ours. Adam represented us and fell; Christ represents us and stands. Adam's trespass led to condemnation for all people; Christ's righteous life leads to justification and life for all who believe (Rom. 5:18). In both cases there is a union between the representative and those represented, and God deems this union sufficient to justify both the imputation of guilt and the imputation of righteousness. We may not fully understand this arrangement, but it is not wise for us to argue with it.

Does Imputation Undermine Holiness?

A third and deeper problem with MacDonald's argument is that it is very wrong and unfair to suggest that the Protestant doctrine of justification by faith is at loggerheads with God's demand that we pursue holiness. In theological terminology, MacDonald is accusing the Protestant doctrine of leading inevitably to antinomianism, or the teaching that Christians need not seek to obey God's Law (Greek *nomos*).

This is an old, tired accusation, and it is quite muddled. Certainly the doctrine of imputed righteousness can be perverted into antinomianism, and perhaps MacDonald had to deal with people who had convinced themselves that because they were justified, their actual behavior was of no concern to God. But no major Protestant theologian has ever drawn that conclusion. The writings of Luther, Calvin, Owen, Edwards, and all other orthodox Protestant theologians up to the present, as well as the major Protestant confessions, are replete with warnings that faith that does not lead to holiness is no saving faith at all. If we are genuinely regenerate, the new nature God has given us will find sin repugnant and will rise up in opposition to it. Knowing that God has already declared us righteous will actually help us in our struggle to be free of sin's power; it will never provide us with an excuse to discharge ourselves from that struggle. Everyone who hopes in Christ purifies himself as He is pure (1 John 3:3).

Moreover, a man of MacDonald's ability should have noticed that the very fact that the Protestant teaching *can* be perverted into antinomianism is a strong argument that it is correct, since Paul had to guard his own doctrine against the same danger. In Romans 1:1–3:20, Paul demonstrates that all people are guilty of sin, liable to punishment, and incapable of justifying themselves by their deeds. In Romans 3–5 he declares that now a righteousness from God has been manifested, a righteousness that is received by faith. His argument culminates with the comparison of Adam and Christ, the purpose of which is to emphasize the truth that Christ's righteousness is imputed to us.

Immediately after Paul has done this, he deals with the objection that this method of justification undermines the Law: "What shall we say then? Are we to continue in sin that grace may abound?" (Rom. 6:1). Paul, of course, shows that this is an unacceptable conclusion: "By no means! How can we who died to sin still live in it?" (v. 2). What is important to us here, though, is that if Paul's doctrine of justification were the same as MacDonald's, there would be no need for him to respond to the objection at all. Neither MacDonald's doctrine that faith is itself righteousness, nor the Roman Catholic doctrine that justification is the infusion of Christ's righteousness into those who believe, is subject to the complaint that it encourages disregard for holiness. Paul's doctrine *was* vulnerable to that complaint. The same accusation MacDonald made against the Protestant theologians was made against Paul. This is good evidence that Protestantism has interpreted Paul correctly.

The Nature of Saving Faith

But the deepest problem in MacDonald's analysis lies in his interpretation of Abraham's faith. On the surface, his reading makes sense. Romans 4:3 reads, "Abraham believed God, and it was counted to him as righteousness." This could indeed mean that God regarded Abraham's faith itself as righteousness. I do not believe MacDonald can point to any biblical evidence for his assertion that, since faith connects us with the God who can make us righteous, it is proper for God to regard a person with faith as *already* righteous. This doctrine is nothing but speculation on MacDonald's part. But it does seem possible to read Romans 4:3 as saying that God counted Abraham's faith as an act of righteousness, and one could then conclude that in *some* way faith fulfills the requirements for justification.

In the end, though, this interpretation has to be rejected. Many reasons can be given; I will offer just two.[6] First, although Paul can speak of Abraham's faith as being counted to him as righteousness, he can also speak of righteousness itself as that which is counted, or credited, to those who believe (Rom. 4:6, 11). In other words, Paul can make either "faith" or "righteousness" the object of the verb "to count" (Greek *logizomai*). He can say that God counts our faith as righteousness (4:3, 9) or that He counts righteousness to us by faith (4:6, 11). While the first form of expression may be compatible with saying that our faith *is* righteousness, the second is not. Both expressions, however, are compatible with the idea that faith is the instrument by which we receive God's (or Christ's) righteousness.

Second, the Bible never suggests that we are justified *because of* or on *account of* faith. It speaks instead of our being justified *by (ek), based on (epi),* or *through (dia)* faith. All of these expressions suggest that our faith is the instrument by which we receive our righteous standing, not that it is the content of righteousness. In Philippians 3:9, for example, Paul declares that the only righteousness God desires is "that which comes through faith in Christ, the righteousness that depends on faith." It is very hard to see how Paul could be speaking of a righteousness that consists *in* faith. Instead, it is a righteousness that he possesses by virtue of being united to Christ *by* faith.

Paul's faith in Christ is not itself his righteousness; rather, it is the means by which Paul gains access to righteousness. I believe Paul would have approved entirely of the following statement by J. C. Ryle:

> True faith has *nothing whatever of merit* about it, and in the highest sense cannot be called "a work." It is but laying hold of a Saviour's hand, leaning on a husband's arm, and receiving a physician's medicine. It brings with it nothing to Christ but a sinful man's soul. It gives nothing, contributes nothing, pays nothing, performs nothing. It only receives, takes, accepts, grasps, and embraces the glorious gift of justification which Christ bestows, and by renewed daily acts enjoys that gift.[7]

In trying to understand the doctrine of imputed righteousness, I have found the following analogy from John Piper very helpful:

> Suppose I say to Barnabus, my teenage son, "Clean up your room before you go to school. You must have a clean room or you won't be able to go watch the game tonight." Suppose he plans poorly and leaves for school without cleaning the room. And suppose I discover the messy room and clean it. His afternoon fills up, and he gets home just before it's time to leave for the game and realizes what he has

done and feels terrible. He apologizes and humbly accepts the consequences. No game.

To which I say, "Barnabus, I am going to credit the clean room to your account because of your apology and submission. Before you left for school this morning I said, 'You must have a clean room or you won't be able to go watch the game tonight.' Well, your room is clean. So you can go to the game."

That's one way to say it, which corresponds to the language of Romans 4:6. Or I could say, "I credit your apology for a clean room," which would correspond to the language of Romans 4:3. What I mean when I say, "I credit your apology for a clean room" is *not* that the apology is the clean room, nor that the clean room *consists of* the apology, nor that he really cleaned the room. I cleaned it. It was pure grace. All I mean is that, in my way of reckoning—in my grace—his apology connects him with the promise given for a clean room. The clean room is his clean room.[8]

That is it exactly. It is not that our faith is righteousness, but that in God's way of reckoning—in His grace—our faith connects us with the promise given for righteousness. We were incapable of "cleaning up our room" for ourselves, but in Christ, God has done it for us. And because the room has indeed been cleaned, God now freely gives to us all the blessings and privileges that depended on having a clean room. Our job is to simply receive those blessings by entrusting ourselves to Christ. "This is the work of God, that you believe in him whom he has sent" (John 6:29).

HE MAKES US HIS CHILDREN

Once when I was in high school, some friends and I let a campfire get out of control at a state park in Iowa. By the time the fire department arrived on the scene to put the blaze out, we had burned an area of dry grass comparable in size to a football field, and the flames were moving into a stand of trees. After it was all over, I went home exhausted, filthy, and humiliated, and waited for the long arm of the law to find me out.

Days passed, yet no punishment was administered. The police did not come to arrest me; the county did not fine me; even the newspaper did not condemn me. I still remember the surprise and gratitude I felt when I realized that I was not going to be held accountable for my actions.

The knowledge that in Christ we have been accounted righteous, so that our sins are *all* forgiven and we are assured the gift of everlasting peace with God, should thrill our hearts and drive us to our knees in praise and thanksgiving. If it does not, then it is almost certain that there remains some defect in our understanding. Perhaps we have not yet grasped the truth that apart from Christ we would be culpable for the millions of sins and transgressions we have committed and would need to suffer eternally to repay our debt to God's justice. Or perhaps we still do not understand the meaning of the Cross and of justification, that "in Christ God was reconciling the world to himself, not counting [our] trespasses against [us]" (2 Cor. 5:19).

If these truths have indeed penetrated our minds and hearts, they cannot help but produce in us a massive sense of relief and gratitude.

A Gift Greater Than Our Justification Before God

But as great as the gift of justification is, there is another gift still greater, and that is our adoption as the children of God. It is wonderful to have our sins canceled and to be clothed in the righteousness of Jesus; it is more wonderful still to be brought into God's family.

Remember, you and I were previously children of wrath, of disobedience, and of the devil (Eph. 2:2–3; John 8:44), but now God has lavished such love on us that we may rightly be called the children of God (1 John 3:1), and Jesus is not ashamed to call us His brothers (Heb. 2:11).

Our Adoption: A Legal Status and a Natural Inclination

There are two important aspects to our adoption. First, there is a legal declaration. We are given the legal status of children. When we believe in the name of Jesus, He gives us the right—the authority— to become children of God (John 1:12).

In addition, we are also given the *nature* of children. This is expressed in Scripture both in terms of the gift of the "Spirit of sonship," whose presence in our hearts stimulates us to look to God as our Father (Rom. 8:15; Gal. 4:6), and by the statement that in our regeneration we are made God's children by nature (John 1:13; 1 Peter 1:3).

The idea is not that we become God—the eternal Son will always be Son in a manner in which we are not—but that we are given both the right and the desire to regard God as our Father. We may and should speak to Him as children to a father ("Our Father in heaven" Matt. 6:9), trust Him in all of life's circumstances ("If you then, who are evil, know how to give good gifts to your children, how much more will your Father who is in heaven give good things to those who ask him!" Matt. 7:11), accept His loving discipline ("It is for discipline that you have to endure. God is treating you as sons" Heb. 12:7), and call to Him in distress ("by whom we cry, 'Abba! Father!'" Rom. 8:15).

True, Paul could speak in Romans 8:23 of our adoption as something for which we "wait eagerly." By this he clearly was referring to the glorification to which we still look forward, when we will be given new bodies in which to love and serve God and one another and will be done with death and suffering forever. But the fact that our adoption is to be consummated in the future should not hinder us from reveling in the filial status and nature that are already ours.

Most of the anxiety, fear, regret, and restlessness we experience in this life would be greatly eased—if not eliminated—if we would meditate daily on the truth that God is to us the most tender, attentive, and protective Father, who has numbered even the hairs on our heads (Luke 12:7).

In this context, I am relieved finally to be able to say a word of praise for the work of George MacDonald. MacDonald's mistake lay in thinking that all people are by nature children of God, regardless of their relationship to Christ. In my view that is a grievous error, for it confuses us at the very outset about the nature of God's justice and ends up diminishing greatly the wonderful things God has done for us in Christ. But I will readily and gladly admit that MacDonald was a master at portraying the meaning of childlike Christian trust in our divine Father. I suspect that it was this understanding of filial trust, together with MacDonald's passionate concern for holiness and his superb imagination, that made his work so very attractive to C. S. Lewis. While I cannot in good conscience recommend MacDonald's sermons, I do believe that Christian readers can benefit from his works of fiction. I wish only that MacDonald's formidable powers as a writer had been employed in the service of a more balanced theology.

HE CONFORMS US TO HIS SON

MacDonald and others have worried that the Protestant emphasis on justification as the imputation of Christ's righteousness will make Christians lazy about seeking holiness. In principle this could indeed happen, and I am sure there are cases where it has happened. Every biblical truth, if ripped from the context of Scripture and made the be-all and end-all of the Christian life, has the potential to lead us into serious error. (MacDonald's own overemphasis on the fatherhood of God has precisely the same effect.) But a reader of the Bible would have to work extremely hard to see only the texts about justification and miss all those that demand that we live a new life. Jesus' Sermon on the Mount is all about holiness.

Many of the New Testament letters have as their basic outline two simple ideas: God has blessed you with stupendous blessings; therefore, you must live like new people. You have received a great calling, Paul writes in Ephesians 4:1; now live accordingly. You have died to sin, he writes in Romans 6:11; now live as those who are alive to God in Christ. The same idea is found in Romans 12:1: You have received God's mercy; now present yourself to Him as a holy, living sacrifice. And the flow of thought in Hebrews is much the same: God has opened a way for you into the Most Holy Place by the blood of Christ; now stir yourselves up to love and good deeds (Heb. 10:19–24).

The idea that *any* of the blessings God has given us in Christ should be regarded as an excuse to ignore the call to holiness is ludicrous. *Because* God has blessed us, we must pursue holiness, both as a demonstration of our gratitude for what He has done for us and as a way of straining forward to the still greater joy that lies before us.

Justification is foundational to the Christian's battle with sin. In Romans 6:1–4 it is our union with Christ in His death—the same union that makes His righteousness ours—that renders it inconceivable that we should continue to live in sin. In Romans 8:3–4 it is God's condemnation of sin in the flesh (that is, in the death of Jesus on our behalf) that makes it possible for the righteous requirements of the law to be fulfilled in us. The Christian reasons in this way: "I am no longer guilty before God but righteous. How then can I continue to live in ways that are a betrayal of my true status?"

Even more clear is the dynamic relationship between adoption and sanctification. Now that we are children of God, we should imitate the behavior of our Father (Matt. 5:44–45). We should seek to live in such a way as to cause other people to give glory to our Father (Matt. 5:16). All our efforts should be turned toward pleasing our Father (Matt. 6:1–18). If we know ourselves to be God's chosen ones, already declared to be holy and beloved, then we must put on "compassion, kindness, humility, meekness, and patience," and in every way live a life worthy of the calling we have received (Col. 3:12; Eph. 4:1). Our goal must be to be perfect, even as our heavenly Father is perfect (Matt. 5:48).

The great mystery of sanctification lies in the cooperation of our wills with God's. We are to bend every effort to be holy. We are to train ourselves to be godly (1 Tim. 4:7). We are to discipline our bodies and keep them under control (1 Cor. 9:27). We are to resist sin to the point of death (Heb. 12:4), and we are told in no uncertain terms that if we will not put our sins to death, then we will not inherit the kingdom of God (1 Cor. 6:9–10). Without holiness, no one will see the Lord (Heb. 12:14). Yet the same Scripture that tells us to work out our salvation in "fear and trembling" also tells us that "it is God who works in you, both to will and to work for his good pleasure" (Phil. 2:12–13). Ultimately, it is God who sanctifies us (1 Thess. 5:23). It is He who transforms us from one degree of glory to another as we behold His glory (2 Cor. 3:18).

We can never be justified in waiting fatalistically for God to change us; we must instead actively work to destroy the power of sin within us. At the same time, we need to do this work in dependence on the Holy Spirit, and we must give credit to Him for any progress He allows us to make. Our driving desire should be to become like Christ in every way (Phil. 3:10).

He Unites Us with Himself Forever

Union with God Now . . . and Forever

The ultimate goal of the Christian life is to be united with God through Christ forever. That union was planned by God from all eternity:

Before the foundation of the world He chose us in Christ and pre-destined "that we should be holy and blameless before him [in] love" (Eph. 1:4). It then became actual when by His grace we first believed in Christ. At that point, though we were dead in our sins, God "made us alive together with Christ . . . and seated us with him in the heavenly places" (Eph. 2:5–6). And it will be made perfect after the return of Christ and the Judgment, when we will be given new, immortal bodies in which to enjoy God and all of His elect creatures to all eternity: "And so we will always be with the Lord" (1 Thess. 4:17). At death, believers are released completely from sin's power and pass into the presence of Christ (Phil. 1:23); they die "in Christ," and so death cannot separate them from Him (1 Thess. 4:16; Rom. 8:38–39).

Nevertheless, the final consummation of their union with Him awaits the day when death is destroyed forever and Jesus hands over the kingdom to God the Father (1 Cor. 15:24; 54–55). It is at that time that, according to Revelation 21:3–4, the dwelling place of God will be with man. "He will dwell with them, and they will be his people, and God himself will be with them as their God. He will wipe every tear from their eyes, and death shall be no more, neither shall there be mourning nor crying nor pain anymore, for the former things have passed away."

A Love Feast in Heaven

In a powerful sermon on 1 Corinthians 13:8–10, Jonathan Edwards describes this perfected world as a world of love, where the love of God flows endlessly "in innumerable streams toward all the created inhabitants of heaven, to all the saints and angels there," who in response love God with a supreme love. Edwards continues:

> Christ loves all His saints in heaven. His love flows out to His whole church there, and to every individual member of it. And they all, with one heart and one soul, unite in love to their common Redeemer. Every heart is wedded to this holy and spiritual husband, and all rejoice in Him, while the angels join them in their love. And the angels and saints all love each other. All the members of the glorious society of heaven are sincerely united. There is not a single secret or open enemy among them all. Not a heart is there that is not full of love, and

not a solitary inhabitant that is not beloved by all the others. And as all are lovely, so all see each other's loveliness with full complacence and delight. Every soul goes out in love to every other; and among all the blessed inhabitants, love is mutual, and full, and eternal.[9]

Edwards argues further that in heaven there will be no envy or jealousy, no discontent, no pride; there will be nothing unseemly or inappropriate, and no internal stirrings of sin to clog the inhabitants' capacity to love God and one another. They will serve God and one another with joy. They will experience perfect peace and tranquility. And their union with God and with one another will grow ever closer throughout all eternity.

In another sermon Edwards uses a spatial analogy to help us grasp this fact. He encourages us to think of union with God as "represented by something at an infinite height above us; and the eternally increasing union of the saints with God, by something that is ascending constantly towards that infinite height, moving upwards with a given velocity, and that is to continue thus to move to all eternity."[10]

To the words of the Revelation, and to Edwards's efforts to describe the state of glory, I would add only the imaginative pictures of C. S. Lewis. In the concluding chapter of *The Last Battle,* the children of Narnia finally find themselves in Aslan's country. Here they can run without ever growing tired, and they can't be afraid even if they want to. Here the cry on every lip is "Further up and further in!"; here they are reunited with those who have gone before them; here everything good from this world is preserved and everything evil purged away; here there is no possibility of their ever being sent out of that glorious land; and here the king tells them that true life is just beginning:

For them it was only the beginning of the real story. All their life in this world and all their adventures in Narnia had been only the cover and the title page: now at last they were beginning Chapter One of the Great Story, which no one on earth has read: which goes on forever: in which every chapter is better than the one before.[11]

In Christ

Apart from Christ, the human condition is bleak. Although progress in medicine and technology may encourage us to feel that the world is getting better, and although our own good health and prosperity may for a time mask from us our mortality and our spiritual misery, the simple fact is that we are all moving swiftly toward the grave. And beyond the grave, when we have shuffled off this mortal coil, what then? Then there is the "fearful expectation of judgment, and a fury of fire that will consume the adversaries" of God (Heb. 10:27). And we are the adversaries! We are ensnared in rebellion. The devil has taken us captive to do his will (2 Tim. 2:26); our minds are set on the flesh and so hostile to God; we cannot submit to His Law, nor can we do anything to please Him.

Those who have read Tolkien's *The Lord of the Rings* trilogy or watched the motion pictures based on the story may have imagined themselves valiantly battling orcs with Frodo and Sam. But it might be better for us to think of ourselves *as* the orcs: doomed creatures serving a dark lord, hopelessly and helplessly committed to evil, the enemies of true righteousness and goodness, destined for destruction.

That is who we are apart from Christ. In Christ it is a very different matter. In Christ there is full forgiveness of sin. In Christ there is the imputation of a righteousness we ourselves could never attain. In Him there is adoption as the children of God. In Him there is the instantaneous transformation of our innermost nature in regeneration and the gradual renewal of our character in sanctification. In Him there is reconciliation of God to us and of us to Him and a union that is ineffably glorious and literally endless in extension. In Him George Herbert wrote, we find

> Softness, and peace, and joy, and love, and bliss,
> Exalted Manna, gladness of the best,
> Heaven in ordinary, man well drest,
> The milky way, the bird of Paradise . . . [12]

To use the imagery of *The Lord of the Rings*, in Christ, the orcs become the sons and daughters of God.

Our culture—even our church culture—has become jaded to the

gospel. We hear of these glorious blessings—this blessed mercy, this merciful redemption—and we feel less excitement over them than we do over the purchase of a new car or the opportunity to watch a new movie or see a sporting event. We yawn in worship and nod while reading the Word of Life. It is time for the church to wake up. It is time to sell everything—*everything*—for the pearl of great price. It is time to "lay aside every weight, and sin which clings so closely, and . . . run with endurance the race that is set before us, looking to Jesus, the founder and perfecter of our faith" (Heb. 12:1–2).

Our God is a great God. The salvation He offers is an incomparable salvation, perfectly suited to the needs of all people everywhere. The heaven He has prepared is a world of love. He has held back from us no good thing.

At God's right hand are pleasures forevermore (Ps. 16:11). Let us throw ourselves into the seeking of those pleasures . . . for ourselves, our children, and all the peoples of the world.

O Lord, how perfect are Your provisions for our needs! We need a stable and abundant physical environment, and You have given us the earth with all its riches and grandeur. We need companionship, and You have given us mothers and fathers, brothers and sisters, husbands and wives, and children and friends. We need purpose, and You have given us work to do, problems to solve, obstacles to overcome.

Most of all, we need salvation—oh, how we need it! We are turned in upon ourselves, barely capable of loving even the members of our own families and utterly unable to love the One in whom we live and move and have our being. We are guilty, condemned, and lost. No good thing dwells in us, and it is only Your hidden grace, poured freely and secretly upon us, that prevents us from exhibiting our depravity in its full horror. If You should leave us to ourselves, we would quickly make earth itself into hell. What we will become if You send us where we deserve is a thought too wretched to contemplate.

But You, O Lord, are merciful and have made so perfect a provision for our redemption from sin. Why should we reject so great a salvation? Why should we not turn and live?

Grant, dear Lord, that not only I but all who are dear to me and all who read this may turn and live, and that we may understand, appropriate, and rejoice in all the riches of Your salvation. In Your great name, amen.

NOTES

1. The sincerity of the offer of the gospel to all people is defended in John Murray's short booklet, *The Free Offer of the Gospel* (Edinburgh: Banner of Truth, 2001).

2. Archibald Alexander, *Thoughts on Religious Experience* (1844; repr., Edinburgh: Banner of Truth, 1967), 22.

3. John Murray, *Redemption Accomplished and Applied* (Grand Rapids: Eerdmans, 1955), 106.

4. Probably the most famous exponent of this idea is the Roman Catholic theologian Karl Rahner, who coined the term "anonymous Christians" to refer to people who have no conscious knowledge of Christ yet are related to Him by "faith." See Rahner's *Foundations of Christian Faith: An Introduction to the Idea of Christianity* (New York: Crossroads, 1994), 311–21.

5. George MacDonald, *Creation in Christ,* ed. Rolland Hein (Wheaton, Ill.: Shaw, 1976), 178–79.

6. For more extensive treatments of this question, see John Murray, *The Epistle to the Romans,* vol. 1 (Grand Rapids: Eerdmans, 1959), 353–59, and John Piper, *Counted Righteous in Christ,* 53–64.

7. J. C. Ryle, *Old Paths* (Cambridge: James Clarke, 1977), 228; quoted by Sinclair Ferguson in *The Christian Life: A Doctrinal Introduction* (Edinburgh: Banner of Truth, 1981), 90.

8. John Piper, *Counted Righteous in Christ,* 63–64.

9. Jonathan Edwards, "Heaven, a World of Love," in *Charity and Its Fruits* (1852; repr., Edinburgh: Banner of Truth, 1991), 333–34.

10. Jonathan Edwards, *The End for Which God Created the World,* as quoted in John Piper, *God's Passion for His Glory: Living the Vision of Jonathan Edwards* (Wheaton, Ill.: Crossway, 1998), 250.

11. C. S. Lewis, *The Last Battle* (New York: Macmillan, 1956), 173–74.

12. George Herbert, "Prayer" *The Temple* (1633) in George Herbert, *The Country Parson, the Temple* (Ramsey, N.J.: Paulist, 1981), 165–66.

9

THE RICHES
OF HIS GLORY

*What if God, desiring to show his wrath and to make known his
power, has endured with much patience vessels of wrath prepared
for destruction, in order to make known the riches of his glory for
vessels of mercy, which he has prepared beforehand for glory —
even us whom he has called, not from the Jews only
but also from the Gentiles?*

+ROMANS 9:22–24

WHY DOESN'T GOD SAVE EVERYBODY? This question has lurked
behind many of the other questions we have asked in this book, and
it is time to face it. If God is all-powerful and all-good, why does He
not use His power to ensure that each and every person will believe
and be redeemed?

The answer most commonly given to this question is that while
God probably does have the raw power to save all, the use of that power
would contradict His respect for our freedom. God wants sons and
daughters, not robots, and so He must in no way compel our wills.
In order to make room for us to come to Him freely, He must allow
us the dignity of not coming at all. By its very nature, freedom rules
out universal salvation.

For simplicity's sake, let's designate this the Arminian view of the universe, and let's remember that we have already seen some reasons to doubt its adequacy.

For one thing, the Arminian idea that human liberty places limits on God's will seems out of sync with what we know of the life of heaven. There the spirits of the righteous are confirmed in holiness so that they cannot sin, yet apparently this is done without any loss of freedom on their part. I suggest that Arminianism has some difficulty explaining this fact.

A deeper problem lies in what we have learned about the fallenness and waywardness of the human will, and about the nature of divine election. If it is the case that all of those—but *only* those—whom the Father has given to the Son come to Him, then there is plainly something wrong with an account of things that portrays God as watching from a distance to see which way we will choose. The Bible teaches that unless a person is regenerated, born again and from above, he or she cannot see the kingdom of God. And once a person has been born anew, he will inevitably respond to Christ in a free act of faith. The relationship between God's sovereignty and human freedom is much more complex than Arminianism allows.

THE ARMINIAN FOCUS ON HUMAN FREEDOM

Although my Arminian friends may take offense at this suggestion, it seems to me that theirs is ultimately, though unintentionally, a human-centered view of the world. In their way of looking at things, there is really nothing in the universe of greater importance than human freedom. They believe that God desires fellowship with His creatures, but He subordinates this desire to His concern not to trample on their free will. He wants to save them but only if they are willing to be saved.

Thus, human freedom is more important than salvation, more important than God's success in redeeming a people for His name, and, in a sense, more important than God Himself.

To me, this stress on human freedom and dignity seems a little too compatible with modernity's emphasis on the autonomy of the individual to be convincing. It fits too neatly with a culture in which what is valued most is for the individual to express himself, please himself, and "be true to" himself. It fits in this culture and it completes it, for it says that my autonomy is so total that, in a sense, even God has no rights over me apart from the acquiescence of my will. In my life, God may be God only if I give Him permission. Unless and until I do so,

> It matters not how strait the gate,
> How charged with punishments the scroll,
> I am the master of my fate:
> I am the captain of my soul.[1]

Now all good Arminians will wince at my suggestion that their doctrine may be properly illustrated by William Henley's self-centered poem "Invictus," but is it not true that Arminianism is, in the end, a faith based on the doctrine of the "unconquerable" human soul?

There is a better and more biblical answer to the question of why God does not save everybody. I will call it the "Calvinistic" answer to distinguish it from the Arminian. It is a humbling and shocking answer, for it dethrones human freedom and puts God squarely at the center of His creation. We may initially find it difficult to grasp or to accept. Ultimately, however, it is a profoundly satisfying answer and one with tremendous power to liberate us from our preoccupation with ourselves. As I try to lay out this answer, I will be leaning heavily on Jonathan Edwards's essay *The End for Which God Created the World*.[2]

GOD'S GREAT END IN CREATING THE UNIVERSE

We start by asking why God created the universe. Christian doctrine says that God, in His triune nature, is eternally perfect and complete. He requires nothing outside of Himself. He is uncreated and self-existent, and so He has no need of matter, energy, or any part of the created order. Inasmuch as created things derive their being entirely from Him, they have nothing to add to Him. "If I were hungry," says God in Psalm 50:12, "I would not tell you, for the world and its fullness are mine."

Nor may we suppose that God created the world in order to ease His loneliness. In His eternal, Trinitarian nature, God experiences the perfect communion and mutual joy of the Father, Son, and Holy Spirit. Although the divine nature is deeply mysterious to us, it is perhaps not an abuse of language to suggest that God exists eternally as a community of delight and satisfaction. As He approached His crucifixion, Jesus asked the Father to glorify Him in the Father's presence with the glory They had shared before the world existed (John 17:5). The idea that creation can be traced back to any need or lack in God is obviously mistaken.

But if God lacks nothing, then why did He create? One might possibly suggest that He created out of love. This makes sense if by "love" we mean the eternal love of the Father and Son for one another and Their desire to share that love with other beings. Nevertheless, we must keep in mind that the decision to create must logically precede love toward that which is created. That is to say, if God did not first have the inclination to create us, we could in no way be objects of His love.

The point can be made with the analogy of human procreation. A loving husband and wife decide to have a child, in order to be able to share with that child the love they enjoy in their marriage. In time the child is conceived and born, and its parents do in fact love it. But at the point when the couple were making the decision to become parents, the child itself did not yet exist as an object of their love. The decision to have a child was one that proceeded from the mutual love of the parents and their desire to extend the circle of their love, but the parents could not properly be said to love the child until the decision to have it had been made. In God's case, there was no time before He intended to create the world, but His decision to create was still *logically* prior to His love toward that which He has created.

God Created to Please Himself

We are forced, then, to say that the inclination to create the universe was an inclination inherent in God Himself. In creating, He was acting to please Himself, not us. Although He did not *need* to create the world, He nevertheless *wanted* to create it. And He wanted it, I believe, for basically the same reason the musician wants to compose music or the writer wants to write a book; that is, He created the world out of a desire to express Himself. In Himself God is perfect in every way—holy, wise, loving, just, and powerful—and He delights in the perfections of His nature. The creation is the result of His desire for an "external" sphere in which to express these perfections.

No, God did not need such a sphere; the creation of the world did not make Him something He was not before. But it pleased Him to create, much as it pleases the artist to paint; and He takes pleasure in what He has made. "And God saw that it was good" (Gen. 1:10). The universe exists for God's good pleasure and for the display of His glory. Or as Edwards put it, God has a propensity to diffuse Himself; He is like a fountain that wishes to overflow.

That God created the universe for Himself is not just a rational inference; it is a biblical doctrine. We are told that "from him and through him and to him are all things" (Rom. 11:36), that "all things were created through him and for him" (Col. 1:16), and that He is the One "for whom and by whom all things exist" (Heb. 2:10). These texts make it very plain that the universe exists for God's pleasure. No higher ground can be given for the created order than God's desire to create. He made all things for Himself.

It is also plain from many passages of Scripture that the pleasure God has in His creation derives from its ability to reflect His glory: "The heavens declare the glory of God, and the sky above proclaims his handiwork"; "May the glory of the Lord endure forever; may the Lord rejoice in his works" (Pss. 19:1; 104:31). The universe and all within it was created by God and for God. It exists as an outward display of His inner and eternal perfections.

Humanity, too, was created as an expression of the Creator's wisdom and goodness. We were made to know Him and enjoy Him forever, and we find the meaning of our lives and the fulfillment of our deepest desires only as we learn to glorify Him in all things. As Augustine put it in his famous prayer in his *Confessions,* "You made us for yourself, and our hearts find no peace until they rest in you."[3] It is the essence of sin and of our misery that we have "fall[en] short" of His glory (Rom. 3:23); that is, we could have had the joy of loving God above all things but instead have turned to idols and fallen into futility.

Yet even our sin will not be allowed finally to mar the glory of God as expressed in His world, because the drama of redemption was itself planned for the display of His holiness and His mercy. It is for the sake of His praise that God defers His anger against sinners (Isa. 48:9, 11). It is for His "name's sake" that He leads His people in "paths of righteousness" (Ps. 23:3). It was for the glory of the Father and the Son that Jesus laid down His life (John 17:1), and it is for the glory of the Father that every knee will be brought to bow and every tongue to confess that Jesus Christ is Lord (Phil. 2: 10–11). In Isaiah 43 God describes His chosen ones as "the people whom I formed for myself, that they might declare my praise" (v. 21). It is for His own sake that He blots out our transgressions (v. 25).

The Bible views *all* of God's works, whether in creation, providence, or redemption, as ultimately intended to display the glory— the wisdom, power, holiness, and love—of the Creator. Recognizing this is the first step toward answering the question of why God does not intend to save all people.

A Self-Centered Tyrant?

But before we carry our argument forward, we must pause to deal with a significant objection. Many people recoil from the doctrine that God does all things for the praise of His glory. We all despise the person who makes himself the center of His universe and requires those around to show him obeisance. Any representation of the character of God that makes Him look like *that* kind of person must, we feel instinctively, be quite false. George MacDonald saw matters that way, and he ridiculed the idea of a God who values above all things His own exaltation:

> How terribly, then have the theologians misrepresented God! Nearly all of them represent Him as a great King on a grand throne, thinking how grand He is, and making it the business of His being and the end of His universe to keep up His glory, wielding the bolts of a Jupiter against them that take His name in vain. They would not allow this, but follow out what they say, and it comes much to this.[4]

To MacDonald, the Calvinistic understanding seemed the very antithesis of the Bible's presentation of God as the Father of Jesus Christ and was, therefore, patently false. It took a God who described Himself as "humble and meek" and turned Him into a sort of Nero or Hitler, a vain, self-centered ruler preoccupied with Himself rather than His subjects.

MacDonald raises a legitimate question. How do we reconcile what the Bible says about God's concern for His glory with what it says about His character? Is there a fatal contradiction between these two, such that we may say *either* that in all things God acts for the praise of His name, *or* that He is kind in all His works, but not both? I do not believe there is any contradiction at all. There are two responses we must make to MacDonald.

God's Righteous Regard for His Own Glory

First, because God is God, behavior that would be vainglorious and contemptible in a human being is the very essence of righteousness in Him. I am a creature. I am not the center of the universe. I exist at God's pleasure, and everything I am and have I owe to Him. If, in spite of my creaturely status, I *pretend* to be the center of all things, exalting myself above other creatures and even above God Himself, then I rightly earn the scorn of my fellow human beings and the wrath of my Creator, for my pretensions are false. The reason MacDonald's sardonic picture of the tyrant on the throne catches our sympathy so quickly is because we instinctively perceive that a human being who behaved in that way would be beneath contempt.

God, however, is not a human being; He is God. He is the Creator. He is the source of all goodness, beauty, and excellence. He is the One for whom we were made. To Him all intelligent beings properly owe their allegiance. It is right that we should make His glory the great concern of our lives; to do anything less is to fall into idolatry. When the biblical writers urge us to "praise the LORD" (e.g., Ps. 103 NIV), or give voice to their desire that all glory and honor be given to God eternally (Rom. 11:36; Eph. 3:21; 1 Tim. 6:16; 2 Tim. 4:18; etc.), or tell us that we must love Him above all else (Deut. 6:5; Matt. 22:37), they are simply expressing their awareness of what is good and right. God *deserves* all honor, glory, praise, and love, because He is God. You and I are not the center of the universe, but He is!

Now let's take one more step. If indeed God is the center of the universe, and if it is right and proper for His creatures to love Him above all things, then it is also right and proper for God to love *Himself* above all things. If God loved some part of the created order more than He loved Himself, then we would have to consider Him an idolater. If He placed any being or any part of His creation on a higher plane of importance than the expression of His glory—if, in biblical terms, He should "give" His glory to another (Isa. 42:8)—then He would be acting unrighteously. God's righteousness consists in His acting in accordance with truth, and the truth is that He is of infinitely greater worth than all created things combined. "Hence it will follow," says Jonathan Edwards, "that the moral rectitude of the disposition, inclination, or affection of God CHIEFLY consists in a regard to HIMSELF, infinitely above His regard to all other beings; in other words, His holiness consists in this."[5]

Now we can see where MacDonald went wrong. If holiness consists in loving God above all things, then one expression of holiness in a creature will be humility. Even Christ Jesus, though by very nature God, took the position of a servant and humbled Himself before God (Phil. 2:5–11). That is, in the Incarnation the Son of God condescended to show us what it is for a creature to be holy. But it would be a great mistake to expect holiness to look precisely the same in the Creator as in the creature. It consists of the same thing—the prizing of God above all else—but its appearance will not be the same.

God does not need to be "humble" in the same way that we do; in fact, He *must* not be humble, if to be humble means to acknowledge the superior greatness of another being. There is no being superior to God. For God, as for us, holiness means loving God above all else. That is why it is proper for God to seek His own glory in all of His acts.

GOD'S *OTHER* GREAT END IN CREATION

To MacDonald we can give a second answer. MacDonald thinks the Calvinistic understanding of the universe makes God not only vainglorious but selfish. But in this he is quite wrong, as he could have learned from Jonathan Edwards. Edwards taught that God's pursuit of His glory and His pursuit of the happiness of His creatures are really not two separate things but one, which means that there is ultimately nothing selfish at all about God's love to Himself. This is an extraordinary insight, and it is what makes Edwards's essay *The End for Which God Created the World* one of the most helpful books I have ever read.

Long before Edwards came on the scene, the Augustinian theological tradition held that God made all things for Himself and that the happiness of the creature lies in glorifying and enjoying God forever. However, I am not sure that any thinker prior to Edwards saw as clearly as he did just *how* God's pursuit of His glory coincides with His commitment to the happiness of His elect creatures. God expresses His glory *by* making His creatures eternally happy in Him, and He makes His creatures happy *by* communicating to them ever greater measures of His glory. Let me do my best to explain.

The universe exists to express God's glory. And how does it do that? Not simply by the mute testimony of inanimate things to the greatness of their Creator, but also by the conscious response of intelligent creatures. God has made human beings and angels capable of knowing Him in ever-increasing measure. He has also made us capable of reflecting His holiness in increasing conformity to His own character. And He has made us capable of participating, in ever-greater degrees, in His own perfect joy in Himself. As He shares with us His knowledge, holiness, and joy, we are made more and more like Him, and we become more and more satisfied in Him. As we grow in conformity to Him, we reflect in ever-greater measure His own internal glory.

In this way, our happiness and God's expression of His glory coincide perfectly. We are ever more conformed to and delighted in God, and our increasing conformity to Him and delight in Him is itself the highest possible expression of His glory. Heaven will consist of a blessed society of beings whose knowledge of, likeness to, and delight in God will increase endlessly. Because God is infinite in His knowledge, holiness, and joy, the union of Creator and creatures will become closer and closer throughout all eternity.

God's supreme regard of His own glory is what moves Him to share Himself with His creatures. Their resulting knowledge of God brings them bliss. As Edwards puts it, "God's esteeming Himself supremely is not contrary to His esteeming human happiness, since He is that happiness."[6] Call God selfish if you like, but understand that His "selfishness" means everlasting and inexpressible joy for billions of created beings!

BUT WHAT ABOUT THE LOST?

However, we have still not answered the question of why God does not save all people. If God has no pleasure in the wicked but desires rather that they turn from their wicked ways and live, and if God is eternally glorified by making His creatures happy, why does He not save us all? Why doesn't He make *all* of His creatures happy? What place can there be for hell in a universe governed by a God of love?

Hell Created to Express the Glory of a Holy God

I have hinted at the answer several times in the course of the book, but now it must be made explicit. If all the universe exists for the glory of God, and if God works out all things in conformity with His will and purpose, then hell, too, exists to bring God glory.

God glorifies Himself primarily in the joy of the redeemed but secondarily in the punishment of the lost. This is the kind of doctrine that would make George MacDonald and his followers howl with fury, but I believe it is both rational and biblical and that, sooner or later, we must face up to it. God *could* save all people, but He does not choose to. Instead, He chooses to leave some people to the punishment their deeds deserve, in order that He may more completely express the fullness of His character. Once again, allow me to quote Jonathan Edwards:

> It is a proper and excellent thing for infinite glory to shine forth; and for the same reason, it is proper that the shining forth of God's glory should be complete; that is, that all parts of his glory should shine forth, that every beauty should be proportionably effulgent, that the beholder may have a proper notion of God. It is not proper that one glory should be exceedingly manifested, and another not at all; for then the effulgence would not answer the reality. . . . Thus it is necessary, that God's awful majesty, his authority and dreadful greatness, justice, and holiness, should be manifested. But this could not be, unless sin and punishment had been decreed; so that the shining forth of God's glory would be very imperfect.[7]

Because the universe exists to display God's glory, and since the full expression of glory requires the revelation of all aspects of God's character, it is fitting for God to so order things, Edwards writes, that not only God's kindness but also His severity may be revealed. We must never say that sin is a good thing in itself. Nor is the suffering of the lost in itself good. Yet we can very properly say that a universe in which sin had never been allowed, or one in which no sinners were justly punished for their sins, would be a poorer universe, because it would be one in which God's character was less fully exhibited. The Arminian view of the universe sees hell as an eternal tribute to the inviolability of human freedom. The Calvinist view sees it as an eternal expression of the holiness of God.

Edwards was not the first to argue in this way. In his great work *The City of God,* Augustine wrote that

> the human race is so apportioned that in some is displayed the efficacy of merciful grace, in the rest the efficacy of just retribution. For both could not be displayed in all; for if all had remained under the punishment of just condemnation, there would have been seen in no one the mercy of redeeming grace. And, on the other hand, if all had been transferred from darkness to light, the severity of retribution would have been manifested in none.[8]

Thomas Aquinas similarly argued that the punishment of the wicked adds to the delight of the saints and increases their gratitude toward God.[9] And the sixteenth-century reformer John Calvin agreed with this interpretation:

> In a word, I acquiesce quietly and willingly in the opinion of Augustine: God who created all things good foreknew that evil would arise out of that good; and He also knew that to make good out of evil would be more appropriate to His omnipotent goodness than not to allow evil at all. So He ordained the life of men and angels that He might first show in it what their free will could do, and then what the blessing of His grace and the judgment of His justice could do.[10]

I know this is not easy to swallow, but before you choke on it, please take time to consider carefully Paul's argument in Romans 9. We have glanced at that argument twice before, but now let us look at it more closely. Paul is trying to explain how it can be that so many of his fellow Jews have not believed in Jesus. Is it the case that God's promise to the Jews has failed (v. 6)? No, because salvation was never promised to all Jews indiscriminately, but only to those who were the "children of the promise" (v. 8). Furthermore, the selection of some and not others to be children of the promise occurred "in order that God's purpose of election might continue" (v. 11). For God claims the right to dispense mercy according to His own sovereign purposes. Salvation does not depend on human will or exertion but on God who has mercy (vv. 15–16).

The Potter and the Clay

Paul illustrates God's sovereignty in salvation by pointing to Pharaoh, whom God raised up for the express purpose of revealing His power in Pharaoh's defeat and destruction. The lesson Paul draws from this example is this: God "has mercy on whomever he wills, and he hardens whomever he wills" (v. 18).

Paul knows that this is tough doctrine. This would be the perfect place for him to defend the inviolability of the human will. Instead, he takes the argument in precisely the opposite direction:

> You will say to me then, "Why does he [God] still find fault? For who can resist his will?" But who are you, O man, to answer back to God? Will what is molded say to its molder, "Why have you made me like this?" Has the potter no right over the clay, to make out of the same lump one vessel for honored use and another for dishonorable use? What if God, desiring to show his wrath and to make known his power, has endured with much patience vessels of wrath prepared for destruction, in order to make known the riches of his glory for vessels of mercy, which he has prepared beforehand for glory—even us whom he has called, not from the Jews only but also from the Gentiles? (Romans 9:19–24)

Paul is insisting that God has the right to do as He wishes with His creatures. He has the right to save some and leave others to their just punishment. Moreover, He has the right to make the punishment of some the means by which He makes known the riches of His glory to those whom He has chosen to save. Those who are lost are condemned to the punishment their deeds have deserved. Those who are saved observe the punishment of the lost, and from it they learn of God's holiness and find their own joy increased as they see the fate from which they have been graciously saved. The eternal punishment of the wicked in hell by no means represents a defeat to God; on the contrary, it contributes to the more perfect expression of His character and the greater joy of His redeemed people.

Again, I realize that this is not easy to accept. It was not easy in Paul's own day, and it has never been easy. We remember Charles Wesley's line about the Calvinistic God "forcing" people into hell. We remember all of George MacDonald's indignation and disgust at precisely the truth we are talking about here. And perhaps we are tempted to respond to this truth in a similarly derisive fashion. But here it is in the book of Romans! How can we accept it?

Making Sense of a Tough Truth

First, let's remind ourselves that sinners deserve punishment. That was the argument of chapter 1. True, we find our involvement in Adam's sin to be a mysterious matter, but we know perfectly well that we are sinners and that sinners deserve to be punished. There is no escaping this truth. We have no grounds for shifting the blame for our own sins to God, and our consciences tell us that He is rightly angry with us for those sins.

Second, let's remember that because sin deserves punishment, salvation is owed to none. Salvation is a gift, and God may very properly bestow it on whom He will. God will never treat any person unjustly. To some He gives justice; to others grace. No person will ever have grounds to accuse God of injustice. "For the word of the Lord is upright, and all his work is done in faithfulness. He loves righteousness and justice; the earth is full of the steadfast love of the Lord" (Ps. 33:4–5).

Third, let us make sure that we do not press the biblical expressions beyond their proper bounds. When the Bible says that God "hardened" Pharaoh's heart, it does not mean that Pharaoh was initially a holy person with a desire to do God's will, and God cruelly forced him into rebellion. The truth is that all human beings are *already* in rebellion, and our hearts are *already* hard. When Scripture speaks of God hardening a person, it means that He withdraws His gracious influence in that person's life and allows him to become even more hardened than he was before. In salvation God actively works to soften the human heart; in reprobation He simply allows the heart to continue in the ways of rebellion. God forces nobody into hell.

Similarly, when Paul defends God's right to act like a potter, making from the same lump of clay some vessels for honored use and others for dishonored, we should take the lump of clay to stand for *fallen* humanity. We should not think of God first deciding to damn a person, and then allowing that person to fall in Adam. Instead, we should think of God looking at humanity as already fallen, and then determining to have mercy on some while leaving the others to their just punishment.

I know it is difficult to stop our speculations at that point. We want to press the matter as far as we possibly can and accuse God of deliberately creating some people for the sole purpose of damning them. But the Bible never teaches such a thing as that. It teaches that we are all sinners, all deserving hell, and that God has chosen to have mercy on some. In our desire for logical consistency we may go that far but no further.

Our Present Defective Vision

One final consideration may help us. In our unregenerate state we are completely blind to the nature of ultimate realities, and even after we have come to faith in Christ, we have to struggle mightily to see spiritual realities clearly. It comes naturally to us to think that human happiness and human freedom are the highest goods in the universe. It also comes naturally to us to think that sin against God is a trivial thing—a peccadillo, really—and that a God of love should not make such a fuss about it.

We are in a spiritual fog, unable—or rather unwilling—to see moral realities as God sees them. This unwillingness lies at the base of our difficulty in believing both in substitutionary atonement and in eternal punishment. We just do not want to believe that God is *that* holy, or that we are *that* bad!

But we will not always remain in this fog. When He brings us out of this life, God will give us the capacity to see things as they are. We will see then that it is absolutely right that the whole universe should exist for God's glory, and that sin should be forgiven only on the basis of the death of the Son of God or else punished everlastingly. And, yes, it is wholly right that God should exercise His prerogatives in apportioning salvation to some while leaving others to their just damnation.

Nothing is illogical or immoral about these truths; our problems with them are the result of our defective vision. This means that while we may well find them hard to accept, we would be wise not to make rash denunciation either of the truths themselves or of those who have perceived them most clearly.

WILL MANY BE SAVED?

There are other questions we would like to ask about God's justice and about His plan for the human race. Probably the most excruciating is why, at most times and places, only a minority of those who hear the gospel respond to it. Jesus warned us to "enter by the narrow gate," adding, "For the gate is wide and the way is easy that leads to destruction, and those who enter by it are many. For the gate is narrow and the way is hard that leads to life, and those who find it are few" (Matt. 7:13–14). The experience of the church through the centuries has borne out this statement. Many are called, but relatively few, apparently, are chosen. This raises the question of whether God's glory in some way requires that a greater number of people be lost than saved.

I do not propose to enter into an extended discussion of this question. Doing so would make the book too long and would also, frankly, lead me into areas in which I do not feel competent to speak with much authority. I will take time here only to give a few personal opinions based upon the reading and thinking I have done over the years.[11]

Death—and Deliverance—of the Young

I suspect, first, that all human beings who die without reaching the age where they can properly be held accountable for their moral acts are elect, and upon death they are regenerated and pass immediately into the presence of the Lord, there to be cared for as they grow to maturity.[12] Notice that I suggest that they are "elect." I do not believe they are saved because they are *innocent,* as that would contradict the truth that Adam's guilt has been imputed to us all. But there are considerations in Scripture that lead me to suspect that God, in His sovereign wisdom and power, has called and is calling millions of individuals from all the peoples of the world by allowing them to die as infants. Chief among these considerations is the fact that the final judgment is to be according to our deeds (Rev. 20:12), which implies that people are condemned on the basis of sins that they themselves have committed.

I find it difficult to imagine God condemning infants to damnation solely on the basis of the sin of Adam. Although the salvation of all who die in infancy is not an explicit doctrine of Scripture, I believe we have grounds to hope that it is true. (But please note: Even if we could be certain of this doctrine, it would never give us the least excuse to condone abortion, infanticide, euthanasia for the mentally handicapped, or neglect of the needs of poor children around the world. We are never justified in doing evil that good may come of it. We are under orders to defend life.)

A Concern for Evangelism and Worldwide Missions

As for persons who have reached the age of accountability, I strongly doubt that they can be saved without hearing the message of the gospel and responding to it. I do not say this because I do not *want* to believe that people may be saved in other ways. I know very well the awkwardness of trying to comfort a new convert who is worried about her grandmother who died a Buddhist. Anybody with half a heart would desire in such a case to be able to offer hope that the loved one was mysteriously saved. But I just do not see any convincing biblical support for this idea. Salvation in large measure *consists* in conscious knowledge of God and of what He has done in Christ (John 17:3), and I see no evidence either that persons can be saved and not know it or that they are given opportunities to believe and repent after death.[13]

I believe that our concern for the lost is to be expressed in wholehearted commitment to evangelism and world missions, not in debating fine shades of inclusivism and pluralism. God's answer to the question of the fate of those who have not heard is to stir up His people to give, sacrifice, preach, suffer, and—if necessary—die, that the gospel may be taken to every corner of the world and persuasively offered to people of every culture.

A Massive Expansion of the Church?

In the end, what percentage of the race will be saved? I have no idea. At present, the dynamic that Jesus talked about certainly seems still to be operative. Even in countries with centuries of exposure to the gospel, only relatively few people show evidence of saving faith in Christ. In the meantime, large tracts of the world have never heard His name. But in spite of this fact, I do not think we should assume too quickly that only a minority will ultimately be saved. Heaven may be populated with billions of people who died in childhood, in the womb, or even in the test tube. And what the future holds for the gospel in this world, nobody knows.

Regardless of which millennial position we may hold, there is room in the theology of most Christians for the possibility—if not the likelihood—of massive expansion in the church in the times ahead.

Paul speaks of the "fullness of the Gentiles" being brought in, followed by the salvation of "all Israel" (Rom. 11:25–26). The latter phrase seems to point to a spiritual awakening on a massive scale among the Jews, and if God still plans to bring in such a great number of Jews, is it not possible that before that time He also intends to save a vast number of Gentiles? If the prophecy of Habakkuk 2:14 is taken as referring not to the ultimate condition beyond the judgment but rather to the millennial rule of Christ on earth, then we can look forward to a time when the vast majority of earth's inhabitants will be believers, for then "the earth will be filled with the knowledge of the glory of the Lord as the waters cover the sea." It may well be that in the end, those who are lost will comprise only a small minority of the human race.

Whatever the truth may be about these matters, we may be sure that the judge of all the earth will do right. God will save the right number of people. The final condition of the human race will be such as to perfectly reflect God's holy, gracious character. He will redeem as large a proportion of humanity as is compatible with making the fullest possible revelation of His glory and producing the greatest possible joy in His people. More than this I cannot say. More than this I do not need to know. We have our marching orders: "Go therefore and make disciples" (Matt. 28:19). We must entrust the final outcome to God.

THE PRACTICAL EFFECTS OF THE CALVINISTIC VIEW

I mentioned at the beginning of the chapter that the Calvinistic view of the universe is more satisfying than the Arminian. I also stated in chapter 4 that I have come gradually to delight in the doctrine of God's sovereignty. Allow me to explain these statements. I do not presume to speak for anyone other than myself, but I believe my feelings are not uncommon among those who have come to similar doctrinal conclusions.

It Makes Sense!

In large part the satisfaction I have in Calvinism is intellectual. In my opinion, the Calvinistic view of the world just makes better sense. It explains the Scriptures better, and it also fits better with my actual experience of the Christian life. I see nothing in the Bible to suggest that the exaltation of human freedom is the highest of God's purposes in the world or that God regards our freedom as constituting any obstacle to the fulfillment of His plans. The Bible seems to me to present God as working out His purposes in sovereign majesty —not as needing to adjust His plans to take account of the foreseen (far less the unforeseen!) actions of His creatures. In some mysterious way far beyond my understanding, our free acts accomplish what God has already determined should take place, and this occurs without our being deprived of our dignity as agents responsible for our own actions.

Further, I believe it is plain in Scripture that the very highest concern of God is the expression of His own glory through His creation and governance of the world.

For all of its difficulties, the Calvinist story line seems to me to be the story line of the Bible. It is also the story line of the Christian life. It is natural to Christians to thank God for our salvation, to pray for the salvation of others, and to believe that God has ordained the course of our lives for us. As individual Christians we do not think that God merely foresaw that we would come into existence, but rather that He deliberately created each of us according to His eternal plan. Both Scripture and the Christian life point to a God who is in full control of His world.

But the pleasures of this doctrine are not intellectual only. I first became convinced of its truth, but then I began to taste its sweetness— the sweetness of knowing that God is in charge of His creation and that He will remain eternally true to His own purposes.

The Adults Are in Charge!

Imagine for a moment a young boy who is the center of his parents' universe. They dote on him shamelessly: They give him every toy he asks for, they bend their rules to protect him from the consequences of his misbehavior, they tremble at his tantrums, and they receive with adoring wonder every precocious pronouncement from his lips and every messy product of his creative genius. Within his own small world, this boy is emperor.

But now suppose that some courageous friend takes these parents aside and warns them that they must change their ways if they do not want to produce a monster, and suppose further that the parents are wise enough to listen to this advice.

Things start changing around the house. Some demands are met with a firm "No!" Tantrums are ignored, or at least not rewarded. Rules are made by the parents, not the child, and when he breaks the rules he suffers for it. Not only that, but the parents begin placing their marriage back at the center of family life: They work at their relationship with one another; they make their decisions together, and instead of assimilating themselves to their child's mentality, they guide him to learn to live in their world.

They do not love their son any less than before. They would gladly lay down their lives for him. But they have decided to live according to the truth that the adults, not the children, should be in charge of the family.

At first the boy doesn't like it. He has lost some of his power, and he tries to wrest it back. He pouts and screams. He holds his breath till his face turns blue.

His parents do not relent, however, and over time the boy actually becomes happier and more secure than he ever was under the old arrangement. He is secretly relieved to live under adult-made rules that cannot be changed by his whining. He experiences the satisfaction that comes from learning to wait and to work for the things he wants.

He is not threatened by his parents' love for one another; he is comforted by it. It makes him happy to know that his very life is a product of that love. Every hug his parents give one another makes him feel just that much more secure, because he knows that their love for him is grounded in their love for one another. Most important, he begins to see that the world he can create for himself is small and pathetic compared to the world his parents inhabit, and he learns to enjoy the process of growing up.

The analogy is far from perfect, but it suggests something of what I have experienced in accepting what I am calling the Calvinistic view of the world. Meditating on this view, I am reminded that the Holy Trinity existed in perfect love and joy before there was a universe, and that the creation, of which I am a part, is a product of that overflowing love and joy. I am reminded also that God's love toward me flows from the joy He has in being God.

Thus, His supreme commitment to Himself and His own glory, far from threatening me or making me insignificant, confirms to me that I am eternally secure. God does not love me because He needs me; He loves me because He has ordained my existence as an expression of His own glory.

Still further, I am reminded that my salvation does not lie in "self-actualization," the boosting of my self-esteem, learning to "be true to" myself, or discovering the depths of my own creativity. My salvation lies in getting *out* of myself and growing deeper in my relationship with God, in whom there is infinite wisdom and infinite joy, at whose right hand are pleasures forevermore. God is not watching with bated breath to see what wonderful new use I will make of my freedom. God is inviting me to lose myself, forget myself, and experience the far superior pleasure of knowing Him. The Calvinist universe feels to me like a family where the adults are in charge and the children are encouraged to grow up.

Now, please do not misunderstand me. I certainly do not mean to suggest that Arminians are narcissistic children who do not want to become mature. I have no idea whether, on the whole, the Arminians or the Calvinists have over the centuries shown the greatest self-denial and the greatest commitment to holiness. Certainly I know that vast numbers of Christians who have disagreed with my theology have been my superiors in every department of the Christian life. I would be happy to have a thousandth part of the zeal, effectiveness, and holiness of John and Charles Wesley, even though they were passionate anti-Calvinists. All I am arguing here is that the Calvinistic view of the universe fits both the Scriptures and our own deepest intuitions, and that its acceptance gives us much encouragement to pursue God with greater focus and vigor.

Let us remember, the universe is not about us; not even about our freedom. It is about God, and that means that our joy is to be found only in Him.

Although he might disagree with much else of what I have written in this book, A. W. Tozer has expressed the truth of our standing before God so beautifully that I wish to give him the final word. "Every soul," he writes,

> belongs to God and exists by His pleasure. God being who and what He is, and we being who and what we are, the only thinkable relation between us is one of full Lordship on His part and complete submission on ours. We owe Him every honor that is in our power to give Him. Our everlasting grief lies in giving Him anything less.[14]

Gracious God, I rejoice that You have made the world for Your own glory, and I rejoice to be a part of Your world. All things are from You, and it is good and right that they should exist for You. I thank You that this truth gives direction to my life. I am Yours; empower me to live accordingly. In Jesus' name, amen.

NOTES

1. William Ernest Henley, "Invictus," *The Oxford Book of English Verse,* ed. A. T. Quiller-Couch (Oxford, England: Clarendon, 1919); http://bartleby.com/101/842.html.

2. Edwards's essay is available in several editions. I am using the one found in John Piper's *God's Passion for His Glory: Living the Vision of Jonathan Edwards* (Wheaton, Ill.: Crossway, 1998), because this edition is readily available and contains much introductory material and many notes that will be helpful to readers who want to sample the book for themselves.

3. Augustine, *Confessions,* trans. R. S. Pine-Coffin, (New York: Penguin, 1981), I.i.

4. George MacDonald, *Creation in Christ,* ed. Rolland Hein (Wheaton, Ill.: Shaw, 1976), 34.

5. Capitals in original; as quoted in John Piper, *God's Passion for His Glory,* 141.

6. As quoted in Piper, *God's Passion,* 169.

7. Jonathan Edwards, *The Works of Jonathan Edwards,* vol. 2, rev. Edward Hickman (1834; repr., Edinburgh: Banner of Truth, 1986), 528.

8. Augustine, *City of God,* book 11, trans. Marcus Dods (New York: Modern Library, 1950), 782–83.

9. Thomas Aquinas, *Summa Theologica: Complete English Edition in 5 Volumes,* trans. the Fathers of the English Dominican Province (Westminster, Md.: Christian Classics, 1981), part 3, Q. 84, A. 1.

10. John Calvin, *Concerning the Eternal Predestination of God,* trans. J. K. S. Reid (London: James Clarke, 1961), VIII.5.

11. I also recommend, as a good introduction to the literature on this issue, Millard J. Erickson's *How Shall They Be Saved? The Destiny of Those Who Do Not Hear of Jesus* (Grand Rapids: Baker, 1996).

12. This would also include those adults without the mental capacity to know right from wrong.

13. A good recent discussion of this issue is found in John Piper, *Let the Nations Be Glad* (Grand Rapids: Baker, 1993), 115–66.

14. A. W. Tozer, *The Pursuit of God* (Camp Hill, Pa.: Christian, 1993), 96.

Conclusion
LOGING A
JUST AND
HOLY GOD

A kind of love may arise from a false notion of God, that men have been educated in or have some way imbibed, as though He were only goodness and mercy, and not revenging justice; or as though the exercises of His goodness were necessary and not free and sovereign; or as though His goodness were dependent on what is in them, and as it were constrained by them. Men on such grounds as these may love a God of their own forming in their imaginations, when they are far from loving such a God as reigns in heaven.

✝JONATHAN EDWARDS
"A Treatise Concerning Religious Affections"

"You may look down with contempt on some who do not know so much as you, and yet they may have twice your holiness and be doing more service to God."

✝CHARLES SPURGEON
Metropolitan Temple Pulpit

MANY YEARS AGO, near the outset of my journey as a Christian, I was told by George MacDonald that if I wanted to understand divine justice, I needed only to observe human fathers and learn from their love for their children. I think essentially the same approach to the study of God is taken by many Christians who have never heard of MacDonald. God, we suppose, is just like us; and so it is unimaginable that He would punish eternally, or exercise His sovereignty in salvation, or require that His Son die in our place before we could be saved. To know God we must just look inward and then project what we see within onto a larger canvas. Throughout this book my goal has been to show why such an approach is too simple, and why it leads us away from the God of the Bible rather than toward Him.

It is still my desire, however, to know God and to love Him, and I hope my readers feel the same. Therefore, let me summarize a few of the lessons I have learned in my journey—lessons about the study of theology and the living of the Christian life. The question I am asking is this: How can we grow in our knowledge of God? In answering this question, we will be able to grow closer to God, so that when our time comes to meet Him face-to-face we will be meeting an old friend and not a stranger. And as we grow in our knowledge of God, we will ensure that our lives will draw people to Christ rather than drive them away from Him.

DEAL WITH YOUR HEART

To grow in our knowledge of the Lord, let's first recognize that knowing God is not a purely intellectual exercise. It involves all of our lives. One Puritan writer, William Ames, defined theology as the doctrine of "living to God," and went on to say that we live to God when we live in accord with His will, to His glory, and with Him working in us.[1] Ames did not mean by this to downplay the importance of intellectual precision in theology, but what is striking about his definition is that it focuses primarily on the state of our hearts and the quality of our relationship with God.

To be a true theologian is not simply to have a head packed with arguments and doctrines but to be a man or woman who lives in accord with the will of God, who lives with the constant desire to glorify God, and who is indwelt by God's Spirit. Jonathan Edwards puts it this way: "Where there is a kind of light without heat, a head stored with notions and speculations, with a cold and unaffected heart, there can be nothing divine in that light, that knowledge is no true spiritual knowledge of divine things."[2]

Even if we adopt a narrower definition of theology and think of it as the purely intellectual dimension of our relationship with God, we cannot escape the fact that theology demands much more of us, on a personal level, than most other intellectual disciplines. It is quite possible for a person to be a superb mathematician yet a rotten human being, but it is very hard to be a good theologian if one's heart is in rebellion against God. A rebellious heart takes offense at all reminders of God's sovereign power and authority, and it seeks constantly to rewrite divine truth to suit its own desires. This rewriting —or at least the drive toward it—occurs mostly at a subconscious level, where it is very hard to detect. We do not feel that we are hostile to God; we feel, rather, that in opposing certain doctrines we are nobly defending Him against misrepresentation. Yet all the while our thinking is being influenced profoundly by a deep-seated unwillingness to acknowledge His authority over us.

As Jeremiah said, "The heart is deceitful above all things, and desperately sick" (Jer. 17:9). This deceitfulness creates problems in all aspects of human life, but it creates greater intellectual problems for the study of theology than for the study of entomology or German grammar. The unredeemed heart seeks to suppress its knowledge of God, and even the renewed Christian heart struggles against its own residual demand for autonomy. This struggle makes theology difficult.

Because this is so, we who want to know God must exercise more than just our minds. We are indeed called to think and to study, but that thinking and studying needs to occur within the context of a life that is being continually offered afresh to God. This offering takes two main forms.

Obedience and Worship

First, we need to strive constantly for complete obedience to God's will. Jesus told us that our knowledge of divine truth is directly linked to obedience: "Whoever has my commands and obeys them, he is the one who loves me. He who loves me will be loved by my Father, and I too will love him and show myself to him" (John 14:21 NIV). Jesus reveals Himself to the obedient and hides Himself from the rebellious. We cannot isolate our intellectual pursuit of God from the rest of our lives. If we want to know God, we must aim at holiness.

This point seems simple enough, but it is often overlooked. I remember hearing, years ago, that the students at a particular seminary were notorious for their sexual immorality. Whether the charge was true I do not know; but if so, then it is only to be assumed that those students emerged from their studies with a theology riddled with prevarication. Whenever our deeds are evil, our hearts will move immediately to suppress whatever part of God's truth would expose them. The result is a twisted, malformed theology built on the rotten foundation of a bad conscience.

This does not mean that we are to go about sniffing out the sins of those who disagree with us theologically. It does mean that we are to be wary of our own deceitfulness—and that of other people—and we are to take it as a given that our theology will never be completely straight until our lives are. To be a good theologian you must want even more to be a good Christian.

Second, we need to continually offer ourselves to God in worship. In worship we humble ourselves before God, and as we do so, we find a deeper satisfaction than can ever be found in rebellion. Our hearts become glad; our minds become clear. If worship is a part of the rhythm of our lives—if we worship with others on a weekly basis and on our own or with our families more frequently—then the habit of worship erodes our rebellion like waves wearing away the shore. As with obedience, the discipline of worship is easily forgotten or set aside in our eagerness to master theology. I have always found it much easier to have my mind filled with arguments about God than my heart filled with love for Him. I have also observed many diligent students of theology who omit worship from their lives altogether. But this is foolishness. We can never think rightly of God if we do not love Him, and it is worship that stirs up and deepens our love.

Here, then, is the first lesson for the person who would be a theologian: Deal with your heart. Obey the Word of God, put your sins to death, and cultivate a spirit of worship. Doing so will very likely make you wiser than all your teachers (Ps. 119:99).

Accept the Imperfect Nature of our Present Knowledge

A second lesson has to do with intellectual humility. As I noted in the introduction, what initially annoyed me about J. I. Packer's book *Knowing God* was that it required one to approach God from many different perspectives, including ones that at first seemed mutually contradictory. I wanted a simpler, more complete knowledge of God's character and ways, and for a time I thought I had found that knowledge in MacDonald's theological method. But MacDonald was mistaken. God is indeed a Father, but that is not all He is.

No single analogy will lead us into a full and perfect knowledge of God. No single divine attribute so completely describes Him that it does not need to be set in careful relationship to other attributes. God is simple in the sense that in Him there is no contradiction, division, or conflict. But our knowledge of God is complex and fragmentary. We see as through a glass, darkly. We do not yet know as we are known. We must accept the limitations of our knowledge and not succumb to the temptation to oversimplify.

What I am thinking of here is the tendency, so evident in theology, for scholars to seize upon one truth and press it to the point that they obscure or deny other, equally important truths. In the effort to highlight God's love, they deny the reality of His wrath. Hoping to emphasize His commitment to our moral responsibility, they deny His sovereign control over us. Wishing to make intelligible His involvement in our lives, they deny His foreknowledge of our actions. MacDonald's decision to make God's fatherhood the touchstone by which all other doctrines were to be measured blinded him to other, equally important aspects of the divine character. Like all who approach theology in this way, MacDonald was reduced finally to flatly refusing to face facts. What the Bible seemed to say it couldn't say; all truth had to be trimmed or stretched to fit onto the bed MacDonald had fashioned for it.

The Unfinished Puzzle

This is not the way to grow in our knowledge of God or our love for Him. If we want to make progress, we are going to have to recognize that theology is like a puzzle whose pieces sometimes do not seem to fit perfectly. We are at times left needing to affirm truths we cannot neatly harmonize. There is but one God, and yet there are Three who are God. The Nicene Creed helps us express the doctrine of the Trinity in such a way as to avoid falling into heresy, but it does not take away the unfathomable mystery of the divine nature. Or again, God is sovereign over His creation and decrees all that takes place, yet

He does so without becoming the author of sin, doing violence to the human will, or taking away the liberty and contingency of secondary causes. How He does this, nobody can say.

And so it goes. We affirm the efficacy of prayer; we deny that God's decrees are changed by our prayers. We affirm that the Bible is God-breathed; we deny that God turned its authors into mere scribes. We affirm that Jesus is fully human; we deny that His humanity cancels His divine nature. We affirm that God is love; we deny that His benevolence is incompatible with the eternal punishment of the wicked.

Are we dissatisfied with the gaps in our knowledge? Of course. But we nevertheless resist the temptation to fill them with our own speculations. We refuse to make the pieces fit by sanding down their sides and lopping off their irregularities. We humble ourselves before the mystery of our God and trust that as we grow into the likeness of and in closeness to Him, our knowledge of Him will also grow.

One day we will see clearly things that are now shrouded in shadow. In the meantime, while we live in semidarkness, we are patient. We learn to admit our ignorance. We confess boldly the truths we see, but we don't pretend to understand that which is still hidden from us.

This attitude is necessary if we want to be true theologians. In many ways, it is the same attitude that must be taken by the serious natural scientist. Scientific progress is never made by those who bend the evidence to fit their theories but by those who are humble enough to believe that nature has more to teach than we have yet learned. But humility is even more important to the theologian than to the scientist, because God is an infinitely higher object of study than His own creation. His thoughts are not our thoughts; His ways are not our ways. His judgments are unsearchable, and His ways beyond tracing out. We can know only that which He has revealed in His Word, and even the truths of the Bible can be found only through hard study.

If we are persistent, reverent, and prayerful we will make progress, because God has expressed His esteem for those who tremble at His Word. But we may be sure that He will laugh to scorn those theologians who think themselves wise enough to reject doctrines the Spirit has taught.

BEWARE THE DEADENING
POWER OF LOVELESS ORTHODOXY

My last comment is more of a warning than a lesson. While I have criticized George MacDonald rather mercilessly in this book, I am convinced that MacDonald was a man of integrity who loved Christ with a deep love. For this reason, I have to assume that he came to his views, at least in part, as a result of interaction with a truly unattractive presentation of the kind of theology I am advocating here. And my guess is that he was not reacting simply to abstract ideas but to people whose lives made those ideas appear ugly. In my view, Calvinist orthodoxy *should* produce humility, gratitude, love, and every other expression of holiness. I am aware that that is not always the case. Let us remember that when orthodoxy instead produces pride, complacency, and a pharisaical attitude toward those of other persuasions, it becomes a great hindrance to our efforts to bring others to the knowledge of Christ.

Consider, for a moment, Longfellow's unflattering portrait of a Calvinistic preacher in "Tales of a Wayside Inn":

> The Parson, too, appeared, a man austere,
> The instinct of whose nature was to kill;
> The wrath of God he preached from year to year,
> And read, with fervor, Edwards on the Will;
> His favorite pastime was to slay the deer
> In Summer on some Adirondac hill;
> E'en now, while walking down the rural lane,
> He lopped the wayside lilies with His cane.[3]

Now this is an unpleasant fellow! He kills animals and plants for the sheer fun of it, and the same destructiveness is shown in his preaching and reading: His theme is divine wrath; his book the philosophical masterpiece of that notorious misanthrope Jonathan Edwards!

This is a grossly unfair caricature, almost certainly a product more of prejudice than of actual experience.[4] But let us not complain of that. Instead, let us take warning from Longfellow's parson. The world is greatly prejudiced against all Christian doctrine, and many Christians are prejudiced against Calvinism. If we are going to be Calvinists, we need to be very, very sure that the caricature does not describe us. If we are going to believe in and proclaim a great gospel, then let us take care to be people of great souls.

The doctrine of universal human guilt must make us humble, not judgmental. The doctrine of eternal punishment must move us to prayer and sacrifice, not to indifference to the fate of our fellow human beings. The mystery of election must stimulate us to gratitude, not complacency. And the truth that God is working out all things for the praise of His glory should cause us to seek every day to know God better, reflect Him more in our attitudes and actions, and rejoice more in His goodness. We should be the most serious, holy, and happy of all people on the face of the earth.

There is no guarantee that such attitudes will attract people to Christ; in some cases, they will instead evoke rejection and anger. But we must at least do what we can to ensure that what people reject is Christ, not some mangled, ugly misrepresentation of Him in our own souls. God wants people to look at us and see a reflection of His Son's face.

So I end with a warning. Pride can stand in the way of your growing in knowledge of God, but growth in knowledge can also produce pride.

Fight that pride by living a Christian life. Pray. Worship. Share your faith. Serve people. Learn from others, including those you disagree with. To your faith add virtue, knowledge, self-control, steadfastness, godliness, brotherly affection, and love, that you may not be unfruitful in the knowledge of Christ (See 2 Peter 1:5–8). Do everything you can to show the world that Jesus is the "joy of man's desiring" and that there is no higher, better, or happier calling than to be His disciple. Don't obsess about the hard doctrines of the faith. Believe them; be unafraid to speak them, but keep your heart grounded in the truth that the Lord is good. "God is light, and in him is no darkness at all" (1 John 1:5).

Dear Father, again I pray that both my reader and I may grow in our knowledge of You. Life in this world is not easy. We often feel that we are walking and suffering in darkness; and when we lift our eyes to look at You, what we see both attracts and terrifies us. But whom have we in heaven but You? And what is the value of earth's joys without You? Who but Jesus can give us the words of eternal life?

So, Father, lead us on. In these few years we have on this earth, expand our minds and our hearts to the fullest possible extent. Let us know; let us see; let us love. Free us from our sins; heal our wounds; set our hearts ablaze. Prepare us for the day when we will rejoice in Your presence forever. And grant that we may bring with us as many others as we can. Amen.

NOTES

1. William Ames, trans. John D. Eusden, *The Marrow of Theology*, 1968, repr., Durham, N.C.: Labyrinth Press, 1983), 77.

2. Jonathan Edwards, *The Religious Affections* (repr., Edinburgh: Banner of Truth 2001), 49; in other editions of *The Religious Affections* this quotation can be found in part 1, sec. 3.

3. "Tales of a Wayside Inn," Henry Wadsworth Longfellow, *Poems and Other Writings*, ed. J. D. McClatchy (New York: Literary Classics, 2000), 441.

4. It is certainly slanderous to drag Edwards into such a picture. Nobody who has any familiarity with Edwards can imagine him lopping lilies with a cane. The reader who would like to get to know the real Edwards could hardly do better than to begin with George Marsden's magisterial biography, *Jonathan Edwards: A Life* (New Haven, Conn.: Yale, 2003).

A LETTER
TO "SEEKERS"

*But he was wounded for our transgressions; he was crushed for
our iniquities; upon him was the chastisement that brought us
peace, and with his stripes we are healed.*

✝ISAIAH 53:5

I UNDERSTAND THE BIBLE to say that until we are reborn we do not,
in the deepest sense, seek God. We may seek His blessings; we may
even seek salvation; but God Himself we reject.

Nevertheless, it is common today to refer to those who are interested in knowing more about the Christian faith as "seekers," and since
it is possible that the reader may fall into that category, I would like
to say a little about the implications of the topic of this book for you.

First, I hope you will not become angry with me for speaking to
you plainly and bluntly about spiritual matters. If I suggest to you that
you are currently lost and in need of Christ, I do not intend by this
any disrespect for you as a person. On the contrary, it is because I care
about you that I speak as I do. I would like to be of service to you.

Are You a Christian?

Let's begin by trying to determine whether you are already a Christian. Many people are deceived about their standing with God, supposing themselves to be Christians when, in fact, they are not. Others are simply uncertain and perhaps feel anxious and worried about how God views them. The Bible tells us that we are to make every effort to make our calling and election sure, and so it is only reasonable to try to determine how we can be certain of our spiritual state. I will first mention some things that do *not* indicate that we are genuinely converted, and then some that do.

False Evidence

On the negative side, a person is not a Christian simply because he or she is born into a Christian family, or baptized into a Christian church, or because he or she joins a church. This is an important point, because millions of people have been deceived with the idea that their baptism or christening as a child, or their membership in a church as an adult, automatically puts them in God's good graces.

Such people often have next to no knowledge of the Christian faith, and nothing in their behavior to suggest that Christ is, in fact, important to them. Yet if you ask them if they are Christians, they will very confidently answer that they are. When I was converted I happened to tell one of my professors that I had become a Christian. His puzzled response was, "Well, what were you before?" He apparently took it for granted that everybody born in America is automatically Christian.

But it is not so. Christian conversion is a spiritual matter. A Christian is a person who has entered into a new relationship with God. Christians have been forgiven their sins, and they have been declared by God to be His children. Their hearts have been changed by His Spirit, and they have within them a love for God and a heartfelt desire to please Him. These things do not come by birth or baptism but only by spiritual rebirth. "Truly, truly, I say to you," said Jesus, "unless one is born again he cannot see the kingdom of God" (John 3:3).

Another way people are deceived is by thinking that because they have raised their hand in an evangelistic meeting or gone forward to kneel at an altar, they can take their salvation for granted. The problem here is that there are many possible motives for responding to an evangelistic appeal other than a true Spirit-wrought change in the heart. Perhaps you raised your hand one day to "receive Christ." You knew that was what your parents wanted you to do, and you didn't want to disappoint them. Or maybe all your friends were going forward, and you didn't want to be left out. Or maybe you were moved by the story of Christ's death, or by some other story the speaker told, and your public response was simply a reaction to the emotional power of the message. Or again, maybe the speaker presented his appeal in such a way that you found yourself desiring some benefit that Christ can bring, and your response was an expression of your desire for that benefit rather than for Christ Himself.

Sad to say, the gospel is often presented in terms such as these: "Are you lonely? Christ can become your best friend. Are you fearful? Christ can take away your fears. Do you want power to overcome your bad habits? Christ can give you power. Now, don't you want Christ?" A person may listen to that type of message and make a public response to it without, perhaps, ever understanding anything at all about his or her own sin, the meaning of Christ's death, and the nature of true faith.

Your decision to go forward and "give your life to Christ" may have been based on a completely inadequate understanding of the commitment you were being asked to make, with the result that you have lived for years in a condition of disappointment, feeling that promises were made to you that have never been fulfilled. Perhaps the problem is that you are not yet a Christian.

One other way we deceive ourselves is by supposing that spiritual "experience" is what shows that we stand in God's good graces. Mormons encourage potential converts to pray that God will show them the truth of Mormon doctrine by causing them to experience a "burning" sensation in their hearts. People involved in New Age religion are inclined to place great emphasis on their ability to make contact with beings in the invisible spirit realm. Some people build a religious faith not on God and Christ but on angels, and they suppose that the experiences they have apparently had of angelic visitations prove that they are at peace with God.

This, too, must be rejected as deceptive and inadequate. It is not that the non-Christian who claims to have had a spiritual experience is necessarily wrong in that belief. The problem, rather, is that apart from the testimony of the Bible, there is no way of being sure that the experience is from God. One popular author claims to be receiving her theology straight from a woman dead several hundred years. I don't know whether she is in contact with a spiritual being, is deluding herself, or is deliberately lying. What I do know is that her theology is completely at odds with the Bible, and so even if she is indeed having some sort of genuine spiritual experience, it has not reconciled her to the true God.

You may think of yourself as a "spiritual" person, but beware: The only spirituality the Bible recognizes as genuine is one that is focused on Jesus Christ and guided by His teaching and that of His apostles. If you put your confidence in your supposed experiences, those experiences may wind up costing you your soul.

True Evidence

Now let's look at the matter from a positive perspective. What constitutes true and adequate evidence that a person is a Christian? In one sense, the answer to this question is both brief and simple: A person is a Christian if he or she believes in Jesus. "Believe in the Lord Jesus, and you will be saved" (Acts 16:31). What connects us to the grace of God is faith. A person who has faith in Christ is, by definition, a believer. And whoever believes in Christ has already passed from death to life and has been forgiven all of his sins.

The problem, of course, is in defining faith. What constitutes true faith, and how does such faith make its presence known? If we don't take time to think about this question, we may deceive ourselves, thinking we believe when really we do not.

So what does faith look like? Well, first, it has an intellectual component to it. In order to believe rightly in Jesus, we have to know who He is, what He did, and what His actions have to do with us. We need to believe that:

- He is the eternal Son of God, fully divine and also fully human;
- He lived a sinless life, and His perfect obedience to God is credited

to those who trust Him, giving them the right to eternal life in God's eyes;

- His death on the cross was for the sins of the world, and all who trust in Him are forgiven their sins on the basis of that death;
- Jesus rose from the dead and now lives forever, and through the Holy Spirit He is present to all of His followers in all places and times; and
- a day of judgment will come, and only those who have placed their faith in Christ will be acquitted and given eternal life in heaven. Others will spend eternity in hell.

Many people who do not believe these things at all nevertheless claim to be Christians, but it is hard to see that there is any basis to their claim. Jesus taught all these doctrines, and it is manifestly dishonest to call oneself a follower of Christ if one denies them.

Faith, of course, requires more than intellectual understanding. The Bible reminds us that even the devils have an intellectual understanding of the gospel, but they obviously are not in a right relationship with God. To intellectual understanding we must add the assent of the will. That is, we must not merely believe that these things are true; we must be willing that they be true. You see, it is possible for a person to become persuaded that Jesus is the only Savior of the world and yet hate that fact. He may be intellectually convinced that without Christ he will perish eternally and yet be unwilling to change his life to bring it into accordance with that truth. His mind is convinced, but his heart is still in rebellion. Such a person is not a Christian.

And there is still more. To intellectual understanding and the assent of the will we must add another element of faith: actual personal trust in Christ. A Christian (1) believes that Jesus is the Savior of the world, (2) has no desire to deny or rebel against that truth, and (3) has placed all of his or her hope for salvation in Jesus alone.

A true follower of Christ is convinced that if God judges him according to his own deeds he will be eternally condemned; so with the hymn writer he says, "Nothing in my hands I bring/simply to Thy cross I cling." And he means it! He would be no more willing to appear before God without the imputed righteousness of Christ than he would be to attempt to swim across the Pacific Ocean. From the heart he says, "Christ is a perfect Savior for sinners. I am a sinner. I will look to Him and Him alone for my salvation."

A Changed Heart

This is faith, and faith is all that is needed to connect us to the salvation offered us in Christ. But because we are so prone to fool ourselves, it is important to know that if our faith is genuine, it will show itself in important and discernible ways. The Bible says of Christians that God has poured out His love into our hearts, and it would be very strange if that outpouring of divine love made no difference in the way we feel and act. If we genuinely believe in Jesus, then we will find, for example, that we have growing pleasure in knowing God through Him. We will enjoy reading the Bible. We will enjoy praying to God in Christ's name. We will enjoy worshiping God and being with the people of God.

Our enjoyment in these things may vary in intensity depending on what else is happening in our lives, but we will have enough pleasure in our relationship with God to convince us that we are His and He is ours.

Similarly, if our faith is genuine, we will have a growing desire to see Christ glorified in our lives, in the lives of other people, and throughout the world. Our reasoning will be something like this: "The God who has saved me is a great and wonderful God, and His Christ is a great and wonderful Savior. I want the world to know that I believe in Jesus, and I want other people to see Jesus in me and come to faith in Him because of me. I also want people everywhere to know about Christ and believe in Him, and I will do everything in my power to spread His fame throughout the world." Again, our passion for God's glory may burn more brightly at some times than at others; but if we are real Christians, it will not burn out.

One more evidence of faith needs to be mentioned: A true Christian will always have a desire for personal holiness. We will want to obey God's Law to the best of our abilities. We will find that we are still unable to comply fully with God's Law, but we will have a heartfelt desire to do so. We will do everything in our power to remove all known sin from our lives, and when we are unable to overcome a sinful habit, we will find ourselves pleading with God to take it away from us.

This means that we will hate sin and love righteousness. Our prayers, once focused on asking God for various physical blessings, such as health, protection, or success, will now center on our holy Lord and our striving to become like Him.

Now let me again make this matter personal: Are you in fact a Christian? Do you believe in Christ, and is the genuine nature of your faith proved by its fruits? Does my description of Christian faith cause you to rejoice and say, "Yes, that's me!" or does it cause uneasiness or even anger in your heart?

Be honest with yourself. There is no sense in ducking the issue or pretending to be what you are not.

A Word of Warning

Let's assume you have answered the question in the negative— either you recognize that you plainly are not a Christian or else you see that you have insufficient evidence to prove that you are a Christian. Please bear with me as I give you a word of warning.

Great Danger

You are in very great danger. You are a sinner, and God is angry with you for your sin. God holds you responsible for your every violation of His Law throughout your life, and He has stated plainly and solemnly that unless your sins are forgiven through Christ, you will pay the penalty for them through an eternity of suffering in hell. God will accept no excuses. You will not get away with blaming your sins on your parents, on Satan, or on God Himself. The sincerity of your false beliefs and wrong way of life will not purchase your forgiveness.

If you do not repent and believe in Christ, you will die in your sins and be lost forever.

Furthermore, your plight is made all the worse because you are morally unable to repent and believe unless God first gives you the power to do so. I do not say that you are physically unable to believe. God has not put any barrier in your way to prevent you from coming to Christ. The problem lies in your own will: You can't come to Christ because you do not want to. Yes, you may well want some of the benefits of being a Christian. You may want to know that your sins are forgiven. You may want assurance that you will go to heaven. You may want the confidence that God will be with you throughout your life and through eternity. You may want the peace of knowing that God hears your prayers.

Not Yet Condemned, But . . .

But your problem is that while you want various things from God, you do not want God Himself. You do not want to submit to His authority in your life. You do not want to suffer the indignity of confessing your sins to Him and admitting your absolute need for Christ's intercession for you. You do not want the inconvenience and shame of being Jesus' disciple.

How can I know this? Because if you did want these things, you would have them already, since nothing stands in your way but your own will. The fact that you do not have them is proof that you do not want them, and your lack of desire for them makes it impossible that you should receive them. You are bound for hell, and it is by your own choice.

God has not yet condemned you, but you are in the process of condemning yourself, and unless God intervenes to save you, you will be lost. God requires you to trust in Christ, but you don't want to trust in Him. God requires you to love Christ, but in your heart of hearts you despise Him.

Now maybe what I am saying is completely untrue of you. Maybe you are a Christian after all. If so, rejoice! But be honest with yourself. Do you love God or not? If not, then do not deceive yourself that He is reconciled to you or that you have it in your power to turn your hatred of Him into love. To put the matter in biblical terms, you are dead in your sins and transgressions. You are by nature an object of God's wrath, without hope and without God in this world (Eph. 2:1–3; 12). God has full power to save you from your guilt and from your enmity toward Him, but only He has that power. If He saves you, you will be saved. If He does not, you will be lost.

LOOK TO CHRIST

What then? If you are in a lost condition and are unable to believe in Christ as your Savior, what are you to do? Should you give up hope of being saved? Should you reason that if it all depends on the action of God, you might as well be passive? By no means! You cannot save yourself, but that does not mean that there is nothing you can do. You can look to Christ, confess to Him your depravity, admit your inability to love Him or even rightly believe in Him, and ask Him to mercifully change your bad heart to a good one.

You could pray such words of humble petition as these:

"Lord Jesus! I am not capable of loving You. I dread the loss of control involved in giving up my life to You. I hate the honesty involved in confessing that I am a sinner who cannot be saved other than by Your death on the cross. I do not want to submit my will to Yours. I do not want the shame of being known as Your follower.

"And yet, I also do not want to perish! I do not want to face an eternity of suffering for my sins. I do not want to experience the implacable and everlasting wrath of almighty God. I do not want to have lived in vain. I do not want to be lost, separated from You forever.

"And so, Lord Jesus, help me! Take away my heart of stone and give me a new heart, a good heart, one that will love You and love God. Change me from within; make me a new person; enable me to believe; cause me to love. If You leave me alone, I will damn myself. If You stand back and do not help me, I will use my free will to make a wreck of my existence. Do not abandon me! Have mercy on me, for the sake of Your own glorious grace. Amen."

THE MEANS OF GRACE

Friend, you cannot save yourself, but you can speak to God in this way. And there is more you can do. You can begin to make use of the means God normally uses to bring people to faith. You can read the Bible. You can pray. You can attend church. You can listen to biblical preaching. You can ask others to pray for you. I cannot guarantee that if you do these things, God will grant you faith and repentance. If I could offer such a guarantee, it would be tantamount to saying that you can, after all, save yourself. God reserves to Himself the right and power to save, and He will not share His glory with us, even if only by granting us the power to save ourselves by confessing that we cannot save ourselves! You are in His hands.

I can, however, tell you this. If you have read this far, and you find within yourself a willingness to pray along the lines I have suggested and to avail yourself of the means of grace I have listed, then it is very, very likely that the Spirit of God is already at work in you and that He plans to display His mercy in you by saving you.

As one great theologian has written, "It is true that no man can regenerate himself, even although he hears and receives God's Word. But God is prepared to come to those who come to him by the way he has told them. He meets souls where he says he will meet them."[1] And the greatest of all theologians, the Lord Jesus Christ Himself, has invited us with these words: "Ask, and it will be given to you; seek, and you will find; knock, and it will be opened to you" (Matt. 7:7).

So take heart! Perhaps this is the very day of your salvation. But do not rest until you are sure. Ask until you know you have received the power to trust Christ. Seek until you have found peace with God. Knock until you know that the door has been opened and you have entered in.

Note

1. John Owen, *The Holy Spirit,* abridg. R. J. K. Law (Edinburgh: Banner of Truth, 1998), 52.

INDEX OF TOPICS

INDEX OF SCRIPTURES

SINCE 1894, Moody Publishers has been dedicated to equip and motivate people to advance the cause of Christ by publishing evangelical Christian literature and other media for all ages, around the world. Because we are a ministry of the Moody Bible Institute of Chicago, a portion of the proceeds from the sale of this book go to train the next generation of Christian leaders.

If we may serve you in any way in your spiritual journey toward understanding Christ and the Christian life, please contact us at www.moodypublishers.com.

*"All Scripture is God-breathed and is useful
for teaching, rebuking, correcting and training in
righteousness, so that the man of God may be
thoroughly equipped for every good work."*
—2 TIMOTHY 3:16, 17

MOODY
PUBLISHERS

THE NAME YOU CAN TRUST®

Sinners in the Hands of a Good God Team

ACQUIRING EDITOR
Greg Thornton

COPY EDITOR
Jim Vincent

BACK COVER COPY
Michele Straubel

COVER DESIGN
Paetzold Associates

INTERIOR DESIGN
Ragont Design

PRINTING AND BINDING
Versa Press, Inc.

*The typeface for the text of this book is
Berkeley*